Income in Kentucky

JOHN L. JOHNSON

INCOME IN KENTUCKY

County Distributions by Amount,
by Type, and by Size

UNIVERSITY OF KENTUCKY PRESS

To my parents

EDITORIAL NOTE

DURING the past few years increasing attention has been given the development of a methodology that would make possible the estimation of county income by type and amount. At the same time, but to a lesser degree, the problem of a size group breakdown of incomes on a county or small area basis has also been studied. Behind this sort of research is the belief that income is one of the best measures of economic well-being and that income estimates on a small area basis make this measure much more meaningful.

A rather comprehensive method of allocating to counties the income received by the individuals of a state has been developed by the Conference on the Measurement of County Income. The conference was the outgrowth of meetings held at the University of Kentucky in June, 1949, to explore the need and possibilities for a study of income by counties. Bureaus of business research, or their counterparts, of the Universities of Alabama, Georgia, Kentucky, Mississippi, North Carolina, Tennessee, and Virginia and the Tennessee Valley Authority organized to undertake a joint study for the purpose of developing a methodology from which could be made actual estimates which would meet demands for local income data.

Recent county income estimates by amount and source have also been made outside the conference area and in different ways from state to state; but for the most part they are based on the allocation method patterned after, or similar to, the conference method. The number of states where, in one manner or another, county income estimates have been made reflects an ever increasing demand by businessmen, government officials, and others for an income breakdown on a county or regional basis. The demand for income estimates by size group on a small area basis is just as keen, but a shortage of adequate data to make such a distribution limits considerably this type of exploration. Some work of note, however, has been done on a county basis but for the most part size group analysis has been confined to large areas.

This study is made as a contribution to the co-operative work of the Conference on the Measurement of County Income (now Southeastern Economic Research Conference), and the procedure developed by the conference has been used in the distribution of income by counties. The Bureau believes that improvements have been made in the distribution of the 1939 and 1947 income data and, at least to that extent, that this study is a further step in the development and use of this type of analysis. These improvements are, of course, incorporated in the estimates for later years.

In addition, for the first time size group distributions of income payments to individuals have been estimated for small areas. The extension of the use of county income data as a basis of size group distributions for small areas presents the first opportunity for a broader and more intensive use of this type of data.

The Bureau is indebted to personnel of the Conference on the Measurement of County Income for numerous ideas on the estimation of income payments by small areas. The following scholars in the field have assisted by reading and criticizing an earlier draft of

all or part of this study: Thomas R. Atkinson, Financial Economist, Federal Reserve Bank at Atlanta;
Lewis C. Copeland, Professor of Statistics, University of Tennessee; A. Ross Eckler, Deputy Director,
Bureau of the Census; John L. Fulmer, Professor of
Economics, Emory University; George Garvy, National Bureau of Economic Research; Robert E. Graham,
Jr., National Income Division, Office of Business Economics, United States Department of Commerce; Frank
A. Hanna, Professor of Economics, Duke University;
and Werner Hochwald, Federal Reserve Bank of St.
Louis. The Bureau's gratitude to business and espe-
cially governmental agencies for generous assistance
is greater than can be expressed. This is particular-
ly the case for the United States Department of Commerce Office of Business Economics and the Kentucky
Departments of Economic Security and of Revenue.
On the Bureau staff itself Mark Frishe has assisted
Mr. Johnson and me in formal editorial revision, and
Charles R. Lockyer critically read the draft.

                        James W. Martin, Director
                        Bureau of Business Research

University of Kentucky

CONTENTS

LIST OF TABLES

LIST OF CHARTS

Chart A
PER CAPITA INCOME OF KENTUCKY COUNTIES, 1952

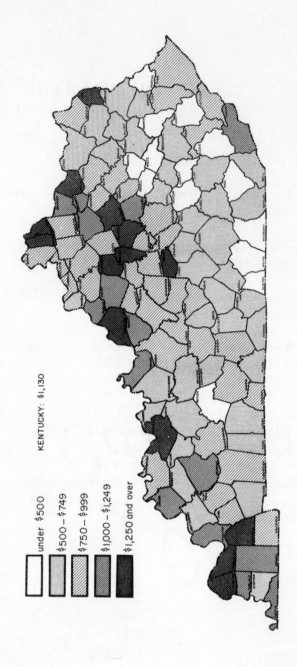

under $500

$500 – $749

$750 – $999

$1,000 – $1,249

$1,250 and over

KENTUCKY: $1,130

CHAPTER I

Introduction

INCOME is the best single index of what is happening
to the economy of a nation, a state, or a county. Although national and state income estimates have been
available for several years, county income estimates
for most states are not now available. Estimates of
total income payments to individuals in each county,
by type and by size, provide both a basis for an understanding of the economy and a point of departure
for the important work that should be done in area
economics. Through county income estimates one
may learn of the economic characteristics or structure of local areas, and a small area approach, supplementing other tools of economic analysis, can ac-
celerate advancement in knowledge of the nation's
economy.

Income estimates provide a framework within
which to study the contribution of each economic activity to total income and the effect of the development
of one activity upon others. Points of weakness in the
area or community economic balance can be detected
if reliable income estimates are available and a
definite plan of resource development that is directed

toward socially desirable goals may quite conceivably
be a direct offshoot of county income data. County
income estimates provide a sound basis for further
research into the differences in living standards between industrially different areas, between urban and
rural areas, and between areas with different per capita incomes. Any comparison of economic well-being
among the counties is difficult; the term is not easily defined. From the estimates of county income,
however, it may be noted that extreme differences
in economic well-being from county to county do exist and continue to exist. County income estimates
and other data constitute a secure foundation upon
which area economic and social trend analyses may
be based.

State and local governments may find many uses
for county income estimates, particularly in the
formulation of plans based on the maximum utilization
of available resources. The estimates may, for
example, help in answering satisfactorily some of
these questions: What is the fiscal capacity of each
county? How may grants-in-aid be best distributed?
What is the need of a particular area for governmental
services? Have the state agricultural and industrial
development boards a statistically sound basis upon
which to make plans? Is there an available income
measure upon which future revenue, expenditure, and
debt policy can be based? These questions and others
need to be answered, and reasonably reliable county
income data are an aid in answering them correctly.

But social scientists and governmental agencies
are not alone in the quest for data upon which further
research and currently sound economic reasoning may
be based. Industrialists, retailers, the men who market services, and those who operate public utilities

can likewise use small area income estimates advan-
tageously. Businessmen are in constant search of data that will help solve their problems of plant location,
sales quotas, type of market, spending power, and future market possibilities. [1]

INCOME PAYMENTS TO INDIVIDUALS DEFINED[2]

Income payments to individuals must not be con-
fused with other measures of income. Gross national
product, for example, measures the nation's output
of goods and services in terms of their market value.
National income may be computed by deducting indirect business taxes and capital consumption allowances (plus other minor adjustments) from gross national product, but it is usually expressed, and is in
fact calculated, in terms of factor shares. Income
payments to individuals report the actual current income receipts of persons from all sources and are
not a measure of output or product.

Briefly, income payments are composed of wage
and salary receipts, income of unincorporated enterprises, rental income, dividends, interest income,
and "other income." Wages and salaries are figured
exclusive of employee social insurance contributions
but inclusive of income in kind, such as board and
lodging furnished hired farm workers.

Income of unincorporated enterprises is divided
into three parts: income from farms, professional
services, and business. Farm proprietors' income
is composed of net cash receipts from the sale of
farm products, the value of food and fuel produced
and consumed on farms, and government payments

under the crop price support and soil conservation
programs. Income from professional services is
made up for the most part of the net income of physicians and surgeons, lawyers, and dentists. Business income, the nonfarm total other than that derived
from professional services, is composed of the net
profit of all unincorporated private business concerns.

The rental income of individuals is composed primarily of returns from rented dwellings and business
and industrial property. The balance of rental income
is derived from royalties paid to persons for the use
of patents, copyrights, and rights to natural resources.

The only part of corporate earnings included in
this concept of income are the dividends paid to individuals. Interest income includes both monetary and
imputed interest. Imputed interest includes, for example, the yearly increase in value of a life insurance
policy in excess of the annual premium or the free
services provided by a commercial bank for its de-
positors.

"Other income," a somewhat large portion of total
income payments, is made up of transfer payments
for which no current productive service is rendered:
industrial pensions, for example, but for the most
part the sum of items such as terminal leave payments
to veterans, payments under the Old-Age and Survivors' Insurance Act, pensions paid by all levels of
government, direct relief, unemployment compensation, and other government transfers.

SUMMARY OF CONTENTS

The major objectives of this study are to distribute
the income payments received by Kentucky residents

in 1950 by (a) county, (b) type, and (c) size group.[3]
The technical procedure, with modifications, per-
fected by the Conference on the Measurement of County Income is used in this study to allocate 1950 income
in Kentucky to the 120 counties in the state.[4] The distribution by county and type is done by assigning to each
county its share of each component of income by using,
in every case, the best practicable allocator. The
final distribution shows the number of recipients and
their total income for each income size group for
counties or county groups.[5]

In addition, there is an analysis of the trend in total and per capita incomes for the state and the counties. A provisional effort is made to isolate the reasons for the difference in county per capita incomes
and to account also for the difference between national
per capita income and per capita income in Kentucky.

The procedure used in each distribution of total
income payments is discussed in considerable detail.
The problems encountered, the reliability of the data,
and a general evaluation of the results complete the
project.

Note: Complete data on each reference may be found
in the Bibliography.

[1]See also Bacon, Income as an Index of the Fiscal
Capacity of Michigan Counties; Leven and others,
America's Capacity to Consume; U.S. Department of
Commerce, National Income and Product of the United
States: 1929-1950; Hochwald and King, "Income Meas-
ures and Their Purpose."

[2]For a complete definition of income payments to
individuals see Schwartz and Graham, "State Income
Payments in 1949," 22-24.

[3]The base year for this study is the census year
1950. In some tables it has been possible to include data for the years 1951 and 1952; however, all analyses
and income allocation, unless otherwise specified,
are based on 1950 data.

[4]Lancaster, County Income Estimates for Seven
Southeastern States; and Copeland, Methods of Estimating Income Payments in Counties.

[5]Important studies in income distribution by size,
both for small areas and for the nation, include Cope-
land, Working Papers on a Method of Estimating Fam-
ily Income Levels in Small Areas; Gilliam, Distri-
bution of Income in Virginia, 1947; Leven and others,
America's Capacity to Consume; Federal Reserve
Board, "Survey of Consumer Finances"; National
Bureau of Economic Research, Studies in Income and
Wealth; National Resources Committee, Consumer
Incomes in the United States; Kuznets, National In-
come: A Summary of Findings; and the United States
Department of Commerce, Income Distribution in the
United States.

CHAPTER II

Income in Kentucky
by Type and Source

THE PICTURE of both total and per capita income payments of Kentucky residents over the past two decades is one of enormous growth. Kentucky per capita income during this period increased much more, percentagewise, than per capita income for the nation as a whole. This growth is in line with a tendency for the per capita incomes of almost every state, high and low alike, to approach the national figure.[1]

Most of this tendency for state per capita incomes to converge at the national average has taken place in the past ten years. These have been years of extremely high employment and rapid industrial growth. An increase in the mobility of labor always accompanies periods of relative prosperity, and there can be little doubt that the movement of the unemployed and underemployed[2] people to the industrial areas of the nation has been an important factor in this tendency toward equality in state per capita incomes. Other factors, of course, have also played important roles. There has been increased industrialization in many of the so-called agricultural states. There has been an increased demand for farm products and an above average increase in farm prices. These and other factors taken in combination seem to emphasize the fact that

greater equality in state per capita incomes is the natural outgrowth of national prosperity.

KENTUCKY INCOME BY TYPE

Internal differences in the economic characteristics
of large areas make it impracticable to consider the

Table 1
INCOME PAYMENTS TO INDIVIDUALS BY TYPE IN
THE UNITED STATES AND KENTUCKY, 1950

Type	Percentage	
	United States	Kentucky
Wages and salaries	64.9	59.8
Agricultural proprietors' income	5.7	10.1
Nonagricultural proprietors' income	11.1	11.7
Property income	11.2	9.4
"Other income"	7.0	9.0

Source: Tables 1 through 5 are computed from unpublished data on
income payments to individuals by source, Office of Business Economics, U.S. Department of Commerce.

Note: Because of rounding, the figures may not add to 100 per cent.

income distribution by type for any state or for the nation as ideal.   Table 1, which gives the percentage distribution of income payments to individuals for Kentucky and the nation by type, should be viewed, therefore, as purely suggestive.

Percentagewise there is considerable difference between the income distributions by type for the nation
and for Kentucky.   Of particular note is the difference
in the amount derived from agriculture.   A further
breakdown of these major types of income sheds more
light on the differences between the economy of Kentucky and the economy of the nation.   Table 2 shows
the percentage distribution of wages and salaries. Ex-

amination of this table, and similar tables to follow,
should be made with reference to the general distribution pattern depicted in Table 1.

With a few exceptions, particularly in mining and
manufacturing, the wage and salary distribution in Kentucky by industrial source follows the national distribution pattern rather closely.   The extreme difference

Table 2
SOURCE OF GROSS WAGES AND SALARIES BY PERCENTAGE
IN THE UNITED STATES AND KENTUCKY, 1950

Source	Percentage	
	United States	Kentucky
Agriculture	1.8	1.9
Mining	2.2	11.5
Manufacturing	34.1	24.5
Construction	5.4	5.1
Transportation	6.9	9.1
Power and gas	1.3	1.4
Communication	1.5	1.2
Trade	18.7	16.3
Finance	3.9	2.7
Government	13.2	15.8
Service	9.0	9.0
Miscellaneous	2.0	1.7

in wage and salary income from mining helps confirm
an earlier statement that no distribution pattern by
type of payment should be considered ideal.

The breakdown of nonagricultural proprietors' income, Table 3, reveals other differences in the source
of income payments to individuals.   Quite naturally it
would be expected that proprietors' income from mining, percentagewise, should be higher in Kentucky than
in the nation.   This is not true of proprietors' income
from manufacturing, construction, and service.   The
greatest percentage of proprietors' income in each case
is the amount derived from trade--much more in Ken-

tucky than in the United States--even though, as will
be indicated later, there is very little difference in
the per capita amounts derived from this source. It

Table 3
SOURCE OF PROPRIETORS' INCOME BY PERCENTAGE
IN THE UNITED STATES AND KENTUCKY, 1950

Source	Percentage	
	United States	Kentucky
Mining, Manufacturing, Construction, and Transportation	22.9	13.1
Trade, Finance, and Service	77.1	86.9

must be remembered, also, that the income of proprietors is only that part of business earnings that is derived from noncorporate activity; it is not a measure
of all business income.

Table 4
SOURCE OF PROPERTY INCOME OF INDIVIDUALS BY PERCENTAGE
IN THE UNITED STATES AND KENTUCKY, 1950

Source	Percentage	
	United States	Kentucky
Interest	43.2	38.7
Dividends	36.7	38.3
Rent	20.1	22.9

In Table 4 the income to individuals from property
is shown by major sources only. Even though the income from property in Kentucky is considerably less,
as a percentage of total income, than the property income for the nation (see Table 1), the distribution by
source is remarkably similar.

The "other income" segment of income payments to
individuals is made up almost wholly of government

transfer payments. These payments have become increasingly important in the past few years, and even
more so in 1950 because of the National Service Life

Table 5
SOURCE OF "OTHER INCOME" BY PERCENTAGE IN
THE UNITED STATES AND KENTUCKY, 1950

Source	Percentage	
	United States	Kentucky
Old-Age and Survivors' Insurance benefits	6.3	5.2
Railroad retirement benefits	2.0	2.8
State unemployment insurance benefits	9.0	5.6
Public assistance payments	15.4	11.4
Federal civilian retirement	1.8	1.6
Workmen's compensation	4.0	2.9
Veterans' pensions and compensation	14.3	23.0
Veterans' subsistence allowances	10.5	12.7
Military reserve pay	1.9	2.2
Military retirement	2.0	2.3
Family allowances and allotments of pay to dependents of military personnel	5.6	7.4
National Service Life Insurance special dividend	17.6	19.4
Unclassified[a]	9.7	3.5

[a]Includes railroad unemployment insurance benefits, railroad sickness benefits, veterans' unemployment allowances, veterans' self-employment allowances, state and local government retirement payments,
state sickness benefits, federal interest payments on veterans' loans,
adjusted service bonds, industrial pensions, mustering-out pay to dis-
charged servicemen, enlisted men's cash terminal leave payments,
state bonuses to veterans, and payments to former prisoners of war
(U.S.) by War Claims Commission.

Insurance special dividend payments to veterans. The
Department of Commerce listed 25 different types of
"other income" payments in 1950. Many of these are
relatively constant or increase gradually from year to
year--retirement pay, for example. Others may increase as the unemployment increases--unemployment

compensation and public assistance payments are of
this type. There are others that can be expected to
fall from year to year, such as the benefits paid to
veterans of World War II under the Servicemen's Re-
adjustment Act. And there are some categories of
"other income" that apply only to some states--state
sickness benefits and state bonuses to veterans are
examples.[3] Table 5 shows the major sources of "other income" in Kentucky and in the United States.

Many factors besides those mentioned have an effect on some of the "other income" components. Some
of these are the welfare policy of the state, the amount
of employment covered by the unemployment insurance
law, seasonality of the industries, the sensitivity of
the major industries to business fluctuations, and the
state and local government retirement systems. The
large amount of payments made by the federal government and the means by which they may be affected by
other elements in the economy result in a dollar distribution of "other income" by county which is closely
correlated to the distribution of population.

INCOME CHANGES IN KENTUCKY

Total income payments to individuals in Kentucky
from 1929 to 1952 have increased more than 240 per
cent--from $964,000,000 to $3,311,000,000.[4] The
changes in Kentucky per capita income since 1929 reflect, perhaps better than does total income, the economic growth of the state. From 1929 to 1952 the per
capita income in Kentucky rose from $371 to $1,135,
reaching a low of $198 in 1932. This rise of 206 per
cent contrasts with the increase in the national per
capita income of only 141 per cent. Kentucky per capita

Table 6
PER CAPITA INCOME IN THE UNITED STATES
AND KENTUCKY, 1929-1952

| Year | Current Dollars | | Constant Dollars[a] | | Kentucky as a percentage of United States |
	United States	Kentucky	United States	Kentucky	
1929	$ 680	$ 371	$555	$303	55
1930	596	303	499	254	51
1931	500	256	460	236	51
1932	380	198	389	203	52
1933	368	199	398	215	54
1934	420	234	439	245	56
1935	460	260	469	265	57
1936	531	307	536	310	58
1937	561	325	546	316	58
1938	509	283	505	281	56
1939	539	297	542	299	55
1940	575	309	574	308	54
1941	693	374	659	356	54
1942	876	487	752	418	56
1943	1,059	627	857	507	59
1944	1,160	704	924	561	61
1945	1,191	760	928	592	64
1946	1,211	778	869	559	64
1947	1,294	821	813	516	63
1948	1,383	912	808	533	66
1949	1,325	867	784	513	65
1950	1,439	917	841	536	64
1951	1,581	1,058	852	570	67
1952	1,639	1,135	864	598	69

Source: Graham, "State Income Payments in 1952," 13.

[a]Current dollars are adjusted to constant dollars by the Consumer Price Index (1935-1939 = 100), prepared by the Bureau of Labor Statistics, U.S. Department of Labor.

income increased from 55 per cent of the national figure in 1929 to 69 per cent in 1952, with the lowest, 51 per cent, in 1930 and 1931. The per capita incomes of the nation and Kentucky are presented in Table 6,

Chart B
PER CAPITA INCOME IN THE UNITED STATES AND KENTUCKY, 1929–1952

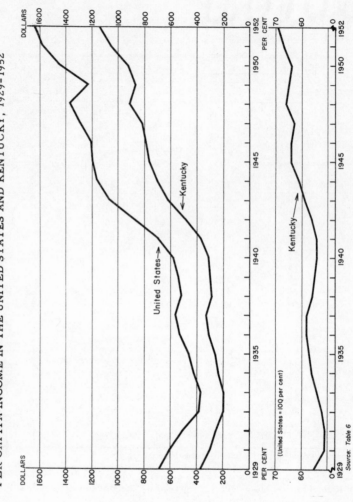

Source: Table 6

both in current dollars and constant dollars (dollars of approximately constant value). The increase in Kentucky per capita income in constant dollars from $303 in 1929 to $598 in 1952, after reaching a low of $203 in 1932, indicates the absolute growth, or growth in terms of purchasing power.

Table 7
RATIO OF THE INDEX OF PRICES RECEIVED TO THE INDEX OF PRICES PAID BY FARMERS IN THE UNITED STATES, 1929-1952

Year	Parity Index	Year	Parity Index
1929	92	1941	93
1930	83	1942	105
1931	67	1943	113
1932	58	1944	108
1933	64	1945	109
1934	75	1946	113
1935	88	1947	115
1936	92	1948	110
1937	93	1949	100
1938	78	1950	100
1939	77	1951	107
1940	81	1952	100

Source: U.S. Department of Agriculture, Bureau of Agricultural Economics.

Note: The record high came in October, 1946, when the parity index reached 122.

Chart B illustrates graphically the extent to which the rate of increase in Kentucky per capita income has exceeded the rate of increase in the national per capita income. The marked tendency toward the long-run convergence of the two per capita income amounts is evident.

There are many causes for this trend toward the equalization of per capita incomes. In part it is because the prices received by farmers have increased more than the prices paid by farmers. This factor

would have more influence on per capita income in
Kentucky than in the nation because of the greater percentage of total income derived from agriculture. Table 7 shows the ratio between prices paid and prices
received by farmers since 1929.

The great difference in this ratio over the years
is, for the most part, due to the fluctuations in the
prices received and the relative stability in the prices
paid.

No source of employment and wage data for the years
prior to 1938 compares favorably with the reliability
of unemployment compensation data that have been
available since that time. In 1938 Kentucky per capita income was 56 per cent of the national figure as
compared to 55 per cent in 1929. Not until 1943 did
Kentucky surpass the 1938 percentage; and for this
reason, and because of the lack of comparable data
for the years prior to 1938, the unemployment compensation commission data are the basis of the following analysis showing how changes in average annual
wage and the degree of industrialization may affect
per capita income.

An idea of the amount of industrialization that has
taken place in Kentucky relative to the nation during
the period 1940 to 1950 can best be realized if it is
measured in terms of employment. In Table 8 the
covered employment in 1940 and 1950 for both the nation and Kentucky is shown as a percentage of total
population.

Percentagewise, Kentucky covered employment is
still considerably less than for the country as a whole;
but from 1940 to 1950 the number of persons engaged
in covered employment increased by nearly 30 per cent,
whereas the increase for the nation was only about 20
per cent. Most of the relative gain in covered employ-

ment in Kentucky has taken place since 1945. This was the same year that Kentucky per capita income climbed to 64 per cent of the national per capita income and, as shown in Table 9, a year when total covered wages continued to advance in Kentucky while they declined in the country as a whole.

Table 8
COVERED EMPLOYMENT AS A PERCENTAGE OF TOTAL
POPULATION IN THE UNITED STATES AND KENTUCKY,
1940 AND 1950

Year	United States	Kentucky
1940	17. 54	9. 34
1950	21. 82	13. 29

Sources: Computed from United States Census of Population: 1950, Vol. II, Part 1, Chap. B, 106; U.S. Department of Labor, "1947 Employment and Wages," Table 3b, and "1950 Average Employment and Total Wages," Table 3b.

No account is taken in Table 9 of the different rates of population growth, and this tends to show Kentucky in a poorer light than if they were incorporated in the index numbers. But the better than average gains made in Kentucky in spite of a lower rate of population growth is a further indication of Kentucky's improved standing as an industrial state. To be considered along with the increase in total covered income, however, is the relative increase in the average wage of covered employees. From 1938 to 1952 the average annual wage of covered employees in Kentucky rose from 80.1 per cent of the national average to 89.9 per cent, as shown in Table 10.

It is extremely difficult to determine with any reasonable degree of exactness the influence of each of the various factors mentioned on the relative increase in Kentucky per capita income. All have played an

Table 9
INDEXES OF TOTAL WAGES EARNED IN COVERED EMPLOYMENT
IN THE UNITED STATES AND KENTUCKY, 1938-1952
(1938 = 100)

Year	Index of Total Covered Wages	
	United States	Kentucky
1938	100	100
1939	111	108
1940	124	121
1941	161	152
1942	209	192
1943	252	220
1944	264	241
1945	254	243
1946	280	272
1947	331	337
1948	367	390
1949	358	375
1950	394	421
1951	453	497
1952	488	552

Sources: Tables 9 and 10 are computed from U.S. Department of Labor, "1947 Employment and Wages," Tables 3a and 3b and "1952 Average Employment and Total Wages," Tables 3a and 3b.

Table 10
AVERAGE ANNUAL WAGES OF COVERED WORKERS IN KENTUCKY
AS A PERCENTAGE OF THE UNITED STATES AVERAGE,
1938-1952

Year	Percentage	Year	Percentage
1938	80. 1	1946	84. 8
1939	81. 4	1947	86. 5
1940	81. 4	1948	86. 6
1941	81. 4	1949	85. 0
1942	79. 8	1950	86. 7
1943	80. 1	1951	88. 1
1944	82. 8	1952	89. 9
1945	82. 8		

important part, but it should not be assumed that there have been no other causes. Some of the other possible reasons why Kentucky has had an increase in per capita income greater percentagewise than the United States may be federal spending policy, increased mechanization on the farms, the greater than average increase in livestock and tobacco prices relative to other farm products (the major sources of cash income to the farmers of Kentucky), the shift from crop to livestock farming, migration of people to the centers of industry within the state, the policies of the state and local governments affecting industrialization, and possibly a greater than average increase in demand for the natural resources of the state.[5]

THE DIFFERENCE IN PER CAPITA INCOME BETWEEN THE UNITED STATES AND KENTUCKY IN 1950

Percentagewise the difference between the per capita incomes of Kentucky and the United States is growing smaller. But nevertheless it is still large and the following analyses are presented as a means of pointing up the origins of this difference. This section is not intended to be a study of cause and effect. There is, for example, no analysis of why the labor force is a smaller percentage of total population in Kentucky than in the nation and no attempt is made to explain the causes of differences in average wages. Primarily the analyses are centered around particular types of income, with variations which show such differences as may result from variations in the distribution of income by type and other factors. It is particularly important to note that the income of farm

proprietors from farm operations adds more to the
per capita income of Kentucky than to the national
figure; but that one factor leading to a lower per capita
income in Kentucky is the larger number of farm
operators in the state relative to the total work force
than in the nation as a whole.

Industry-Mix, Average Wages, and Per Capita Income[6]

Kentucky per capita income, as reported by the
Department of Commerce, was $917 in 1950. Per
capita income, after adjustments for interstate employee commuting, was $932. About 60 per cent of
the total was income from wages and salaries, somewhat less than the national figure of 65 per cent. This
analysis, however, is devoted wholly to the type of
industry and average wage. The percentage of total
income represented by wage and salaries is not considered even though the amount of each type of income
received in any economy is an important factor in explaining per capita income level.[7]

In the first part of this analysis only the wages and
salaries of employees covered by the state unemployment insurance laws will be considered. Covered
wages and salaries in Kentucky in 1950 amounted to
65 per cent of all wages and salaries earned in the
state.[8] For the nation as a whole, covered wages and
salaries were 72 per cent of the total.[9]

If all the workers covered by the Kentucky Unemployment Insurance law in 1950 had received annual
wages equal to the average for all workers covered
by unemployment compensation laws in the nation, average covered income in Kentucky would have been

about $417 per year higher for the average worker
and Kentucky per capita income about $55 higher.
Covered wages and salaries in Kentucky, if employees had been paid at the national average compensation rate, would have been $1,277,100,000 or, as shown
in Table 11, $163,200,000 more than they actually
were. This difference divided by the state's population in 1950 is $55. The problem here is to determine

Table 11
THE EFFECT OF COVERED WAGES ON INCOME PAYMENTS
TO INDIVIDUALS IN KENTUCKY, 1950

	Average Annual Covered Wage	Average Covered Employment in Kentucky	Col. 1 X Col. 2 (millions)
United States	$3,136		$1,227.1
Kentucky	2,719	391,284	1,063.9
Difference in Column 3			$ 163.2

Sources: Tables 11 to 15 are computed from unpublished data on
income and average employment, Kentucky Department of Economic
Security; and U.S. Department of Labor, "1950 Average Employment
and Total Wages," Table 3.

whether this $55 per capita is the result of differences
in industry-mix (composition of industry in terms of
number of workers and average wage), differences in
average annual wages in the particular industries, or
both.

Shown in Table 12 are the average annual wages
in covered employment in the United States and Kentucky by major industry group. Also shown is the
percentage distribution of covered employment. Covered wages and salaries in agriculture and miscellaneous industries are omitted because they comprise such
a small percentage of the total. There are considerable

differences in the average wage by industry between
the United States and Kentucky, and in each instance
the Kentucky average wage is lower. But a dissimilar
industrial makeup is also apparent, and one must take
account of both average wages and type of industry
in order to determine the net effect of covered employment on per capita income.

Table 12
AVERAGE WAGE AND PERCENTAGE OF TOTAL COVERED
EMPLOYMENT BY MAJOR INDUSTRY IN THE UNITED
STATES AND KENTUCKY, 1950

Industry	Percentage Distribu- tion of Employment		Annual Average Wage	
	U.S.	Kentucky	U.S.	Kentucky
All covered industries[a]	100.0	100.0	$3,136	$2,719
Mining	2.7	15.6	$3,471	$2,911
Construction	6.3	6.3	3,496	2,972
Manufacturing	44.9	35.3	3,313	2,933
Public utilities and transportation	7.6	7.0	3,273	2,862
Trade	24.9	24.8	2,867	2,384
Finance	4.7	3.2	3,201	2,843
Service	8.6	7.5	2,483	2,037

[a]Includes a small amount of covered wages and salaries in agriculture and miscellaneous industries.

As stated before, the term industry-mix is used to
denote the composition of industrial activity in terms
of number of workers by industry and average wage.
To determine whether or not the industry-mix in Kentucky is favorable or unfavorable in relation to the
industry-mix of the United States as a whole, the number of covered workers by industry in Kentucky and
the average annual wage in the nation must be the
standards. If, for example, all the covered employ-

ment in Kentucky were in mining, manufacturing, public utilities and transportation, or finance, or any combination of these, the results would be a favorable industry-mix because all of these industries have a higher average country-wide wage than all covered

Table 13
INDUSTRY-MIX BY MAJOR INDUSTRY GROUP
IN KENTUCKY, 1950

Industry	(1) Average Covered Employment in Kentucky	(2) Average Annual Wage in the United States	(3) Col. 1 X Col. 2 (thousands)
All covered industry	391,284	$3,136	$1,227,067[a]
Mining	61,049	$3,471	$ 211,901
Construction	24,747	3,496	86,515
Manufacturing	138,120	3,313	457,592
Public utilities and transportation	27,446	3,273	89,831
Trade	96,855	2,867	277,683
Finance	12,673	3,201	40,566
Service	29,452	2,483	73,129
Total Column 3			$1,239,232[a]

[a]Includes a small amount of covered wages and salaries in agriculture and miscellaneous industries.

industries for the nation combined. Similarly, if all the covered employment in Kentucky were in trade and service, the industry-mix would be unfavorable. Differences in wage rates within the state do not enter into these computations. In Table 13 the industry-mix for Kentucky is computed. The average covered employment in the state is multiplied by the average covered wage in the nation for all covered employment and for each of the major industry groups separately. The sum of the products for the major in-

dustry groups is greater than the product of total
covered employment and the average covered wage in
the nation. Kentucky, therefore, has a differentially
favorable industry-mix of 1 per cent.

The amount of favorable industry-mix in the covered
industries in Kentucky can be measured by the following method: Subtract the product of all covered employment in Kentucky and average covered wage in the
United States from the total of column 3 and divide
by the former ($1,239,232,000 minus $1,227,067,000
divided by $1,227,067,000). The favorable industry-
mix indicates that Kentucky has relatively more high
wage industries than the nation; and this can readily
be confirmed by referring again to Table 12. The
three industries with the highest average wage are
mining, construction, and manufacturing. In these
three groups Kentucky has 57.2 per cent of all covered employment, whereas the whole country has
only 53.9 per cent in the same three industries. This,
along with the average annual wages in the nation,
accounts for the favorable industry-mix in Kentucky.

The analysis, however, should be carried further.
In the foregoing discussion all covered employment
was taken as a unit with major industries as subgroups. Another and probably better method of analysis
would be to inspect each of these major industry groups
separately. How much of the $380 difference in average
wages in manufacturing, for example, can be accounted
for by differences in wages and how much by differences
in the type of manufacturing? To find the answer manufacturing must be broken down into type of activity--
machinery, chemicals, tobacco, etc.--and analyzed in
the same way covered employment as a whole has been
examined. And so with all other major industries. For
illustration an analysis of the industry-mix in trade

is shown in Table 14 for employment covered by unemployment insurance.

Analysis of each of the seven major industries in

Table 14
COMPUTING THE INDUSTRY-MIX IN TRADE FOR KENTUCKY, 1950

Industry	(1) Average Covered Employment in Kentucky	(2) Average Annual Wage in the United States	(3) Col. 1 X Col. 2 (thousands)
All trade	96,855	$2,867	$277,683
Full-service and limited function wholesalers	14,889	$3,634	$ 54,107
Other wholesale distributors	9,499	3,976	37,768
Wholesale and retail trade combined, n.e.c.	5,365	3,306	17,737
Retail general merchandise	15,363	2,129	32,708
Retail food and liquor store	10,044	2,626	26,376
Retail automotive	9,885	3,705	36,624
Retail apparel and accessories	5,378	3,423	13,031
Retail trade, n.e.c.	13,094	2,716	35,563
Eating and drinking places	11,645	1,768	20,588
Retail filling stations	1,693	2,321	3,929
Total Column 3[a]			$278,431

[a]Since the total of column 3 is greater than the product of all covered employment in trade and average annual wage for the nation there is a favorable industry-mix in trade in Kentucky of 0.3 per cent.

a similar manner reveals that there is a favorable industry-mix in trade, finance, construction, and public utilities and transportation, and an unfavorable industry-mix in mining, manufacturing, and service. Column 5 in Table 15 shows the industry-

Table 15
DIFFERENCES IN COVERED ANNUAL WAGES BY MAJOR
INDUSTRY COMPONENT IN KENTUCKY, 1950

Industry	(1) Average Covered Employment in Kentucky	(2) Total Wages for Year (thousands)	(3) Amount Computed from National Average (thousands)	(4) Amount Computed from Industry-Mix (thousands)	(5) Percentage Difference Attributable to Industry-Mix	(6) Percentage Difference Attributable to Average Wages
All covered industry[a]	391,284	$1,063,887	$1,227,067	$1,239,232	1.0	-14.1
Mining	61,049	$ 177,688	$ 211,901	$ 202,711	-4.3	-12.3
Construction	24,747	73,549	86,515	86,956	0.5	-15.4
Manufacturing	138,120	405,093	457,592	435,487	-4.8	- 7.0
Public utilities and transportation	27,446	78,550	89,831	90,238	0.5	-13.0
Trade	96,855	231,354	277,683	278,431	0.3	-16.9
Finance	12,673	36,019	40,566	40,596	0.1	-11.3
Service	29,452	59,992	73,129	70,141	-4.1	-14.5

[a] Covered wages and employment in agriculture and miscellaneous are included in the totals.

Column 1, average employment, and column 2, total wages, are from unpublished data on income and average employment, Kentucky Department of Economic Security.

Column 3 is the product of average employment and average national wage in Table 11.

Column 4 shows amounts computed from the industry-mix in each component.

Column 5 is column 4 minus column 3 expressed as a percentage of column 3.

Column 6 is column 2 minus column 4 expressed as a percentage of column 4.

mix differentials for each of the major industry groups.

It was pointed out earlier that per capita income in Kentucky would be about $55 greater if all employees working in covered employment were compensated at the average wage for all covered employees in the nation. In spite of the fact that Kentucky, in total covered employment, has a favorable industry-mix--

Table 16
DIFFERENCES IN INCOME ATTRIBUTABLE TO
INDUSTRY-MIX IN KENTUCKY, 1950

Industry	Difference in Amounts Computed from National Average Wage and Covered Employment in Kentucky[a] (thousands)
Mining	$ - 9,190
Construction	441
Manufacturing	-22,105
Public utilities and transportation	407
Trade	748
Finance	30
Service	- 2,988
Total	$ - 32,657

[a]Column 3 subtracted from column 4, Table 15.

a relatively large percentage of workers in industries that pay the highest annual wage--the unfavorable industry-mix in mining, manufacturing, and service results in a net negative effect on average annual wages. This total negative effect--the total of column 3 subtracted from the total of column 4 (Table 15)--is $32,700,000. In Table 16 the net contribution of each major industry group to this total amount attributable to the industry-mix difference is shown.

The per capita effect of the unfavorable industry-mix in mining, manufacturing, and service, which is only partly offset by the favorable industry-mix in the other four groups, can now be easily calculated. Dividing $32,657,000 by the population of Kentucky, an estimate of the effect of industry-mix on Kentucky's per capita income is obtained. This amount, $11, is about 20 per cent of the total difference of $55 that is caused by lower wages and industry-mix combined. However, the relative effect on per capita income of average annual wages in the major industry groups is different from the effect of industry-mix. Whereas manufacturing has the most unfavorable industry-mix of the major industries, the average annual wage in this industry is nearer the national average, percentagewise, than the average wage in any other industry.

From this analysis it can be concluded with reasonable certainty that differences in wages are about four times as important as differences in industry-mix in accounting for the lower than average yearly income per employee in covered industries in Kentucky. Covered wages and salaries, however, amount to only about 65 per cent of all wages and salaries earned in the state. In order to project the analysis to cover all wage earners in the state and to measure the impact of all wage and salary incomes on per capita income, the earnings of noncovered workers must be included. The assumption may be made that noncovered employees, whose wage and salary income was $581,000,000 in 1950, are paid below the country-wide average to the same extent as covered employees. In that event they would have received 15.3 per cent more if they had been paid at the national average for their efforts. It may be assumed, too, that about 20 per cent of this wage differential is a result of an unfavorable industry-mix, while 80 per cent is the result of lower than average wages. These assumptions are subject to some error, but too little data are available for precise cal-

culations. This $581,000,000 in noncovered wages
and salaries, therefore, is $88,900,000 less than it
would be if Kentucky workers received wages equal to
the average for the nation. On a per capita basis this
amounts to $30. The net difference in per capita in-
come between the United States as a whole and Kentucky as a result of industry-mix and wage rates,
then, is $85. If the industry-mix and wage rate per-
centages (20 per cent and 80 per cent respectively)
are applied to this difference we can conclude that
Kentucky per capita income is lower than the national
per capita income by $17 as a result of an unfavorable
industry-mix and by $68 because of differences in av-
erage annual wages in the same industries.

Proprietors' Income in Agriculture and
Per Capita Income

It is not at all unusual to hear Kentucky referred
to as an agricultural state. But in 1950 the net income
of agricultural proprietors from farm operations was
only $272,100,000, [10] that is, 10.1 per cent of total
state income payments to individuals. This income
was earned by 218,476 farm operators, [11] an average
of $1,245 each. For the same year, in the country as
a whole, 5,382,134 farm operators [12] had a net income
from agricultural operations of $12,416,000,000, [13]
an average of $2,307 per operator. If each farmer in
Kentucky had profited from his operations on a level
with the average farmer in the country as a whole the
net farm income for the state in 1950 would have been
$504,000,000, and per capita income would have been
$79 greater. [14]
This general view of the comparative economic

status of United States farmers and Kentucky farmers, which shows an extreme difference in the average yearly income of the two groups, raises questions related to cause. No effort will be made here
to analyze the problem in detail; net productivity per
farm acre and the difference in average farm size
will be the only considerations. The relative importance of these two factors is clearly portrayed in Ta-

Table 17
A COMPARISON OF FARMS IN THE UNITED STATES AND
KENTUCKY BY NET RETURN PER ACRE AND BY SIZE,
1950

	Net Income from Farm Operations (millions)	Number of Acres in Farms	Average Net Return per Farm Acre	Average Farm Size
United States	$12,416.0	1,158,564,600	$10.72	215.3
Kentucky	272.1	19,441,774	14.00	89.0

Sources: Computed from unpublished data on income payments to
individuals by source, Office of Business Economics, U.S. Department of Commerce; United States Census of Agriculture: 1950, Vol. V,
Part 8, Table 1; and ibid., Vol. I, Part 19, State Table 1.

ble 17. It is not the author's contention, however,
that the many factors which lie behind these two aspects under consideration, such as soil fertility, degree of mechanization, and social heritage, are unimportant.

Even though the net return per acre in 1950 was
greater in Kentucky than it was for the country as a
whole by $3.28, the much smaller average farm size
in Kentucky more than outweighs this advantage. The
average farm in the United States is more than twice
as large as the average farm in the state. In this
connection it might be well to point out that the average

size of farm in both the nation and the state is growing. The rates of increase, however, are not the
same. From 1940 to 1950 the average farm in Kentucky changed in size from 80 acres to 89 acres, an
increase of 11 per cent. [15] During the same period
the average farm for the nation as a whole increased
from 174 acres to 215 acres, a gain of 24 per cent. [16]
This substantial difference in growth rates, if it is
an indication of future farm size differences, should,
perhaps, be explored further. It may eventually cause
an even greater income differential between farm operators in Kentucky and in the nation as a whole unless the gap between net income per acre becomes
even greater.

Nonagricultural Proprietors' Income and Per Capita Income

The net income of proprietors engaged in nonagricultural activity in 1950 was $316,400,000 or 11.1 per
cent of all income payments to individuals in Kentucky
for that year. [17] On a per capita basis this is $107 to
Kentucky residents as compared to $161 for the nation
as a whole from this type of payment. The total amount
of this component that accrued to persons in the various classes of proprietary activity is shown in Table
18 on a per capita basis.

It must be kept in mind that proprietors' income
is exclusive of all corporate activity. It has also been
shown that in all industries the Kentucky average wage
is lower than the national average wage, and there is
some tendency in business activity for proprietors' income to follow the pattern of wages and salaries in
the same industry. [18] Such a proposition, however, is

rather tenuous and difficult to prove. But for proprietors' income in mining, transportation, and finance, in which contributions of proprietors' income
to per capita income in both the state and the country as a whole is rather small, the factor listed above
is considered as a satisfactory explanation of differ-

Table 18
CONTRIBUTIONS OF NONAGRICULTURAL PROPRIETORS'
INCOME TO THE TOTAL PER CAPITA INCOMES OF
THE UNITED STATES AND KENTUCKY, 1950

Class	United States	Kentucky
Mining	$ 2	$ 2
Manufacturing	10	3
Construction	21	5
Transportation	4	4
Wholesale trade	9	4
Retail trade	65	64
Finance	6	3
Service	44	23
Total	$161	$107

Source: Computed from unpublished data on income payments to
individuals by source, Office of Business Economics, U.S. Department of Commerce; and United States Census of Population: 1950,
Vol. II, Part 17, Chap. B, Table 12.
    Note: Because of rounding, the figures may not add to the totals.

ences when used in conjunction with the probability
that there may also be fewer proprietary firms relative to the population.
    The difference between the state and the nation in
dollar income per capita from proprietary manufacturing operations is rather extreme, though small, and
is suggestive of a dearth of small manufacturing industries in the state. Assuming most noncorporate
activity in manufacturing is concentrated in small
firms, Table 19 bears out this contention. Along with
the other factor mentioned above, plus an added em-

phasis on the small firm data, the difference in the
contribution to the per capita incomes from proprietors' income in manufacturing is largely explained.

It may be seen from Table 19 that there are fewer
than half the number of small manufacturing firms
relative to the population in Kentucky than there are
in the United States. A similar but less extreme
situation exists also in the construction industries.

Table 19
NUMBER OF FIRMS IN MANUFACTURING AND CONSTRUCTION
EMPLOYING FEWER THAN 20 PERSONS FOR EACH 1,000
PERSONS LIVING IN THE UNITED STATES AND IN
KENTUCKY, 1948

	Manufacturing	Construction
United States	1.246	1.326
Kentucky	0.620	0.763

Sources: Computed from United States Census of Population: 1950,
Vol. II, Part 1, Chap. B, Tables 34 and 59; U.S. Department of Commerce, "Business Establishments, Employment, and Taxable Payrolls,
by Industry Groups under Old-Age and Survivors Insurance Program,
1948," Part 1, 10 and 46.

To be coupled with the firm-size data in construction
is another important factor that may be interpreted as
a reason for the extreme difference in the contribution
of proprietary income in the construction industry to
the per capita incomes of Kentucky and the nation. In
1950 heavy construction in Kentucky accounted for 33.7
per cent[19] of total covered pay rolls in this industry
and in the country as a whole accounted for only 20.8
per cent.[20]   In the same year the covered pay rolls
in the state from special-trade contractors amounted
to 32.8 per cent[21] of all construction pay rolls and in
the nation 42.0 per cent.[22] The heavy construction
industry is composed mainly of large firms, and

special-trade construction is composed almost entirely of small firms. The firm-size data in Table 19 and
the pay roll data given above were, in all probability,
both important factors in determining the amount of
income per capita that was derived from proprietary
activity in construction.

The most important source of nonfarm proprietors' income, for both Kentucky and the United States,
is net income from trade, especially retail trade.
There is likewise considerable uniformity in the net
contribution from this source to per capita income in
the two areas. But in spite of the uniformity in retail
activity there is considerable disparity, percentagewise, in the net contributions to per capita incomes
from the wholesale trade sector. The ratios of proprietors in wholesale trade per 1,000 population in
1948 were 1.119 for the country as a whole and 0.657
for Kentucky. [23] This difference alone probably accounts for much of the disparity in per capita income
contributions from proprietary wholesale trade operations.

Next to retail trade, the service industries make
the largest contribution to state and national per
capita income payments from proprietary sources.
There is, however, considerable difference between
the per capita dollar amounts obtained from this
source (see Table 18). Much of this difference can
be attributed to the fact that there are fewer than two-
thirds the number of service establishments per 1,000
population in Kentucky than in the nation as a whole. [24]
Also the average Kentucky service establishment in
1948 did nearly 11 per cent less business than the
average for the nation. [25] Along with other reasons
mentioned above that apply to proprietors' income as
a whole, these two facts probably account for most of

the difference between state and national per capita
return from service proprietors' income.

But proprietors' income in service includes the income of professional self-employed--physicians, den-

Table 20
AVERAGE INCOME OF PHYSICIANS, DENTISTS, AND
LAWYERS BY REGION AND FOR KENTUCKY

Region	Physicians		Dentists		Lawyers
	Nonfederal Physicians Per 100,000 Civilian Population	Average Income	Number Per 100,000 Civilian Population	Average Income	Average Income
United States	121	$11,058	53	$6,912	$7,532
New England	151	9,442	65	5,891	6,981
Middle East	158	9,772	70	6,075	8,779
Southeast	83	11,159	28	7,117	6,566
Southwest	94	12,228	33	8,439	6,177
Central	118	12,012	59	6,673	7,040
Northwest	107	11,257	53	6,834	5,933
Kentucky	84	10,744	32	(NA)	5,190

Sources: Weinfeld, "Income of Physicians, 1929-49," 19 (data
shown are for 1949); "Income of Dentists, 1929-48," 13 (data shown
are for 1948); "Income of Lawyers, 1929-48," 23 (data shown are for
1947). Number of lawyers per 100,000 civilian population not available.

Note: (NA) denotes not available.

tists, lawyers, accountants, etc. --and not only the income of service establishments as classified in the
Census of Business. The physicians, dentists, and
lawyers in combination had a total income in Kentucky
in 1950 greater than that of all other service proprietors. It is evident, then, that state differences in the
average income of those engaged in these professions
may be important in a discussion of why nonfarm pro-

prietors' income in Kentucky, on a per capita basis,
is so low relative to the nation.

In Table 20 are shown the average net incomes for
physicians, dentists, and lawyers by region and for
physicians and lawyers in Kentucky. Although the average for Kentucky in these two categories is lower
than the national average as well as the regional, a
more important factor is the low number of physicians
and dentists per 100,000 population. These two factors, in combination, account for much of the difference between the national and Kentucky per capita incomes derived from proprietary activity in the service trades.

Property Income and Per Capita Income

It is quite likely that property income is distributed among a greater number of people than is any other income component. Everyone who carries life insurance, collects dividends on stock, draws interest
on a bank account or government bonds, or receives
rents or royalties shares in the net income from property. As shown in Table 21, however, there are tre-
mendous differences in the per capita income from
rents, dividends, and interest from state to state.

For the most part property income is the return
from wealth accumulated some time in the past. This
fact is suggested in Table 21. In the selected group
of states, those that have had a high per capita income
for the ten years prior to 1950 also have a high per
capita property income. [26] The percentage range between the lowest to the highest in per capita property
income in 1950 is much greater than for per capita

incomes in the ten previous years. This would indicate that the poorer the state, from the standpoint of
per capita income, the less it receives in property
income as a percentage of total income; or, to put it

Table 21
THE RATIO OF STATE TO NATIONAL PER CAPITA INCOME,
1940-1949 AVERAGE, AND OF STATE TO NATIONAL PER
CAPITA INCOME FROM PROPERTY, 1950, FOR
SELECTED STATES

State	Per Capita Income		Per Capita Property Income	
	Amount[a]	Percentage of U.S.	Amount[a]	Percentage of U.S.
United States	$1,086	100	$160	100
Illinois	$1,319	121	$214	134
Ohio	1,206	111	171	107
Indiana	1,085	100	125	78
Tennessee	713	66	77	48
Kentucky	644	61	87	54
Alabama	632	58	58	36
Mississippi	512	47	49	31

Sources: Computed from Statistical Abstract of the United States:
1951, 28; Graham, "State Income Payments in 1950," 20; Schwartz,
"State Income Payments in 1944," 17-18.

[a]Average total income divided by average population for ten years,
1940-1949.

another way, the percentage of total income that is
derived from property tends to get proportionately
larger as we go up the state per capita income scale
and proportionately smaller as we go down the income
scale. Savings and therefore the income derived from
savings--property income--is dependent upon the level of income. It is quite probable, then, that 1950
per capita income from property in Kentucky was $73
below the national figure because average income in

Kentucky has been consistently lower than in the nation. Personal savings are owned primarily by persons with large incomes. The property income of
counties (Table 42) may be compared with the distributions of income by size (Table 44) for verification
of this factor.

"Other Income" and Per Capita Income

As shown in Table 5 "other income" is made up
almost entirely of government transfer payments. At
the same time there are many different categories of
recipients--veterans, the unemployed, the retired,
the needy, and others. The federal government, as
in the case of most payments to veterans, railroad
workers, and social security beneficiaries, generally
has direct control over the amounts paid, and place
of residence is not a factor in determining the eligi-
bility of recipients. In some instances the state has
control over the disbursements even though the federal government may contribute to the program. Public assistance payments--aid to dependent children,
aid to the blind, and old age assistance payments--
are of this type. In other instances, for example,
state bonuses to veterans, the state or local governments have complete control and operate without federal aid.

As explained in the discussion of sources of income
there are many reasons for differences in "other income" per capita payments from state to state. Table
22 shows the per capita contribution of "other income,"
divided into groups according to degree of control exercised by the federal government.

The difference of $19 per capita in "other income"

between Kentucky and the nation comes in the categories where the federal government exercises only
partial or no control over the amount and size of payments. Differences are to be found in each type of
payment not subject to complete federal control; for
example, public assistance--$6 per capita; work-

Table 22
CONTRIBUTION OF "OTHER INCOME" PAYMENTS TO PER CAPITA
INCOME IN THE UNITED STATES AND KENTUCKY BY DEGREE
OF FEDERAL CONTROL, 1950

Degree of Federal Government Control	United States	Kentucky
Complete	$ 64	$64
Partial[a]	16	10
None[b]	21	8
Total	$101	$82

Sources: Computed from unpublished data on income payments to
individuals by source, Office of Business Economics, U.S. Department
of Commerce; and United States Census of Population: 1950, Vol. II,
Part 1, Chap. B, Table 34.

[a]State control over payments, but federal funds contributed through
grants-in-aid.

[b]Includes a small amount of industrial pensions--less than 1 per
cent of all "other income."

men's compensation--$3 per capita; unemployment
insurance benefits--$4 per capita; and state and local
government retirement payments--$3 per capita.

Other Factors and Per Capita
Income

The difference between Kentucky and national per
capita income in 1950, as estimated by the Department of Commerce, was $522. So far in the analysis

factors accounting for $310 of this difference have
been discussed. But three important items have yet
to be considered: (a) the difference in the ratio of
farm proprietors to private wage and salary earners,
(b) the difference in the size of the labor force as a
percentage of total population, and (c) the differences
that are the result of the residents of one state working in another.

An estimate of the effect on per capita income of
the different average returns from farm operations
for Kentucky farmers and for all farmers in the nation has been made. The difference in the average
earnings of employed persons has also received consideration in this attempt to explain the total difference in per capita income between the state and the
United States. But in neither analysis was the relative number of persons deriving income from these
two sources taken into account. For every 1,000 private wage and salary earners in the Kentucky labor
force in 1950 there were 289 farm proprietors,[27]
whereas on a national basis the ratio was 1,000 to 108.[28]
Because the purpose of this analysis is to determine
why Kentucky per capita income is lower than that of
the nation, and because the effects on per capita income of the different average earnings of the two
groups of income receivers under consideration have
already been computed, the computations here must
necessarily be made by using the national averages
for each group as the basis of measurement. If the
ratio of civilian wage earners in Kentucky to farm
proprietors were equal to that of the nation--1,000
to 108--and if the total number of persons in the two
groups remains constant--there would be an addition
to the wage and salary receiver group of 97,300 persons
and an equal deduction from the farm proprietor group.

This number multiplied by the difference in average income, $186, is equal to $18,100,000; this amount divided by total state population amounts to $6 per capita.

Even if every person in the labor force in Kentucky had had an income equal to the average for the nation in 1950, Kentucky per capita income would still be under the national figure by $161. In the United States 39.85 per cent of the total population in 1950 were in the labor force. [29] In Kentucky the labor force was only 34.41 per cent of the population. [30] Assuming there would be no difference in average earnings, Kentucky income would have been $475,000,000 greater in 1950 if 39.85 per cent, the national percentage, of the population had been employed.

The Department of Commerce in some instances makes adjustments for the income earned by individuals in states other than their state of residence, [31] but did not make an adjustment that affected the 1950 Kentucky income estimate. It is estimated that Kentucky total income has been understated by the Department of Commerce by $70,400,000 because interstate situs adjustments have not been included. [32] This amounts to $24 per capita.

Summary of Differences in the Per Capita Incomes of the United States and Kentucky

In Table 23 the various factors so far discussed are presented in summary form. In most instances no effort has been made to show causes for these differences. The per capita income of any state is the net result of cause and effect relationships that go far deeper into the socio-economic background of the state than this examination intends.

The percentage of total population in the labor force is more important than any other factor in explaining the difference between the Kentucky and na-

Table 23
A SUMMARY ANALYSIS OF THE DIFFERENCE BETWEEN THE
NATIONAL AND KENTUCKY PER CAPITA INCOMES, 1950

Factors	Amount of Difference
Industry-mix	$- 17
Average wage levels	- 68
Income per farm operator from farm operations	- 79
Nonagricultural proprietary activity	- 54
Income from property	- 73
Nonfederal portion of "other income"	- 19
Difference in the ratios of farm operators to private wage and salary workers	- 6
Percentage of population in the labor force	- 161
Interstate situs adjustments	- 15
Statistical discrepancy and other factors[a]	- 30
Total	$- 522

[a]Bureau of the Census data, as published in both the 1950 Census of Population and the 1950 Census of Agriculture have been used extensively in this analysis. The census enumeration dates (which may not be typical of the whole year), sampling methods, and differences of definition probably cause part of this unexplained difference.

tional per capita incomes in 1950. This element alone accounted for more than 30 per cent of the $522 differential. Income per farm operator from farm operations, income from property, and average wage levels together accounted for another 42 per cent--15 per cent, 14 per cent, and 13 per cent respectively. Absolute accuracy in an analysis of this sort is, of course, impossible, but there is no doubt that the amounts as stated are close approximations.

[1]Wardwell, Regional Trends in the United States Economy, 3.

[2]Underemployment is sometimes referred to as "concealed unemployment." Either term may be used when referring to employed persons who are qualified to hold more productive positions, or to regularly employed persons working less than full time.

[3]Even though Kentucky has not paid a bonus to veterans of World War II the Department of Commerce allocated a small amount to the state on the basis that Kentucky is the current residence of veterans who receive bonuses from other states.

[4]Graham, "State Income Payments in 1952," 12.

[5]See Wardwell, 31-37.

[6]Adapted from Johnson, "The Effects of Industry-Mix and Wage Rates on Per Capita Income in Kentucky." See also Hanna, "Contribution of Manufacturing Wages to Regional Differences in Per Capita Income"; and Wardwell, 31-37.

[7]Fulmer, "Factors Influencing State Per Capita Income Differentials," 259-78.

[8]Unpublished data on income and average employment, Kentucky Department of Economic Security.

[9]U.S. Department of Labor, "1950 Average Employment and Total Wages," Table 2.

[10]Unpublished data on income payments to individuals by source, Office of Business Economics, U.S. Department of Commerce

[11]United States Census of Agriculture: 1950, Vol. I, Part 19, State Table 1.

[12] Ibid. , Vol. V, Part 8, Table 1.

[13] Unpublished data, U.S. Department of Commerce.

[14] See also Ducoff and Hagood, Differentials in Productivity and in Farm Income of Agricultural Workers by Size of Enterprise and by Regions, 5.

[15] United States Census of Agriculture: 1950, Vol. I, Part 19, State Table 1.

[16] Ibid., Vol. V, Part 8, Table 1.

[17] Unpublished data, U.S. Department of Commerce.

[18] Copeland, Methods for Estimating Income Payments in Counties, 13.

[19] Unpublished data, Kentucky Department of Economic Security.

[20] "1950 Average Employment and Total Wages," Table 4a.

[21] Unpublished data, Kentucky Department of Economic Security.

[22] "1950 Average Employment and Total Wages," Table 4a.

[23] Computed from United States Census of Population: 1950, Vol. II, Part 1, Chap. B, Table 34; and United States Census of Business: 1948, Vol. V, Wholesale Trade, Area Statistics, 0. 02 and 16. 02

[24] Computed from United States Census of Population: 1950, Vol. II, Part 1, Chap. B, Table 34; and United States Census of Business: 1948, Vol. VII, Service Trades, Area Statistics, 3. 08.

[25] Ibid.

[26]It should be pointed out that even though the average income for only ten years was chosen as the basis
for comparison, there has been little change in the
ranking of the states in per capita income since 1929.
This is the earliest year for which comparable statistics are available.

[27]United States Census of Population: 1950, Vol.
II, Part 17, Chap. B, Table 29.

[28]Ibid. , Vol. II, Part 1, Chap. B, Table 53.

[29]United States Census of Population: 1950, Vol.
II, Part 1, Chap. B, Table 53.

[30]Ibid. , Vol. II, Part 19, Chap. B, Table 25.

[31]Graham, "State Income Payments in 1950," 20.

[32]A complete discussion of the procedure used in
estimating the interstate and intercounty situs adjustments will be found in Appendix 1.

CHAPTER III

Income in Kentucky
Distributed by County

THE METHOD used to estimate the total income of each county in the state may be described briefly: Each component of income in the state is distributed to the counties by an allocator based on the best available series of related data. The procedure developed by the Conference on the Measurement of County Income is used extensively in this study.[1] This method involves allocating to the counties each component of the four major income types--wages and salaries, proprietors' income, property income, and other income, and has the advantage of resulting not only in an estimate of total income for each county but also in an estimate of county income by type of payment. The allocators are derived from three major sources-- gross wages and salaries reported to the Kentucky Department of Economic Security, Bureau of the Census reports, and Kentucky income tax returns. These, however, are not the only sources of data. Pay roll and retirement statistics from all levels of government, other commercial and agricultural statistics, industrial directories, and direct correspondence are all important in providing suitable allocators.

Many of the allocators are based on a "county where earned" rather than on a "county of residence" series

of data. Because income payments to individuals implies income received by the residents of a particular
area, a series of situs adjustments are required to
reallocate the earnings of persons who do not reside
in the county where they are employed.

A detailed description of the allocation procedure
is presented in outline form in Appendix 1. In the
main it consists of the income components to be allocated; the allocators and their source; the weights
assigned to the county allocators, when used; and a
summary of the advantages and limitations of the allocators employed. Also included in Appendix 1 are
tables showing the total income payments by county
for the years 1939, 1947, 1950-1952, and county per
capita incomes in terms of both current dollars and
constant purchasing power dollars for the same years.
In other tables county income payments for 1952 are
distributed by type of payment, and county per capita
income payments for the above five years are shown
as a percentage of the national figure. Another table
in this section shows the net income per farm acre
from farm operations in each county for the same five
years.

In Table 24 a summary of income payments by county in 1950 is presented. Shown in this table are the
county totals for that year, county per capita incomes,
and a comparison of the per capita income of each with
the national figure.

The last column in Table 24 is based on total income payments by county and the total number of income receiving units (families and unrelated individuals) reported by the census;[2] and although the percentage difference between the highest and the lowest
county figures so measured is enormous, it is considerably less than the percentage difference between

Table 24
INCOME PAYMENTS TO INDIVIDUALS BY COUNTY, 1950

| | Total (thousands) | Per Capita | | Average for Families and Un-related Individuals[c] |
		Amount	Percentage of U.S. Per Capita	
UNITED STATES				
KENTUCKY				
Adair	$ 7,709	$ 438	30.4	$1,576
Allen	6,219	451	31.3	1,519
Anderson	7,623	849	59.0	2,850
Ballard	4,799	562	39.1	1,839
Barren	19,740	694	48.2	2,303
Bath	6,134	589	40.9	2,187
Bell	26,554	558	38.8	2,297
Boone	11,865	912	63.4	3,086
Bourbon	18,477	1,041	72.3	3,356
Boyd	60,937[a]	1,232[a]	85.8[a]	4,198
Boyle	19,744[a]	1,037[a]	72.3[a]	3,344
Bracken	6,738	800	55.6	2,612
Breathitt	8,788	440	30.6	1,984
Breckinridge	8,614	555	38.6	1,895
Bullitt	9,354	824	57.3	2,852
Butler	4,162	368	25.6	1,248
Caldwell	9,218	698	48.5	2,114
Calloway	13,805	685	47.6	1,947
Campbell	95,998	1,260	87.6	4,111
Carlisle	3,870	624	43.4	2,162
Carroll	7,221	848	58.9	2,645
Carter	11,544	512	35.6	2,128
Casey	7,239	415	28.8	1,678[b]
Christian	29,429[b]	816[b]	56.9[b]	2,798[b]
Clark	19,819	1,049	72.9	3,379
Clay	9,749	422	29.3	2,023
Clinton	4,414	416	28.9	1,685
Crittenden	5,583	516	35.9	1,858
Cumberland	4,262	458	31.8	1,688
Daviess	66,404	1,160	80.6	3,783
Edmonson	3,922	418	29.0	1,713
Elliott	3,085	435	30.2	1,928
Estill	8,162	556	38.6	2,134

Table 24--continued

	Total (thousands)	Per Capita		Average for Families and Un-related Individuals[c]
		Amount	Percentage of U.S. Per Capita	
Fayette	$134,748[a]	$1,413[a]	98.1[a]	$3,812
Fleming	8,559	716	49.8	2,529
Floyd	40,613	759	52.7	3,358
Franklin	28,592[a]	1,142[a]	79.4[a]	3,271
Fulton	11,804	864	60.0	2,838
Gallatin	2,468	622	43.2	2,083
Garrard	7,635	692	48.1	2,382
Grant	6,129	625	43.4	2,147
Graves	26,134	833	57.9	2,611
Grayson	8,459	496	34.5	1,786
Green	5,737	509	35.4	1,757
Greenup	16,123	648	45.0	2,471
Hancock	2,635	439	30.5	1,468
Hardin	23,378[b]	685[b]	47.6[b]	3,008[b]
Harlan	69,242	965	67.1	3,906
Harrison	11,748	855	59.4	2,751
Hart	9,081	593	41.2	2,100
Henderson	27,468	894	62.1	2,947
Henry	8,777	770	53.5	2,529
Hickman	4,281	550	38.2	1,857
Hopkins	41,150	1,060	73.7	3,508
Jackson	5,257	401	27.9	1,555
Jefferson	799,413[a]	1,667[a]	115.6[a]	5,001
Jessamine	9,628	773	53.7	2,140
Johnson	12,805	537	37.3	2,303
Kenton	147,904	1,419	98.6	4,405
Knott	6,667	328	22.8	1,618
Knox	11,710	385	26.8	1,604
LaRue	7,204	724	50.3	2,370
Laurel	12,078	468	32.5	1,928
Lawrence	6,266	435	30.2	1,731
Lee	4,085	467	32.5	1,795
Leslie	5,826	375	26.1	1,793
Letcher	26,147	662	46.0	2,861
Lewis	6,535	483	33.6	1,783

Table 24--continued

| | Total (thousands) | Per Capita | | Average for Families and Un-related Individuals[c] |
		Amount	Percentage of U.S. Per Capita	
Lincoln	$10,213	$ 547	38.0	$2,006
Livingston	4,260	593	41.2	2,130
Logan	13,661	612	42.5	2,266
Lyon	3,493[a]	607[a]	42.5[a]	2,073
McCracken	55,278	1,125	78.2	3,381
McCreary	7,629	458	31.8	2,111
McLean	4,849	484	33.6	1,813
Madison	26,200	840	58.4	2,410
Magoffin	4,576	331	23.0	1,493
Marion	12,402	721	50.1	2,642
Marshall	8,488	634	44.1	2,111
Martin	3,996	342	23.8	1,722
Mason	21,313	1,153	80.1	3,671
Meade	7,203	764	53.1	2,708
Menifee	1,802	376	26.1	1,653
Mercer	10,947	748	52.0	2,606
Metcalfe	5,081	516	35.9	1,805
Monroe	6,117	444	30.9	1,636
Montgomery	10,358	795	55.2	2,652
Morgan	6,529	479	33.3	1,975
Muhlenberg	21,456	660	45.9	2,424
Nelson	14,943	765	53.2	2,683
Nicholas	5,811	772	53.6	2,416
Ohio	11,329	544	37.8	1,824
Oldham	7,728[a]	854[a]	59.5[a]	2,726
Owen	6,659	683	47.5	2,261
Owsley	2,282	312	21.7	1,278
Pendleton	6,734	701	48.7	2,193
Perry	40,449	869	60.4	3,975
Pike	59,787	737	51.2	3,207
Powell	2,531	372	25.9	1,511
Pulaski	21,837	568	39.5	2,130
Robertson	2,280	791	55.0	2,492
Rockcastle	6,255	449	31.2	1,859
Rowan	7,678	604	42.0	2,118

Table 24--continued

| | Total (thousands) | Per Capita | | Average for Families and Un-related Individuals[c] |
		Amount	Percentage of U.S. Per Capita	
Russell	$ 6,059	$ 442	30.7	$1,782
Scott	13,554	895	62.2	2,557
Shelby	16,198[a]	912[a]	63.2[a]	3,127
Simpson	7,756	664	46.1	2,119
Spencer	4,698	763	53.0	2,553
Taylor	10,072	699	48.6	2,427
Todd	7,304	567	39.4	1,998
Trigg	5,202	537	37.3	1,885
Trimble	2,733	531	36.9	1,786
Union	10,410	699	49.6	2,371
Warren	36,441	852	59.2	2,601
Washington	9,341	731	50.8	2,797
Wayne	6,318	383	26.6	1,591
Webster	9,718	625	43.4	2,002
Whitley	18,620	583	40.5	2,242
Wolfe	3,195	420	29.2	1,751
Woodford	13,178	1,175	81.7	4,018

[a] Such institutional population as inmates of homes for delinquent or dependent children, homes and schools for the mentally or physically handicapped, places providing specialized medical care, homes for the aged, and federal and state prisons are excluded. As the inmates in the state prisons in Lyon and Oldham counties received certain wages, these payments are excluded.

[b] The military payroll has not been included in the designated counties for the years shown. Military payroll data are not readily obtainable, and military population data are confidential since the Korean conflict began. For many purposes comparability between counties is better maintained through exclusion of the payroll of military personnel living in military camps.

[c] Total families and unrelated individuals from United States Census of Population: 1950, Vol. II, Part 17, Chap. B, Table 45.

the highest and the lowest counties on the per capita
income scale. The lowest, in terms of income per
receiving unit, is Butler County. The figure for this
county is only 25.0 per cent of that for the highest--
Jefferson County. The most important factor, exclusive of per capita income, in determining county differences in this series is the percentage of total population in the labor force. These differences have been
adequately pointed up before. Not only is there some
tendency for the income range, percentagewise, between the lowest and highest counties to close up when
measured by census receiving units; but there is
also a tendency, quite pronounced, for counties to fall
in a different order on the income scale. Average
income to the families and unrelated individuals in
Floyd County, for example, is $3,358, thirteenth larg-
est in amount; on a per capita basis Floyd County
ranks fortieth. And while there are only two counties
with per capita incomes greater than that of Fayette,
this county ranks eighth when figured on a census receiving unit basis.

Two methods of analysis will be employed in exam-
ining the differences in county per capita incomes. The
first will be an analysis of county income payments
by type and source to point up the reasons for county
per capita income differences. The second will be an
analysis of relationships between county per capita incomes and other economic and social phenomena.

COUNTY AND NATIONAL PER CAPITA
INCOME DIFFERENCES IN 1950

This analysis of differences in county per capita
incomes will necessarily be quite similar to the dis-

cussion in Chapter II on why Kentucky per capita income differs from that of the nation. The range between the highest and lowest counties on the per capita income scale, as indicated in Table 24, is enormous--from a low of $312 in Owsley County to a high of $1,667 in Jefferson County. State per capita income, exclusive of Jefferson County, in 1950 was $801. Behind this, and all other county per capita income differences, are differences in agricultural productivity per acre, farm size, differences in industrial composition and average wages, differences in the size of the work force as a percentage of total population, differences in property ownership, etc. There will be no effort to explain why wages are high or low, or why farms are large or small; but the mere fact that these and other important social and economic phenomena are not analyzed should not render them unworthy of careful consideration--they fall outside the scope of this project.

Time and space will not permit a detailed analysis of all Kentucky counties in this section. And with very few exceptions it is impossible to identify particular counties with the detail necessary to make this analysis without disclosing confidential information. Jefferson County, the largest in the state from a population standpoint, will be completely examined. Other counties will be used in the analysis on a selective basis and identified whenever proper.

Industry-Mix, [3] Average Wages, and County Per Capita Income

In 1950 nearly 37 per cent of all the covered employees in the state worked in Jefferson County and

received 42 per cent of the wages and salaries paid to
workers in covered employment. [4] It is obvious, then,
that from the state data the economic picture of Jefferson County cannot be brought into focus. Net wage
and salary payments amounted to 71.4 per cent of all
individual income in the county in 1950, and about 70
per cent of this was earned in covered employment.
Table 25 shows the industry-mix and wage rate analysis for Jefferson County and the rest of the state.

In Jefferson County, as in Kentucky as a whole,
the percentage difference in average annual wages that
may be attributable to differences in industry-mix are
much smaller than the differences attributable to wage
rates. There is remarkable balance in Jefferson County industries, assuming the national industry-mix to
be perfect, even though the average annual wages,
with the exception of those paid in manufacturing and
public utilities and transportation, do not compare
favorably with the average annual wages for the nation. By using the same procedure as that used in
Chapter II to find the effect of industry-mix and average annual wages in covered employment on per capita
income, we find that Jefferson County per capita income would have been $2 higher if the industry-mix
were identical with that for the nation, and $17 higher
still if all covered employees had received annual wages
comparable to the national average for the industry
in which they were employed. Covered wages and
salaries were about 70 per cent of all wage and salary
income for the county in 1950. By using the same technique employed in Chapter II in the analysis of state
per capita income, per capita income in Jefferson
County would have been about $27 higher if there had
been no difference in industry-mix and wage rates
between the county and the nation.

The other half of Table 25 presents quite a different picture--a picture of less uniformity in industry-
mix and of wages that are well below the national average.   The combined effect of industry-mix and low
wage rates on the per capita income of Kentucky, exclusive of Jefferson County, amounts to about $117.
Of this amount, $23 may be attributed to industry-
mix and $94 to wage rates. If the industry-mix and
average annual wages of all workers, covered and noncovered, outside Jefferson County were on a par with
the nation, the 1950 per capita income in these 119
counties, as a group, would have been $918 instead
of $801.

To show the industry-mix and wage rate contrasts
between the counties of Kentucky, two other counties,
which we shall call "A" and "B," have been selected
for analysis and the data are presented in Table 26.
County "A" is one of Kentucky's many coal mining
counties and County "B" is a better than average agricultural county with some industrial development. In
all probability they are fairly representative of these
two types of county economic structure.

Revealed in Table 26 are further extremes in both
industry-mix and average wages. These extremes,
in one form or another, probably exist in most of the
state's counties. If we exclude mining from a comparison of the two counties, there is a marked simi-
larity in their wage rates and in both instances an industry-mix that is conducive to low incomes. It should
be added, however, that the per capita incomes of the
two counties are far apart--that of County "A," the
coal producing county, is well below the state figure,
while the per capita income of County "B" is considerably above.

County "A" is a prime example of a county with a

Table 25

DIFFERENCES IN COVERED ANNUAL WAGES BY MAJOR INDUSTRY COMPONENT IN JEFFERSON COUNTY AND IN ALL OTHER COUNTIES IN KENTUCKY, 1950

Industry	(1) Average Covered Employment in Kentucky	(2) Total Wages for Year (thousands)	(3) Amount Computed from National Average (thousands)	(4) Amount Computed from Industry-Mix (thousands)	(5) Percentage Difference Attributable to Industry-Mix	(6) Percentage Difference Attributable to Average Wages
Jefferson County[a]	144,464	$442,349	$453,039	$452,118	-0.2	- 2.2
Construction	7,682	$ 24,613	$ 26,856	$ 27,022	0.6	- 8.9
Manufacturing	69,025	231,099	228,680	226,354	-1.0	2.1
Public utilities and transportation	10,859	34,752	35,541	35,397	-0.4	- 1.8
Trade	37,458	103,119	107,392	108,829	1.3	- 5.2
Finance	7,002	20,164	22,413	22,741	1.5	-11.3
Service	12,051	27,237	29,923	29,426	-1.7	- 7.4
All other counties[b]	247,151	$622,759	$775,177	$788,263	1.7	-21.0
Mining[c]	61,049	$177,688	$211,901	$202,711	-4.3	-12.3
Construction	17,065	48,936	59,659	59,934	0.5	-18.4
Manufacturing	69,095	173,994	228,912	209,133	-8.6	-16.8
Public utilities and transportation	16,587	43,798	54,290	54,841	1.0	-20.3
Trade	59,397	128,235	170,291	169,602	-0.4	-24.4
Finance	5,671	15,855	18,153	17,855	-1.6	-11.2
Service	17,401	32,755	43,206	40,715	-5.8	-19.6

Sources: Tables 25 and 26 are computed from U.S. Department of Labor, "1950 Average Employment and Total Wages," Table 4; and unpublished data on income and average employment, Kentucky Department of Economic Security.

[a]Covered wages and employment in agriculture, mining, and miscellaneous industries are included in the Jefferson County totals and in the computations.

[b]Covered wages and employment in agriculture and miscellaneous industries are included in the "all other counties" totals and in the computations.

[c]Includes a small amount of mining in Jefferson County.

Column 1, average employment, and column 2, total wages, are from unpublished data on income and average employment, Kentucky Department of Economic Security.

Column 3 is the product of average employment and average national wage in Table 11.

Column 4 shows amounts computed from the industry-mix in each component.

Column 5 is column 4 minus column 3 expressed as a percentage of column 3.

Column 6 is column 2 minus column 4 expressed as a percentage of column 4.

Table 26
DIFFERENCES IN COVERED ANNUAL WAGES BY MAJOR INDUSTRY
COMPONENT IN TWO KENTUCKY COUNTIES, 1950

Industry	(1) Average Covered Employment in Kentucky	(2) Total Wages for Year (thousands)	(3) Amount Computed from National Average (thousands)	(4) Amount Computed from Industry-Mix (thousands)	(5) Percentage Difference Attributable to Industry-Mix	(6) Percentage Difference Attributable to Average Wages
County "A"	4,803	$13,868	$15,065	$16,250	7.9	-14.7
Mining	3,946	$12,157	$13,697	$13,092	-4.4	-7.1
Manufacturing	182	362	603	511	-15.3	-29.2
Trade	464	908	1,330	1,228	-7.7	-26.1
Service	100	153	248	222	-10.5	-31.1
All Other[a]	111	288	372	360	-3.2	-20.0
County "B"	2,914	$5,991	$9,135	$8,958	-1.9	-33.1
Construction	186	$466	$650	$657	1.1	-29.1
Manufacturing	967	1,776	3,204	2,592	-19.1	-31.5
Public utilities and transportation	269	684	880	883	0.0	-22.5
Trade	1,136	2,404	3,257	3,185	-2.2	-24.5
Service	258	386	641	576	-10.1	-33.0
All Other[b]	98	275	326	319	-2.1	-13.8

predominance of high wage industries (employment
in mining accounts for more than 80 per cent of all
covered employment) and therefore a favorable industry-mix. But in this same county when the industry-mix is computed for the separate major industrial classifications it is, in each instance, unfavorable. If counties "A" and "B" are at all typical,
industrially, of other Kentucky counties, they would
seem to indicate that the "rural county" industries
are not only low wage industries (unfavorable industry-mix), but that the wages in these industries are
low relative to the national average.

Proprietors' Income in Agriculture
and County Per Capita Income

It was pointed out in Chapter II that the average
farm operator in the United States made a net profit
of $2,307 from farm operations in 1950, and in the
same year the average farm operator in Kentucky
made a net profit of only $1,245. It has also been
shown that state per capita income would have been
$79 greater if Kentucky farmers had profited from
operations equally with all farmers in the nation. It
should be remembered that this analysis does not take
into account the number of farmers relative to total
population--only the relative productivity per farm
operator.

In this analysis four counties will be examined to
find how much, if at all, the productivity of farm operators affects county per capita income. The counties selected are from different parts of the state and
have quite different types of farming. Harrison County lies in the bluegrass area, is a large producer of

burley tobacco, and in 1950 had a net income per farm acre of $21.[5] Knott is an eastern Kentucky county, rather mountainous, grows virtually no tobacco, and had a net return per farm acre in 1950 of $6. Logan County in the southwestern part of the state has a more diversified type of agriculture than either of the two mentioned above. Average income per farm acre in 1950 was $13, just slightly below the state average. Jefferson County is highly urbanized and less than 1

Table 27
A COMPARISON OF THE NET PRODUCTIVITY OF THE AVERAGE FARM OPERATOR IN THE NATION TO THE AVERAGE FARM OPERATOR IN FOUR KENTUCKY COUNTIES, 1950

	Number of Farm Operators	Average Net Return Per Farm Operator
United States	5,382,134	$2,307
Harrison County	2,011	$2,090
Knott County	1,683	373
Logan County	3,052	1,413
Jefferson County	2,673	770

Sources: Computed from net income to farm proprietors from agricultural activity, and "Number of farm proprietors," United States Census of Agriculture: 1950, Vol. I, Part 19, County Table 1.

per cent of all income in the county in 1950 was derived from agriculture. The average net income per acre was $13, derived primarily from the sale of livestock and livestock products. Table 27 is a comparison of these four counties with the national average.

Table 27 shows the extreme differences in the average income of farm proprietors from agricultural operations that exist from one county to another. If the farmers in these four counties had profited from their operations equally with the average farmer for the nation, Harrison County income would have been

$437, 377 greater, Knott County income $3, 254, 681
greater, Logan County income $2, 727, 964 greater,
and Jefferson County income $4, 109, 611 greater. Di-
viding these amounts by the county populations the per
capita amounts are, in the same order, $32, $160,
$122, and $8. For the state as a whole, exclusive of

Table 28
A COMPARISON OF FARMS IN THE UNITED STATES AND IN
FOUR KENTUCKY COUNTIES BY NET RETURN PER ACRE
AND BY SIZE, 1950

	Net Farm Income (thousands)	Number of Acres in Farms (thousands)	Average Net Return per Farm Acre	Average Farm Size
United States	$12, 416, 000	1, 158, 566	$11	215. 3
Harrison County	$4, 202[a]	198	$21	98. 4
Knott County	628[a]	105	6	62. 5
Logan County	4, 313[a]	324	13	106. 0
Jefferson County	2, 057[a]	158	13	59. 1

Sources: Computed from unpublished data on income payments to individuals by source, Office of Business Economics, U.S. Department of
Commerce; United States Census of Agriculture: 1950, Vol. I, Chap.
19, County Table 1; and ibid., Vol. I, Chap. 1, Table 1.

[a]Computed by the author.

Jefferson County, the net effect on per capita income
of this factor is $93.

Using again the same procedure as that used in the
Kentucky per capita income analysis--a comparison
of farm productivity and farm size--it is possible to
see clearly why these differences exist. In Table 28
these comparisons are made.

From this table it will be noticed that the average
size farm in all four counties in the analysis is much
smaller than the average size farm for the nation, but
only in Knott County is the average return per acre

less than the national average. The average net return per farm acre, although greater than the national average in the other three counties, is more than
offset by the much smaller average farm size.

Nonagricultural Proprietors' Income and
County Per Capita Income

It has already been shown in Table 18 that nonagricultural proprietors' income for the country as a whole
was $161 per capita in 1950. The same year total income
in Jefferson County from this source was $75,972,000--
$157 per capita. These amounts are not much differ-
ent, only $4, but considering the state figures exclu-
sive of Jefferson County, the picture is not the same.
Per capita income from all sources of nonagricultural
proprietors' income for the state was $107 in 1950.
When the computations are made for the state, exclusive of Jefferson County, per capita return from this
source is only $94, or $67 less than the national average.

Property Income and County Per
Capita Income

Property income--income in the form of dividends,
interest, rents, and royalties--as explained in Chapter II, is largely dependent upon past incomes, or more
precisely, upon past savings. The per capita return
from property in 1950 was $160 for the nation and, by
using the same procedure, was estimated to be $207
per capita in Jefferson County. Jefferson County, in
this respect, compares favorably with the United States

but this component of income on a per capita basis
for the rest of Kentucky, in 1950, was only $63. This
pattern of income from property in Kentucky is to be
expected because of the great spread in per capita return from property between high and low income states
(see Table 20).

"Other Income" and County Per
Capita Income

Income payments per capita from "other income,"
as shown in Table 22, do not vary a great deal between
the state and the nation. The income per capita, on a
national basis, from this source in 1950 was $101. In
Jefferson County the per capita return from "other
income" was $104, and for the rest of the state, $78.
Reference to the sources of "other income" payments
(Table 5) may help explain why Jefferson County per
capita income of this type is so high relative to the
state amount ($82), and why it is slightly higher than
the national average. In most urban areas, especially those that are experiencing rather rapid growth,
there is a concentration of population between the ages
of 20 and 40 years. Veterans' payments, which are
a large part of "other income," went primarily to persons in this age group in 1950. In the industrial centers there are also more retired persons eligible to
receive private or government retirement benefits.
In Harrison, Knott, and Logan Counties, for example,
the average per capita returns from "other income"
in 1950 were $72, $68, and $59 respectively. These
counties have entirely different types of economy from
that in Jefferson County, and from observation only
would be expected to receive less per capita from

"other income" payments. The factors which result
in a high per capita income from "other income" payments in the urban counties, then, are relatively more
important in these counties than the factors which are
most important in many of the low income counties,
for example, public assistance payments.

Other Factors and County Per
Capita Income

Following the same procedural outline as is used
in the analysis of state per capita income there are
still three points to be considered: (a) the difference
in the ratio of farm proprietors to private wage and
salary earners, (b) the difference in the size of the
labor force as a percentage of total population, and
(c) the differences that are the result of the residents
of one county working in another.

As in the analysis of state per capita income the
employment figures for both of the groups (farm proprietors and wage and salary earners) to be considered here are taken from the same source, the 1950
Census of Population. The ratio for the nation of private wage and salary earners to farm proprietors was,
in Chapter II, calculated to be 1,000 to 108. In Jefferson County the 1950 ratio was 1,000 to 9, and again
using the national figures because the differences in
per capita income as a result of differences in average
farm income per farm operator have already been determined, Jefferson County would have 15,700 more
farmers with an average income $186 less than the
average private wage and salary earner. This would
be a total of $2,920,000 less income or $6 per capita.
Exclusive of Jefferson County the state ratio of farm

proprietors to private wage and salary workers is much greater than for the nation as a whole (1,000 to 240). If this ratio were equal to that of the nation (1,000 to 108) the income of Kentucky residents outside Jefferson County would be $19,500,000 greater-- $8 per capita.

The most important factor in the analysis of the difference between state and national per capita incomes is the difference in the size of the labor force as a percentage of total population. This is likewise an extremely important factor in the analysis of county differences in per capita income. In the United States there was 39.85 per cent of the total population in the labor force in 1950. In Jefferson County there was 41.17 per cent and in the rest of the state 33.08 per cent. If, in Jefferson County, in 1950 the ratio of labor force to total population had been 39.85 per cent the earned income would have been $19,023,000 less than it was or $39 per capita. If, in the rest of the state, on the other hand, the percentage of total population in the labor force had been equal to the national figure, income would have been $494,000,000 greater, $201 per capita. [6]

In Chapter II when the situs factor was taken into account in making the estimates of the relationship of the various factors considered to the total difference in state and national per capita income, the situs adjustment amount had not been added to the Kentucky total nor had it been included in the state per capita income figure. The county and state total and per capita incomes, as estimated in Chapter III, have been made with the situs adjustment worked in. An estimate of the differences in per capita income as a result of this factor, then, need not be made in this part of the present analysis. It cannot be overemphasized,

however, that accounting for the workers who reside
in one county and work in another is very important
in county income estimation when the estimates are
derived by employing the allocation procedure.

Summary of County Per Capita
Income Differences

In Table 29 the various factors discussed in the
preceding analysis are summarized. Assuming, with
references to Kentucky exclusive of Jefferson County,
the national per capita income to be a desirable goal,
and assuming further that the source distribution of
income in the United States to be a desirable standard,
it is possible from Table 29 to get an approximate idea
of where effort should be concentrated if this goal is
to be achieved. By going somewhat further it is also
within the realm of feasibility to get some idea of just
how difficult it would be to eliminate all of the $638
per capita differential. As for the state as a whole,
the most important factor is the percentage of total
population in the labor force. This element alone accounts for over 31 per cent of the total difference. The
other most important factors are per capita income
from property, average wage levels, and the income
per farm operator from farm operations which, in the
same order, account for 15. 2 per cent, 14. 7 per cent,
and 14. 6 per cent of the total difference.

Jefferson County, with a per capita income well
above the national figure, makes an interesting contrast with the remainder of the state. The item "statistical discrepancy and other factors" accounts for
more than half the total of all items that together show
why Jefferson County per capita income is above the

national level. The "other factors" part of this item
which by all odds is greater than the "statistical discrepancy" part, although not easily computed, maybe
readily explained. There is strong evidence that most

Table 29
A SUMMARY ANALYSIS OF THE DIFFERENCE BETWEEN THE PER
CAPITA INCOMES OF THE NATION AND JEFFERSON COUNTY
AND KENTUCKY EXCLUSIVE OF JEFFERSON COUNTY, 1950

| Factors | Amount of Difference | |
	Jefferson County	Remainder of Kentucky
Industry-mix	$- 3	$- 23
Average wage levels	- 24	- 94
Income per farm operator from farm operations	- 8	- 93
Nonagricultural proprietary activity	- 4	- 67
Income from property	47	- 97
"Other income" payments	3	- 23
Difference in the ratios of farm operators to civilian wage and salary workers	6	- 8
Percentage of population in the labor force	61	-198
Statistical discrepancy and other factors	133	- 35
Totals	$ 211[a]	$-638[a]

[a]The per capita incomes upon which this table is based are $1,650
for Jefferson County and $801 for the remainder of the state. These are
slightly lower than the final estimates because in these computations institutional population has not been deducted. By not deducting institutional population the per capita estimates for the nation, the state, and
Jefferson County are conceptually the same.

of this item should be included in "percentage of population in the labor force." Because all labor force and
population figures in the latter element are taken from
the 1950 Census of Population, and because there was
a considerable increase in employment soon after the
census enumeration dates, these data are not representative of Jefferson County for the entire year. Covered employment alone increased by 12,000 between

April 15, 1950, and the end of the year, an increase
of about 8. 7 per cent. [7] Assuming the bulk of "other
factors," then, to represent a dollar difference created by relative labor force size, the percentage of
population in the labor force is by far the most important element in explaining the difference between
Jefferson County per capita income and national per
capita income. The other factor that looms large in
this respect, as would be expected from earlier discussions on the subject, is income derived from property.

Even though the average income of farmers from
farm operations, on a per farmer basis, is ordinarily
an important determinant of per capita income, it is
not significant in Jefferson County because of the small
number of farmers relative to total population. Average wage levels appear to be the most important negative factor in Jefferson County even though, it will be
remembered, manufacturing wages and salaries in 1950
were above the national average.

RELATIONSHIPS BETWEEN COUNTY PER CAPITA INCOMES AND OTHER DATA

In the foregoing discussion the same technique used
to account for the difference between the per capita
incomes of the United States and Kentucky is used to
account for differences in the per capita incomes of
the nation and Jefferson County and the remainder of
the state. This technique could likewise be used to
account for the difference between the national per capita income and that of any, or all, of the counties.
In this part of the analysis there is no attempt to measure with exactness the influence of any of the factors

mentioned. Rather it is a discussion of generalities--
a discussion of factors usually associated with per
capita income levels. And frequently in studies of
income most of the factors that are discussed here
have not only been discussed along with levels of income but have been referred to as having a cause or
effect relationship on income levels.

Table 30 is a presentation of data commonly cited
as having causal relationships with levels of per capita income. The counties of the state have been divided
according to per capita income into four equal groups
of 30 each. This has been done for two reasons: (a) it
will simplify the analysis and make the points clear
and understandable, and (b) it will eliminate any dis-
tortion caused by single counties that may be out of
line with the general trend.

Although there is considerable difference in the
weighted per capita incomes of the first three groups,
the greatest difference in this respect is between the
third and fourth group. These 30 counties with a per
capita income of over $800 each have a weighted av-
erage per capita income of $1,283, but only three
counties in this group have per capita incomes that
exceed this amount. And well over 40 per cent of the
total income received by the residents of the counties
in this group went to a single county--Jefferson--
where per capita income in 1950 was $1,667.

The counties in Group IV not only enjoyed over two-
thirds of the total income but also have more than half
of the total state population. There seems to be a rather pronounced tendency in Kentucky for high income
levels to concentrate in the counties that have a high
urban population. There are 20 counties in the state
that have an urban population amounting to 36.8 per
cent or more of total population, the proportion for

the state as a whole. Sixteen of these counties are in
Group IV, and of the 15 counties that have a per capita
income greater than that of the entire state, only three
have a percentage of urban population below the state
figure.

From day-to-day observations and from data presented in many studies of income, there is a reasonable certainty that the per capita income of the nonwhite people of any given area is below that of the
white population of the same area. [8] However, the percentage of nonwhite population in Kentucky is much
greater in Group IV of Table 30 than it is in any other
group, and over eight times the percentage in Group
I. Does this prove, then, that other studies are wrong
in this important aspect, that a concentration of nonwhite population is conducive to high per capita income
rather than the reverse? Obviously not. These statistics show only that the nonwhite population is concentrated in some, or all, of the high per capita in-
some counties and nothing more.

The population per household may be important in
explaining the low per capita incomes in the counties
in Group I. Of the individual counties in this group
only eight have an average population per household
of fewer than four persons, while in Group IV only two
counties have an average of over four. The variations
in average household population are probably a partial
explanation of why the percentage of total population
in the civilian work force is lowest in the lowest per
capita income group.

The percentage of total population in the civilian
work force is one of the important factors in explaining per capita income levels. Primarily it is dependent upon the employment opportunities available to
women in urban areas and upon the age composition

Table 30

A COMPENDIUM OF RELATIONSHIPS BETWEEN PER CAPITA INCOMES
BY GROUPS OF COUNTIES AND OTHER DATA, 1950

	Counties Ranked According to Per Capita Income and Divided into Groups of Thirty			
	Group I	Group II	Group III	Group IV
Range of per capita incomes (dollars)	$312--$479	$483--$625	$634--$800	$811--$1,667
Per capita income (weighted)	$414	$558	$713	$1,283
Total income (millions of dollars)[a]	$171.4	$256.7	$405.9	$1,875.2
Total population[b]	414,166	459,940	569,602	1,462,078
Number of counties with urban population greater than 36.8 per cent[c]	0	1	3	16
Percentage of population nonwhite[d]	1.26%	4.07%	4.60%	10.31%
Population per household (not weighted)[e]	4.28%	3.68%	3.66%	3.49%
Percentage women are of the civilian labor force[b]	10.6 %	15.1 %	16.5 %	27.1 %
Percentage of total population in the civilian labor force[b]	27.4 %	31.0 %	30.7 %	38.3 %
Wages and salaries in manufacturing as a percentage of total income	2.4 %	5.9 %	5.7 %	20.7 %
Years of school completed, average for males 25 years old and over[f]	6.9 yrs.	7.7 yrs.	8.0 yrs.	8.4 yrs.
Percentage of total civilian labor force in agriculture[b]	52.0 %	43.3 %	34.8 %	11.4 %
Proprietors' income in agriculture per acre in farms[g]	$10	$12	$17	$17
Proprietors' income in agriculture as a percentage of total income	26.6 %	24.7 %	19.7 %	4.4 %

[a]Total income payments less the military pay in Hardin and Christian Counties and the pay to prisoners in state prisons.

[b]Total population less the military population of Hardin and Christian Counties and the inmates of state and federal institutions. Source: United States Census of Population: 1950, Vol. II, Part 17, Chap. B, Table 43.

[c]Ibid., Vol. I, Part 17, Chap. A, Table 5. Kentucky urban population in 1950 was 36.8 per cent of total population.

[d]Total nonwhite population less the nonwhite military population in Hardin and Christian Counties. United States Census of Population: 1950, Vol. II, Part 17, Chap. B, Table 44.

[e]Ibid., Table 12.

[f]Ibid., Table 42.

[g]Net income from farm operations divided by total acres of "Land in Farms," United States Census of Agriculture: 1950, Vol. I, Part 19, County Table 1.

of the population. [9] Table 30 shows the civilian labor
force in the highest per capita income counties to be
27. 1 per cent women and in the lowest per capita income counties to be only 10. 6 per cent women. In
Groups II and III the percentage of the civilian labor
force composed of women is 15. 1 per cent and 16. 5 per
cent respectively. Because the relative size of the
labor force seems to be an important factor in determining the level of per capita income, and because the
size of the labor force is largely dependent on the employment opportunities for women, there would appear
again to be a rather close relationship between a high
degree of urbanization and a high per capita income.
It is in the urbanized areas where women are afforded
job opportunities.

The amount of manufacturing activity is usually
considered a good index of relative per capita incomes.
Kentucky counties are no exception to this generalization. Of all the income received by the individuals
residing in the high income counties in 1950, more than
20 per cent was in the form of manufacturing wages
and salaries, but at the same time only 2. 4 per cent
of total income in Group I was derived from this source.
Income from this source in each of the other two per
capita income groups was, percentagewise, more than
double the amount in Group I but far below the Group
IV figure. Oddly enough, also, there was little difference in this component between the two middle groups
of counties, with Group II having slightly more on a
percentage basis. As important as this factor may be
in explaining per capita levels, it in no way accounts
for the difference of $155 between these two groups.
The same statement also applies to most of the factors discussed up to this point.

It will be noticed that there is a constant rise in

the average number of years of school completed by
the male population 25 years old and over from the
lowest to the highest per capita income group. Whether this is a cause of high income levels or a result
of high income levels is open to debate. In Group I
the male population over 25 years of age had completed an average of 8.0 years of school or more in only
two counties, while in 19 counties they had completed
an average of 7.0 years of school or less. In Group
II, 13 counties had an average of 8.0 years or more
and only three had an average of 7.0 years of school
or less. In Group III, 21 counties had an average of
8.0 years or more, and in Group IV only three counties had an average below the 8.0 year level.

There are three factors listed in Table 30 that have
to do with agricultural activity in the state. It is in
these three series where differences between Group
II and Group III show up best. There is considerable
difference, for example, in the percentage of the civilian labor force employed in agriculture among the
per capita income groups. The range is from 52.0
per cent in Group I to 11.4 per cent in Group IV. But
from the second to third groups we find a decline from
43.3 per cent to 34.8 per cent. In actual numbers
there is extremely little difference in this category
between groups. The number of persons engaged in
agricultural activity from the lowest to the highest per
capita income groups in that order were 58,983;
61,680; 60,920; and 64,013. In another series of agricultural data, the percentage of the total income represented by agricultural proprietors' income is shown.
The range here is from 26.6 per cent in Group I to
4.4 per cent in Group IV with a decline from 24.7 per
cent to 19.7 per cent from the second to third group.
As a means of adding to the fact that income in agri-

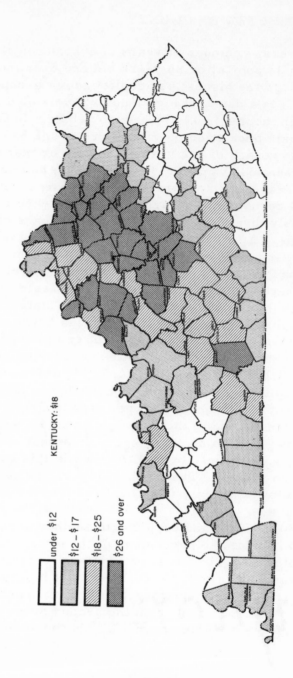

Chart C
NET INCOME PER FARM ACRE IN KENTUCKY COUNTIES, 1952

KENTUCKY: $18

under $12

$12 – $17

$18 – $25

$26 and over

culture is an important factor in determining per capita income levels, the average net income per farm acre in each per capita income group is shown. Here again there is an extreme difference from Group II to Group III, $12 per acre to $17 per acre, while from the lowest per capita income group to the highest the range is only slightly greater, from $10 per acre to $17 per acre. The data on net income per farm acre for all Kentucky counties is shown in Table 43, Appendix 1, and graphically in Chart C.

As stated before, Table 30 is a compendium of generalities which are frequently associated with per capita income levels as having causal relationships. But even though no claim has been made here that such a relationship does exist between the data shown and per capita income levels, the writer believes that all the factors discussed are of considerable importance. Another word of caution on the use of such data, however, may not be out of order. In an analysis of per capita income levels it is a dangerous practice to try to establish a cause and effect relationship from too little data. If, for example, the proverbial "Man from Mars" were shown the group per capita incomes and the series showing the percentage of nonwhite population by group he would immediately infer that the latter is a cause of high per capita income. Or if he were shown only the percentages derived from manufacturing wages and salaries or percentage of population in the civilian work force for Groups II and III only, his reactions would again, obviously, be incorrect.

---

[1]Copeland, Methods for Estimating Income Payments in Counties.

[2]United States Census of Population: 1950, Vol. II,

Part 17, Chap. B, Table 45. For a complete definition of "family" and "unrelated individual" see ibid., ix.

[3]See Chap. II for the definition of industry-mix.

[4]Unpublished data on income and average employment, Kentucky Department of Economic Security.

[5]Net agricultural proprietors' income (see Table 28), divided by "Number of Acres in Farms," United States Census of Agriculture: 1950, Vol. I, Part 19, County Table 1.

[6]These computations, of course, are based on national average earnings, because the effect of differences in average earnings was considered previously. If in Kentucky, or in Jefferson County, the percentage of all persons employed were the same as in the nation, and if each person received the average amount of earnings as each person in the national labor force, the per capita income from wages and salaries and proprietors' income would be equal.

[7]Unpublished data on income and average employment, Kentucky Department of Economic Security.

[8]See United States Census of Population: 1950, Vol. II, Part 17, Chap. B, Table 32a; and Lancaster, County Income Estimates for Seven Southeastern States, 57.

[9]The composition of the population according to age is, to a large degree, indicated by average family size.

CHAPTER IV

Income in Kentucky Distributed by Size

MOST distributions of income by size are made by using one of two important methods, or a combination of the two. The first, and most often employed, is the sampling method. The second may be referred to as the allocation method. Each procedure has its merits and its limitations. Before using any size distribution of incomes for any type of economic or social analysis the user should first thoroughly familiarize himself with the basic data from which the distribution was made, the assumptions that were necessarily utilized when the desired facts were not available, and the statistical procedure followed. Knowing these things the person who may use a size distribution of incomes for further research will be able to select the proper series, if more than one is available, and recognize the conceptual and statistical limitations of the series selected.

In this study no mention is made of cause and effect relationships; the concern is solely with the problems of definition and statistical procedure. The term "income," unless otherwise specified, is always used within the conceptual framework of the United States Department of Commerce definition of "income payments to individuals." State per capita incomes, as

published yearly in the August issue of the Survey of
Current Business, are based on this concept as are
the county total and per capita incomes as previously
estimated. One of the prime purposes of this study
is to provide state and county income distributions by
size based on this concept of income. The income receiving unit will be the individual; the total number of
recipients will be the total number of individuals with
income. This is in contrast to the 1950 census estimates for counties which break down the recipients
into two groups, families and unrelated individuals.

Income size distributions will not be made for each
county but for forty county groups (see Table 32). These
groups range in size of from one to ten counties each.
By combining counties that have but few high incomes
(over $10,000) into groups, it is possible to show the
incomes received over a greater range of income sizes
without having so few recipients in the highest income
class that the income of known persons would be revealed. Most of the county groups are based on per
capita income level; for example, the ten counties
with the lowest per capita incomes in 1950 comprise
County Group 1. [1] Although per capita income is the
primary consideration in grouping the counties, other
factors taken into account are type of industry, geographic location, and population.

THE PRACTICAL VALUE OF A SIZE
DISTRIBUTION OF INCOME

The practical value of any distribution of income
by size must necessarily depend upon the bases of the
distribution itself--the statistical data used, the many
necessary assumptions made where accurate data are

not available, the concept of income, the time period
covered, the recipient unit, and other factors. There
are many types of analysis that can be made from income distribution data, and for particular types of
analyses a series prepared in one manner will provide a better analytical tool than a distribution compiled by some other method. But it is not an unknown
circumstance to have the same size distribution of income offered as proof for diametrically opposed points
of view.[2] The practical value of a size distribution
as discussed here under four major headings--taxa-
tion, market analysis, economic theory, and general
well-being--is an attempt to put emphasis on certain
types of analysis for which this distribution is particularly suitable.

Taxation

Some of the uses in tax research for which an income size distribution is particularly suitable are as
a measure of fiscal capacity; as a measure of tax load,
debt load, and tax load projections; as a means of estimating incidence and effects of proposed tax legislation and similarly, as a basis upon which some tax
laws may be built; and as an analysis of federal-state
and state-local fiscal relationships. Among these suggested uses in the fields of tax administration and tax
policy there is considerable overlapping. Fiscal capacity, for example, has meaning and importance in itself, but its value in tax administration and tax policy
determination is immeasurably increased when employed in conjunction with other factors such as state-
local fiscal relationships. In one of the most intensive reports on state and local taxation the following
statement stands out as one of great importance. "The

committee further suggests that no future legislation
be enacted which would have the effect either of adding to the costs of local government or depleting local
tax revenues without first carefully analyzing the ex-
tra burden that such legislation would impose."[3]

There is a general feeling among most persons in-
terested in fiscal policy problems, and in tax programs
particularly, that some reliable measure of fiscal capacity is desirable.[4] But there is no unanimity among
these same persons as to how fiscal capacity should
be measured. Prior to the availability of income statistics it was common practice to use property tax
assessments as the measure. Income statistics, particularly a size distribution of income, may be used
to supplement the older methods or may be used alone.
If used alone there is always the problem of determining a level, perhaps a subsistence level, of income
below which no direct tax should be extracted. It could
be assumed, then, that all income above that particular level is a measure of the fiscal capacity of a county or a state. And, dependent of course on the pre-
conceptions of the estimator, it may be that rather
than a minimum level-of-living standard, a standard
based on the minimum level of services that a unit of
government should provide would furnish better estimates of fiscal capacity. A known fact, however, is
this: There have been many misgivings as a consequence of using other measures, and to supplement
these with measures based on the incomes of individuals who reside in the county or state may prove fruit-
ful.

It is a relatively simple problem to determine the
load of a particular tax on any group of persons if data are available. It is usually possible to find out, for
example, how much in property taxes are paid by the

residents of a county or of a state. The primary incidence of some other taxes may also be determined.
But to relate the tax load to income payments for each
income classification is usually not an easy matter.
In 1950 Kentucky residents paid about $14,000,000 in
state income taxes, and gross income reported was
more than $1,000,000,000. [5] The effective rate on
reported income was, therefore, about 1.4 per cent,
but if total income payments are used as a basis of
computation, the effective rate is about 0.5 per cent.
A size breakdown of incomes for the state and the counties provides a means of calculating the tax load for
all persons in any county above a particular income
level, and also provides a means of relating the effective income tax rates of the income size groups
one to the other.

Because income taxes paid to the federal government are allowed as a deduction in the process of determining the net income subject to state income taxes
in Kentucky, the amount of federal income tax paid by
the residents of each county and by each income size
group may also be determined. It is possible, then,
to determine the net load of either the state or federal
income tax by county and by size group or the combined load of both taxes with a reasonable degree of
accuracy.

With this information available, modifications of
the current tax structure of the state or the counties
may be undertaken on a relatively sound basis. The
potential economic effects of a new tax, from the standpoint of either legal or economic incidence, may be
studied in greater detail than possible up to now. Among
the many avenues of exploration that are opened up--
and the reader will become increasingly aware of these
as the methodology of determining the amount of in-

come and number of recipients is read--are the effects of changing the income tax base (that is, of bringing currently nontaxable sources of income into the
taxable category, of deleting some sources of income
currently taxable), or of changing the tax rates.

With income data by size group for the state and
the counties available, a more understanding and
comprehensive analysis of the whole gamut of federal-
state and state-local fiscal relationships is possible.
This is neither the time nor the place to make a lengthy
analysis of this or other fiscal problems and relationships. But with the advent of the enormously enlarged
grant-in-aid programs over the past few years, and
the current interest in such programs, it would seem
significant that income distributions by size are now
available on a small area basis. "Whenever grant-
in-aid programs are being considered, careful investigations should be made to assure the use of the most
descriptive data available. It is important, however,
that any index used in determining the allocation of
grants should be free from bias."[6] In this project
there is concerted effort to keep the procedure of estimation statistically sound and free from bias. Only
by adhering to these standards is it possible to obtain
what may be a partial solution to the two most important problems that face the grant-in-aid policy mak-
ers--the measurements of financial need and of fiscal
capacity.

Market Analysis

The distribution of income by size in this project
is a distribution of the incomes of all income recipients[7] rather than one of spending units or of families
and individuals. One feature of the data presented here,

however, may in some types of analyses be of more
value than that to be found elsewhere, because two of
the most important series in current use do not give
the size breakdown of incomes above $10,000. [8]

Generally speaking there are three important types
of consumer purchases--convenience goods, service
goods, and fashion goods. Convenience goods are
those which are bought rather regularly from day to
day at some convenient location, including such items
as food, drugs, and other goods (usually low cost
standardized products) which are consumed regularly
in the normal pattern of living. Service goods, in general, are the rather expensive durable goods that may
require considerable service either in installation or
in maintenance. Fashion goods are those which are
not, as a rule, frequently bought and which usually
have a relatively high unit value. Included in this
list are clothing (exclusive, of course, of low price
standardized articles) and house furnishings. [9]

Spending habits, as a general rule, are determined
in part by the size of individual incomes. It is quite
possible, then, that a detailed breakdown, showing
the income recipients by size group in the income levels above $10,000, would be a boon to persons inter-
ested in market analysis for luxury goods. It should
not be inferred from this that there is no value in the
statistics for analysis other than in the shopping goods
category. One feature of the size distribution of incomes as presented here, not incorporated in the other size distributions cited above, is the inclusion of
imputed, as well as the cash, income of individuals.
It may, therefore, be a better approximation of the
living standards of persons and hence a better source
of data for market analysis. [10]

Included under the general heading of market anal-

ysis are things other than those already mentioned.
For example, advertising is a vital part of the whole
marketing process. Knowing where the potential markets for a particular good are located is important beyond measure, and from the income size data for small
areas these markets may be located and exploited.
The determination of sales quotas, the answer to the
question of whether or not to expand operations and
where, and trends in market behavior for a particular good in an area with a given income size distri-
bution--these and other market research problems
may be implemented if income size distribution data
are available.

A related field, but in a somewhat different sphere
of economic activity, is finance--and in particular
the area of consumer finance. By knowing the number of income recipients and the amount of their incomes the eternal question faced by consumer finance
agencies may, in part, be answered; that is, can this
area support a greater amount of consumer credit?
Particular interest in this respect has already been
expressed by persons connected with housing finance.
And here is a tie-up of fiscal policy and business. It
is not only important that the financial institutions
know when housing credit has been expanded to a relatively safe limit, but both businessmen and government personnel want to know how to proceed with further housing developments when it is established that
they are necessary and desirable.

General Well-being

Well-being is a commonly accepted term and may
imply several identifiable measures. Of these measures the most comprehensive is income. This is not

to say that physical condition or state of mind, for example, are unimportant, but frequently the amount of
an individual's income is a prerequisite to good health
and happiness. It is conceivable, then, that a fairly
reliable measure of the relative well-being of the people in any community may be had by finding their average income. Averages, however, do not always
tell the whole story. But a size distribution of incomes for any area will provide another dimension
with which the well-being of the community may be
measured.

An income size distribution may mean different
things at different times. The income distribution
pattern has changed over recent years, and to compare an income distribution for 1950 with one for 1938
would not be sound unless the time differences are tak-
en into account. In 1950 nearly $13,000,000 was paid
to well over 50,000 Kentucky residents in the form of
Old-Age and Survivors' Insurance benefits. These
persons, most of whom had a total income of less
than $1,000, account for many of the income recipi-
ents in the 0--$999 size group. In the lower income
classes there are also many retired persons other
than those who receive Old-Age and Survivors' Insurance. Many of these individuals, even though their
incomes are small, may live rather well on past savings and other types of retirement income. There are
many persons who received small incomes for 1950
because they were among those thousands who were
not in the labor force the whole year or who were part-
time workers. [11]

Not only should a researcher exercise caution
when comparing income distribution data for different years, he should also recognize that in a given
year identical incomes may represent different levels

of economic well-being in different geographic areas;
in other words, the cost of maintaining a given standard of living may vary from place to place. In October, 1950, the annual cost of a "modest but adequate"
standard of living for an urban worker's family of
four persons ranged in different cities from $3,453
in New Orleans to $3,933 in Milwaukee. [12] The dif-
ference in cost for identical standards between these
two cities cannot be explained wholly by their location.   Other Southern cities have an annual budget cost
nearer that of Milwaukee than that of New Orleans.
A factor in area budget cost analysis is the cost of housing.   The rental cost for identical housing varies widely
from county to county, city to city, and state to state. [13]

A further look into area differences may be help-
ful.   Some goods and many services are priced and
marketed on a small area basis.   Rent has already
been mentioned as an important factor to be considered   when comparing the income levels of different
areas.   There is considerable difference in building
costs from one area to another largely because of
different wage rates, but another factor which affects
rent levels, particularly on a small area basis, is
the current change (increase or decrease) in population.   The market area for many personal and business services is small and the price, therefore, is
a matter of local determination.   There is frequently
considerable variation in the price of amusements,
medical services, local public transportation, laundry
and dry cleaning services, and public utility services
(household electricity and gas rates)--to mention only
a few.

The preceding paragraphs are merely warnings
pertaining to the interpretation of income size distribution data.   These data, if they are used as a meas-

ure of individual well-being, should be used with the
time and place limitations clearly in mind. Fortu-
nately there is nothing inherent in the limitations as
they are reviewed here that would detract seriously
from the value of the size distributions as a measure
of the relative well-being of the residents of different
areas.

The Economy of the State and Economic Theory

There are different measures and methods of analysis that may be used to show an over-all economic
picture of a nation, a state, or a county. One of these
measures is a breakdown of total income by source
and type. But the importance of income as a standard
of measurement is enormously enhanced when another dimension is added--the breakdown of incomes by
size. From these two series of data it is possible
to isolate particular regions or areas that may be referred to as being economically blighted. These blighted areas are of two kinds. First, there are the particular counties or geographic regions where, even in
times of high level income and employment, the residents have a pitifully low average income. These
are the areas where economic deprivation is normal,
rather than a condition to be suffered in a time of general economic depression. And there are those economically blighted areas that cannot be geographically
defined--the low income segments of the income size
distributions--and are a consequence of many social
and economic factors which will not be explained at
this time. It is enough to say that income distributions by size will put some emphasis on the magnitude of these problem areas, both in the state as a
whole and in the counties.

It is only reasonable to assume that as additions
are made to the store of knowledge relevant to the
economy of the state, a better examination may not
only be made of the problem areas, geographically
speaking, but also of the more prosperous counties.
Knowing as much as possible of the economic super-
structure upon which the high income counties rely
is a step toward remedying the situation in the poorer areas of the state. Income statistics alone, of
course, are only a part of the analytical tools required. But other data coupled with reliable income
statistics will serve as a basis for area analysis.

Quite frequently in economic literature may be
found reference to the "pure science of economics."
The phrase is high-sounding, but there are sometimes conflicting opinions on just what constitutes the
"pure science." Prior to the great depression of the
1930's and the subsequent pronouncement of the economic doctrines of Keynes, there were few persons
of note in the field of economic thinking who expound-
ed such abstractions as "aggregate demand," "level
of income," "income size distributions," "full employment," and other such terms as today are rather
commonplace. Another landmark was reached when
inquiry into consumer spending habits disclosed that
there was an instability in this function that could not
be explained by changes in aggregate income. "Consumer spending is the most uncertain factor determining the general inflationary outlook for 1952. . . .
A few years ago a statement of this character would
have invited ridicule. Today it hardly causes a rip-
ple. Few, if any, economists are any longer disposed
to question the capacity of consumers to change their
rates of spending and saving without prior notice. In-
deed, there is some danger that the whimsical char-

acter of consumer spending will now be as roundly
exaggerated as was its mathematical determinacy only a short time back."[14]

There is a possibility that income size distribution on a small area basis used in conjunction with total and per capita income estimates will be of considerable value for further inquiry relative to the consumption function. And this value should be enhanced
by the fact that the same concept of income is used
throughout. There are marked differences in consumption patterns between income groups and between
different geographic areas.

Part of the area difference is undoubtedly a result of
different average incomes and distribution patterns.
One possible type of inquiry, and one that would produce much needed information on a small area basis,
would be into the different consumption levels relative to the per capita income level and a known pattern
of income distribution by size. It is conceivable, and
in the mind of the author highly probable, that there
are many counties in Kentucky where total consumption is at a higher level than total income. There is
a possibility, in other words, that capital consumption (dissaving) may be in some counties the rule
rather than the exception.

Even though this section is intended primarily as
an outline of suggestions pertaining to the use of income distributions by size, it would be wise, perhaps,
to go one step further with the discussion related to
consumer spending. In answer to the question of pro-
spective consumer spending in 1953 one economist
said: "It is eloquent testimony to the American economic system that this question must be raised. In
most of the world people are forced by the requirements of subsistence to spend up to the limit of their

income; they cannot afford the luxury of not spending if they want to stay alive. In the United States
items representing things generally considered to
be 'basic necessities' account for only 63 per cent of
total consumer spending. Furthermore, many items
included in the food and clothing classes hardly represent 'necessitous' expenditures--for example, cav-
iar and mink coats, which are, of course, included
in food and clothing.

"The American consumer's standard of living has
thus been raised to the point where he can, if he
chooses, do a considerable amount of 'not spending.
And not infrequently he chooses to do just that. "[15]

The basic necessities referred to include food,
clothing, housing, medical, and funeral expenses,
about which the quotation contains the kind of gener-
ality that gives no hint of the detail in the extremely
complex problem of levels of consumption. Analyses
of this type are important, but consumers should not
be referred to as singular. Even at best there are
many groups of consumers, and spending habits are
different from one group to the next. And likewise,
there is nothing sacred in the "63 per cent." There
is even some doubt about whether this figure includes
all of the day-to-day "necessities" or excludes all lux-
uries. The main point, however, is this: In a good
many counties in Kentucky the average income falls
far short of the "63 per cent"; in other words, the average person in these counties does not have enough
income to supply himself with the necessities which
Mr. McCracken seems to assume are a part of the
"American consumer's standard of living." But reference to only the low income counties does not complete the criticism. In every county in the country,
in all probability, there are many persons who spend

their whole incomes on consumer goods, and many
others who must dissave (consume capital) to furnish
themselves with the necessities of life.

Some mention should also be made of the use of
income distribution data relevant to savings and investment. It is probably true that savings and, as a
consequence of savings, investment come about partly as a result of the inequality of incomes. And it is
probably true also that extremes in inequality may
stifle investment just as the extreme in income equality would probably destroy incentive. Assuming these
two statements to be true, it automatically follows
that there is some optimum distribution of income--
a size distribution that would have the net effect of
maintaining total income and employment at a high
level, but short of the point where there would be excessive inflationary pressures. There are numerous
ramifications to be considered along with the income
distribution pattern, of course, which need not be discussed here.

ALLOCATING THE TOTAL INCOME AND
THE TOTAL NUMBER OF RECIPIENTS
TO THE INCOME SIZE GROUPS

Briefly, the procedure used to allocate the income
and the recipients to the various size groups is as follows. The first part of the procedure has to do only
with allocation of taxable incomes as defined in the
Kentucky income tax law. [16] The data as to income
and number of returns tabulated by the Kentucky Department of Revenue are then adjusted for estimated
underreporting and noncompliance (failure to file a
return). Nontaxable cash income is allocated to the

various income classes in the manner outlined in Appendix 2. After completing this procedure the income allocated is roughly comparable in concept to income as defined by the census, and it is possible to use census data to allocate the remaining recipients and their cash income to the size groups between 0 and $3,000. All recipients are, at this point, accounted for, but still remaining is the problem of allocating imputed income items that are a part of income payments to individuals. The final adjustment is made for the purpose of deducting the social insurance "premiums" paid by wage earners (social security tax, etc.). The several steps in the allocation procedure, which are discussed in detail in Appendix 2, are used to determine the income distribution in each county or group of counties.

More than 1,200,000 persons received income in Kentucky in 1950--more than 40 per cent of the total population. The figures shown in Table 31 are the totals of the 40 individual counties and county groups for which separate distributions were made.

It must be remembered that this is a distribution of individuals and not of families or spending units. Similarly, too much emphasis cannot be put on the fact that also included in this distribution are persons who are voluntarily retired, persons who had income for only a part of the year, and persons whose only source of income is in the form of government assistance.

The income data in Table 31, of course, include all payments to individuals as defined earlier, including various types of imputed income but exclusive of transfer payments between individuals. Such transfer payments are primarily contributions from one individual to the support of another, for example, alimo-

Table 31
DISTRIBUTION OF INCOME AND INCOME RECIPIENTS
IN KENTUCKY, 1950

| Income Size Group | Recipients | | Income | | | Average Income Per Recipient |
	Number (in thousands)	Percentage	Amount (in millions)	Percentage		
Under $ 1,000	343.1	28.547	$214.0	7.905		$ 624
$ 1,000 - 1,999	332.7	27.688	494.5	18.262		1,486
2,000 - 2,999	269.6	22.432	666.7	24.624		2,473
3,000 - 3,999	128.6	10.700	439.7	16.240		3,420
4,000 - 4,999	61.8	5.144	273.8	10.111		4,429
5,000 - 6,999	38.5	3.202	220.2	8.134		5,725
7,000 - 9,999	13.7	1.143	111.4	4.114		8,108
10,000 - 14,999	6.8	0.565	81.3	3.003		11,982
15,000 - 24,999	4.1	0.344	78.4	2.895		18,976
25,000 - 49,999	2.2	0.185	74.6	2.756		33,649
50,000 and over	0.6	0.050	52.9	1.955		87,636
State	1,201.7	100.000	$2,707.6	100.000		$2,253

Note: Percentages and averages were calculated prior to rounding the amounts. Because of rounding, the figures may not add to the totals.

ny and other voluntary support payments. These
things are of varying importance, as is pointed out
in the section dealing with uses of size distribution
data, depending on the use to which the data are put.

Table 32 shows the counties and county groups by
reference group number and the income per capita
and per recipient in each group. The primary considerations in grouping the counties were size and per
capita income level. Considerable variation will be
noted between the two income series: not in the difference in amount, which is necessarily larger on a
recipient basis, but in the trend in income per recipient from county group 1 to county group 40. There
is much less percentage difference in income per recipient between these two groups than there is in income per capita. But most outstanding is that income
per recipient does not follow the per capita pattern of
increasing size from county groups 1 through 40. This
is because of the variations in the relative number of
income recipients from county to county. In other
words, there is considerable variation from the state
average of 40 per cent (40 income recipients per 100
population) from one county group to another, and the
variation is not necessarily a function of per capita
income. Primarily it is a function of the type of industry and urban development. Notice in particular
county groups 15, 24, and 27. The counties in these
three groups had in 1950 a relatively high income per
recipient, but at the same time relatively few income
receivers. County group 1 is a case where not only
the average income per recipient was low but the proportion of persons receiving income was also low relative to the state average.

Table 32
PER CAPITA AND PER RECIPIENT INCOMES FOR
KENTUCKY COUNTIES, 1950 (by group)

County Group	Counties	Income Per Capita	Income Per Recipient
1.	Butler, Knott, Knox, Leslie, Magoffin, Martin, Menifee, Owsley, Powell, Wayne	$360	$1,310
2.	Adair, Casey, Clay, Clinton, Edmonson, Elliott, Hancock, Jackson, Lawrence, Wolfe	423	1,367
3.	Allen, Breathitt, Cumberland, Laurel, Lee, McCreary, Monroe, Morgan, Rockcastle, Russell	456	1,455
4.	Carter, Crittenden, Grayson, Green, Johnson, Lewis, McLean, Metcalfe, Trigg, Trimble	512	1,551
5.	Breckinridge, Estill, Hickman, Lincoln, Ohio	550	1,578
6.	Bell	558	1,792
7.	Ballard, Pulaski, Todd, Whitley	572	1,724
8.	Bath, Hart, Livingston, Lyon, Rowan	597	1,616
9.	Carlisle, Gallatin, Grant, Logan, Webster	619	1,746
10.	Letcher, Muhlenberg	661	1,948
11.	Greenup, Hardin, Marshall, Simpson	663	2,033
12.	Barren, Calloway, Garrard, Owen	689	1,827
13.	Caldwell, Fleming, Pendleton, Taylor, Union	702	1,848
14.	LaRue, Marion, Mercer, Washington	731	1,894
15.	Floyd, Pike	746	2,306
16.	Henry, Meade, Nelson, Spencer	766	1,910
17.	Bracken, Jessamine, Montgomery, Nicholas, Robertson	790	1,909
18.	Christian	816	2,045
19.	Graves	833	1,990
20.	Bullitt, Carrol	834	2,037
21.	Madison	840	1,919
22.	Warren	852	1,865
23.	Anderson, Fulton, Harrison, Oldham	856	2,210
24.	Perry	869	2,581
25.	Henderson	894	2,214

Table 32--continued

County Group	Counties	Income Per Capita	Income Per Recipient
26.	Boone, Scott, Shelby	$ 906	$2,188
27.	Harlan	965	2,639
28.	Boyle	1,037	2,268
29.	Bourbon	1,041	2,243
30.	Clark	1,049	2,348
31.	Hopkins	1,060	2,426
32.	McCracken	1,125	2,550
33.	Franklin, Woodford	1,152	2,340
34.	Mason	1,153	2,142
35.	Daviess	1,160	2,331
36.	Boyd	1,232	2,792
37.	Campbell	1,260	2,697
38.	Fayette	1,413	2,787
39.	Kenton	1,419	2,715
40.	Jefferson	1,667	2,874

[1]There are four groups of ten counties, five groups of five counties, six groups of four counties, one group of three counties, four groups of two counties, and 20 groups of one county each.

[2]Brady, "Research on the Size Distribution of Income," in Studies in Income and Wealth, Vol. XIII, 6.

[3]California Legislature, State and Local Government Finance in California, Part 2, 390.

[4]Bacon, Income as an Index of the Fiscal Capacity

of Michigan Counties, 17-27; and Martin, "Income
and the measurement of the Relative Capacities of
States," in Studies in Income and Wealth, Vol. III,
456-61.

[5]Unpublished data taken from state income tax return statistics, Kentucky Department of Revenue.

[6]Mountin and Greve, The Role of Grants-in-Aid
in Financing Public Health Programs, 25. This is
an excellent, but brief, discussion on the measurement of financial need and fiscal capacity.

[7]The method used to calculate the total number
of income recipients for the state and the counties is
discussed in detail in Appendix 2.

[8]United States Census of Population: 1950, and
the "Survey of Consumer Finances," a continuing survey of consumer finances conducted by the Institute
for Social Research at the University of Michigan, under the general supervision of the Board of Governors
of the Federal Reserve System.

[9]Coolsen, Myers, and Martin, Paducah and Western Kentucky Income, Labor, and Retail Trade Patterns, 45.

[10]See also the discussion on the evaluation of the
census data and the discussion of possible errors in
the estimates as they are presented in this study.

[11]This brief discussion of low income persons is
by no means complete. It is merely a warning as to
how the data should be interpreted and, by the same
token, used in an analysis of the well-being of the people in any area.

[12]U.S. Department of Labor, Family Budget of

<u>City Workers</u>: <u>October</u>, <u>1950</u>, 2. This bulletin presents budget costs for 30 large cities, none of which are in Kentucky; but it is nevertheless a sound reminder that even among cities of comparable size there may be considerable difference in living costs.

[13] Leven and others, <u>America's Capacity to Consume</u>, 223.

[14] Burns, <u>The Instability of Consumer Spending</u>, 9, quoting <u>The Economic Report of the President</u>, January 16, 1952, 20.

[15] McCracken, "A Policy for Prosperity in 1953," 7.

[16] <u>Kentucky Revised Statutes</u>, secs. 141.180 and 141.250-141.270. Very briefly the Kentucky individual income tax law provides that married persons living together with a gross income of more than $2,500 or a net income (gross income less allowable deductions) of $2,000 or more must file a return. All other persons with a gross income of $1,500 or more, or a net income of $1,000 or more, are required to file a return. Taxable income includes capital gains or losses (taxable 100 per cent) if the assets are held for two years or less and does not include capital gains or losses if the assets are held over two years. Interest received from United States Government bonds, and the bonds of Kentucky and the local governments of the state are not taxable. Also the dividends paid by National and Kentucky banks and trust companies are not taxable as individual income. For a complete analysis of the Kentucky income tax see Lockyer, <u>An Analysis of the Kentucky Income Tax</u>.

CHAPTER V

Conclusions

THE PURPOSE of this project is to provide an estimate of Kentucky income by county and to distribute
the income to the residents of each county by type and
by size. It is a many-sided purpose, not only involving the income distributions as such but extending into many other social and economic areas. Some of
these areas have been touched upon; none have been
fully developed. Some have only been mentioned. Others have been intentionally passed over. New pur-
poses--or uses--are constantly developing, and particularly in the area of income trends.

Trends represent one of three things--growth, stag-
nation, or decline. The United States today is, for
both capital and labor, the most mobile nation in the
world. It is the "country on wheels." But, as may
have been noticed in passing over the trends of county
per capita incomes, mobility of labor and capital has
not been the great equalizer of economic well-being.
It has been pointed out in some detail that the nation
as a whole may enjoy good economic health, although
a state, or more likely a county (or many counties),
may, in an economic sense, be declining. It has been
shown, also, that in Kentucky there are many counties
that seem to exist in a perpetual state of depression.

Closely associated with such counties, as has also

been indicated, are such things as land values in
terms of relative productivity, type of nonagricultural economy, population changes, and level of education. It is possible that an increased store of economic knowledge may provide a means of getting closer to the cause and effect relationships associated
with low income areas. From the material assem-
bled in the preceding pages the income differences between counties are carefully spelled out. In two
chapters there is also a brief analysis of the reasons
for differences in per capita incomes. Little was said
of why these differences develop or of why they per-
sist. In a study of this type that is as it should be;
but this detracts nothing from the fact that the "why"
aspect should be explored further.

In 1950 the income received by the residents of
Jefferson County alone accounted for more than 25
per cent of all income received in the state; and this
by about one-sixth of the state's population. It seems
only natural that there are differences in per capita
income from county to county. This in itself is the
sign of a dynamic economic structure--a sign of change
in the demand for and use of resources, natural and
human. In an economy such as ours there is a con-
tinual change in the allocation of resources. But
possibly a better insight into the economy of counties,
that it is hoped this study provides, may bring about
orderly economic changes a little more rapidly.

Income estimates alone, no matter how accurate,
cannot be used as the only yardstick for measuring
the relative well-being of persons in different areas
or in different occupations. There are advantages in
living on a farm, according to many people, that do
not accrue to nonfarmers. Other advantages may accrue to persons residing in small towns and in cities.

The value of living in a particular place is not considered as income, but there is little doubt that this factor alone would create some differences in county per capita income and in the size distribution of income if all other income determining factors could be overcome.

But even holding to a strict income concept, identical dollar incomes in different areas do not necessarily mean comparable living standards. This is clearly shown in the United States Department of Labor studies of consumer prices. Among large cities the difference in the cost of living was more than 10 per cent in 1950. [1] There are no comparable cost of living statistics for Kentucky counties, but because of the differences in local markets it is quite likely differences in cost of living from county to county do exist and that these differences are considerable. [2]

Not much can be said of the differences in the size distribution of income among counties or between a county and the state. There is no measure against which to check except the subjective standards of each individual. An ideal distribution of incomes by size is nonexistent. But the fact that there should be income differentials among persons has been accepted almost universally in this country. As in the case of per capita incomes, further research needs to be done on the causes of variations in the distribution of income by size. Parts of these two explorations would be similar--that is, the causes of a per capita income of a given size would also be related to size distribution. But why, for example, may there be such differences in distribution by size for counties with about equal per capita incomes?

A part of the value of the income size distributions presented here rests on the fact that the concept of

income is the same as that used by the Department
of Commerce in measuring the per capita and total
incomes of states. This is the same concept, of
course, upon which the county total and per capita income estimates are based. This standardization of
income concept adds to the value of the statistics for
purposes of comparative analysis. As states and regions are now related to the nation in the income studies currently published by the Department of Commerce, it is now possible to relate counties to the national and state figures on a comparable basis.

COUNTY AND STATE PER CAPITA
INCOME

Kentucky's position as a state on the per capita
income scale was highest in 1932 and again in 1936,
when this state ranked ahead of nine others, and lowest in 1942 and 1943, when only three states has less
income per capita than did Kentucky. But it is pointed up in Chapter II that in the nation as a whole there
is a pronounced tendency for the regional differences
in per capita income, percentagewise, to become
smaller. In other words, the general trend in state
per capita incomes, high and low alike, is toward the
national figure.

Kentucky per capita income, which was 55 per
cent of the national figure in 1929, climbed to 69 per
cent in 1952.[3] The rise, in percentage amounts, however, has not been uniform throughout the years (see
Chart D). There are several reasons for this, but
primarily it is a result of the economy of Kentucky
being different from the economy of the nation.

Also shown in Chart D is the trend line, fitted by

Chart D
TREND OF KENTUCKY PER CAPITA INCOME RELATIVE TO THAT OF THE UNITED
STATES, 1929-1952 (U. S. per capita income = 100)

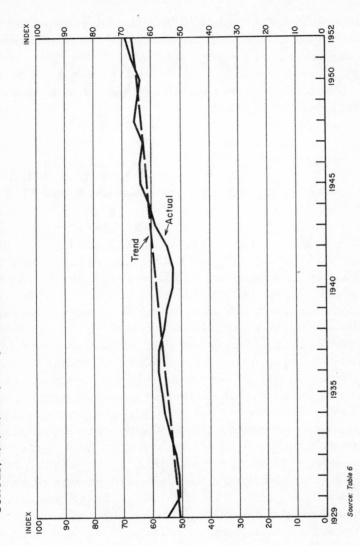

Source: Table 6

the least squares method, of the increase in Kentucky
per capita income relative to the per capita income
of the nation. The computed formula for this line
is Y = 58.26 + .65X, with 1940 as the origin year.
An extension of this trend line, and this must not be
interpreted as a forecast but as a simple linear pro-
jection, would intersect the line representing the national average about 64 years from the year of origin,
or about the year 2004.

Kentucky per capita income, measured in dollars
of constant purchasing power and using 1935-1939 dollar value as a base, increased from $303 in 1929 to
$536 in 1950 (see Table 6). The lowest figure for
these years by this measure is $203 in 1932 and the
highest is $592, the 1945 amount. In 1951, after
reaching a postwar low of $513 in 1949, the Kentucky
constant-dollar per capita income reached $574,[4] the
second highest point since 1929. The per capita income of Kentucky residents since 1929, adjusted to
show the amounts in dollars of constant purchasing
power, is graphically presented in Chart E.

Chart E also shows the trend line in real income
(income measured in dollars of constant purchasing
power). This trend line is again computed by the
least squares method from 1929 through 1951. The
derived formula for the trend is Y = $387 + $18X,
with 1940 the base year. If this trend line is pro-
jected, the indicated real per capita income of Kentucky residents in 1960 is $747. There are many
other means of computing a trend line, of course, and
it must be realized that a real per capita income of
$747 in 1960, measured in terms of the 1935-1939
purchasing power of a dollar, is based only on the pro-
jection of one type--a straight line trend computed by
the method of least squares. If the real per capita

Chart E
KENTUCKY PER CAPITA INCOME MEASURED IN DOLLARS OF
CONSTANT PURCHASING POWER, 1929-1952
(adjusted by the Consumer Price Index, 1935-1939 = 100)

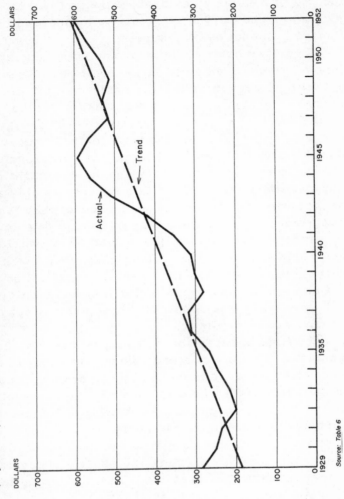

Source: Table 6

income of Kentucky residents happens to be the pro-
jected amount in 1960, it would be an increase over
the 1951 amount by 30 per cent.

These two brief reviews of Kentucky per capita
income trends lead up to these questions. Is the present outlook regarding the per capita income of Kentucky residents favorable? Is it likely that the trends
of the past 23 years will continue? There are, of
course, no conclusive answers to these questions;
positive answers may be had only in retrospect.

The economy of Kentucky should be thought of, for
purposes of an analysis of this nature, as only a part
of the national economy. The demand for the resources
and products of the state are, in a large degree, the
demands of the national market and of the world market. It is assumed here, then, that these markets
will continue to follow the general trends of the present and that a condition of relatively full employment
will prevail in this country. These assumptions may
or may not be realistic.

The first observation that may be made is that the
Kentucky economy is more volatile than that of the nation. Or, to put it another way, an economic decline
in the nation as a whole is conducive to a proportionately greater decline in the economy of Kentucky; con-
versely, an economic rise at the national level is conducive to a proportionately greater economic rise within the state. [5] This fact may be readily recognized by
referring again to Chart E. The per capita income
of the nation, of course, is always represented as 100
per cent. The relative fluctuations in Kentucky per
capita income may be followed from year to year and
the above statement verified. It is reasonable to conclude, then, that the economic condition of the nation
has somewhat of a dual impact on the state. Ken-

tucky prospers as does the nation, but to a greater
degree.

There are, however, three important phenomena
currently existing that could, and probably will, have
an adverse effect on the per capita income of the state.
The first of these is that corollary to full employment,
the migration of labor. There is a definite tendency
for migration to increase during periods of prosperity. Exactly how migration affects per capita income
has not been determined. Migrants, as a general
rule, have more education than nonmigrants; they are
usually in the younger work force age groups, have
few, if any, dependents, and migrate to areas where
the opportunity for employment (from an economic
standpoint) is greatest.[6]

"Outmigration tends to relieve the pressure of the
population on the limited resources of the area. At
the same time, because of its selective nature, migration tends to drain off young adults, leaving a high
proportion of children, aged, and disabled, thereby
increasing the dependency burden upon the families
and upon the... economy of the area."[7] This quotation puts emphasis on the problem of weighing the advantages of emigration against the disadvantages. If
the migrants are either unemployed or working on a
part time basis, the net effect will probably be a higher per capita income; or, to put it another way, there
will be fewer persons to share the same amount of income.

It is pointed up in Chapter II, Table 23, that the
percentage of total population in the work force is the
most important element in accounting for the differences in state and national per capita income. The
population of Kentucky since the census was taken in
1950 has been declining.[8] It is likely that the net emi-

gration during this period has been about 120,000,[9] and it is also likely that more than 50 per cent of this loss in population represents a decline in the work force. If these estimates are sound, Kentucky is in a worse position now, relative to the percentage of population in the work force, than in 1950, the year on which the estimates in Table 23 are based. On the other hand, if there had not been a decline in total population during the two year period, and if the amount of available work had followed the same course, the per capita income of Kentucky residents today would have been higher than if there had been no net emigration.

This leads up to the other two points that will be considered here, and it is quite probable that these should be considered as a part of the migration-population problem. It was pointed up in previous chapters that approximately 25 per cent of the total work force in Kentucky in 1950 was employed in agriculture, either as farm proprietors or as farm laborers, and it was also pointed up that this is considerably above the national average. Because there is a constant decline in the farm population, in absolute as well as in relative numbers,[10] it is axiomatic that the number of new nonfarm employment opportunities would have to expand more rapidly in Kentucky than in the nation as a whole if the persons leaving farms for other types of employment are to be absorbed into the employed work force of the state. This assumes, of course, that the movement of persons from farm to nonfarm activity in Kentucky follows the national pattern.[11]

The other thing that looms large as a threat to the economy of the state and particularly to the economy of several Kentucky counties is the decline of employment in coal mining. "Employment in bituminous coal

mining was at the low level of 37,500 in June, 1953,
down by one-fifth or 9,400 workers from last year
and a nightmarish 31,500 lower than in June, 1948. In
addition, a short work week is also the rule in many
fields."[12] In June, 1950, the approximate employment in Kentucky coal mines was 59,600,[13] a decline
from 1948 but considerably above the level three years
later. In order for Kentucky to maintain even a constant work force from midyear 1950 to 1953, approximately 22,100 new jobs were needed to absorb the excess work force in the mining counties, assuming all
other employment conditions have remained constant.

As noted above, however, there are persons other
than coal miners that are faced with the task of seeking new jobs. A rough estimate of the number of persons that left Kentucky in search of employment over
the past three years may run as high as 75,000. But
migration is not an instantaneous thing. The short
run impact of underemployment, as in farming, and
of the combination of unemployment and underemployment, as in the coal mining industry, is in the direction of a lower per capita income. In a general but
real way there is also a tendency for per capita income to be depressed in any area where the natural
increase in the work force is not matched by job opportunities.

The immediate outlook for Kentucky, taking into
account migration, farming, and the coal industry, is
not particularly bright. The increase of employment
in manufacturing (134,600[14] to 156,300[15] from June,
1950, to June, 1953) has been far short of the necessary minimum amount needed to absorb the unemployed or underemployed workers in the state. And
added to those who find it necessary or desirable to
seek new employment is the natural increase in the

labor force. With employment available in other states,
there is the natural tendency for persons seeking work
to leave Kentucky. Manufacturing, of course, is not
the only industry showing a net increase in employment over the past three years. The Department of
Economic Security reports increases in trade, finance, service, and transportation, as well as a few
other industries; but outside of trade (employment in
trade increased by 11,800 from June, 1950, to June,
1953) the rise of employment has been rather small.

A partial list of new industries in Kentucky for
1950-1952 indicates the current rate of investment per
employee in the state to be about $15,000 in manu-
facturing establishments. [16] The investment cost per
employee varies considerably for the different manufacturing industries, but the above figure appears to
be a fair estimate of the current average. It was previously estimated that the net loss to the work force
in Kentucky since June, 1950, was 75,000. Assuming
further that an increase of 50,000 employees in manufacturing over the actual increase, with the secondary
and tertiary employment effects in other industries,
would have resulted in neither a net loss nor a net gain
in the growth of the labor force relative to the nation,
the deficit in the required manufacturing investment
during this period based on the assumptions discussed
above was about $750,000,000.

Just as Kentucky is not a typical state from an
economic point of view, neither is any other state.
But within Kentucky it is even more true that no county is a typical county. It is not erroneous to say that
the per capita income of Kentucky residents in 1950
is estimated to be $932, but it is misleading. In 1950
only 15 of the state's 120 counties enjoyed a per capita
income of $932 or more, and the residents of 27 coun-

ties received an average of less than half this amount.

In 1950 in Kentucky more than half of the total population of 69 counties lived on farms. The median net decline in population of these counties from 1940 to 1950 was 9.4 per cent. Also, in 1950 there were 13 counties with more than 25 per cent of the employed work force (not population) in coal mining. These counties had a median net increase in population of 1.3 per cent during the same decade. But in 1950 only six counties had more than 25 per cent of the employed work force in manufacturing industries; and these counties, during the same ten year period, had a median net increase in population of more than 9.0 per cent. [17] On July 1, 1952, the same 69 counties with 50 per cent or more of the total population on farms in 1950 showed a median population decline from the 1950 figures of 4.4 per cent; the same 13 mining counties showed a median population decline of 6.8 per cent; and the six counties with over 25 per cent of the 1950 employed work force in manufacturing had a median population increase of 2.7 per cent.[18] This trend in population changes has, without doubt, had an effect on county per capita incomes, but just what effect is not now known. In Table 46, Appendix 3, it is shown that the counties lowest in per capita income in 1950 suffered a substantial population loss in the previous ten year period, while the counties with the highest per capita income increased in population. There is, however, relatively little difference in the rank position of counties on the per capita income scale between 1939 and 1950. A conclusion that may be drawn from this, then, is that migration during this period had the net effect of perpetuating existing county per capita income differences, but it may also be concluded that if there had been no population loss

in the low income farm counties it is quite likely that
county per capita income differences would have become more extreme.

The situation in the coal producing counties is somewhat different. These counties, as is shown above,
had a small increase in population during the 1940's.
Since 1950, however, there has been a substantial decrease in the demand for coal and as a consequence
substantial decrease in employment. The changes in
population, production, employment, and earnings in
these counties have been more abrupt than in most of
the farm counties. It is quite likely that most of the
economic consequences of the emigration suffered by
the coal producing counties since 1950 are more severe than would have been the case if population decreases had come about gradually.

The following is a summary of the possible economic effects of emigration on the low income farm
counties since 1950.

1. There has been a rather constant decline in
farm population--both in absolute numbers and relative to total population--over the past several decades.
A net loss in population would not come as a shock,
then, to most of the farm counties, and in few instances would the nonfarm economy be geared to an
increasing population.

2. The possibility of constant, or even increased,
per capita income in the farm counties relative to the
more urban counties would not be surprising--assum-
ing a constant price level--because of the increasing
productivity per farm worker and the fixed number of
acres. There would, in other words, be a given amount
of production (income) to divide among fewer persons.

3. Even though there may be relatively the same
total income in the predominantly farm counties from

year to year, the markets for consumer goods and for
farm capital equipment may change considerably. Increased expenditure on such items as electric power, tractors, and improved housing should be expected as population decreases and farm size increases
(see Table 17), but at the same time there may also
be a decrease in the purchase of various food, clothing, or service items, particularly those which are
purchased rather regularly even though the income of
persons may change.

The effects of emigration on the coal producing
counties may be expected to be somewhat different.
The following points serve as illustration.

1. Decreases in the production of coal--assum-
ing a constant production level per man per day--is
a corollary of decreased employment. This may be
in the form of a decrease in the number of employees,
in the length of the work week, or both. Many Kentucky counties since 1950 have suffered from both unemployment and employment on a part time basis. Unemployment compensation payments relieve the shock
of income loss to some degree, but the relief is only
temporary, and unemployment appears now to be a
continuing thing. Emigration does not, in general,
follow decreased employment unless there are job opportunities elsewhere, and even then the time lag may
be considerable.

In the first stages of declining employment there
is probably a decline in per capita income which will
continue to be abnormally low until such time as emigration or employment in other industries produces
a force great enough to raise per capita income.

2. The effect of the loss of wages in the coal mining industry on other phases of the economy will probably be more severe than is the loss of farm popula-

tion. In the latter instance there is not necessarily
a decline in total income. A decrease in wages and
salaries from mining, whether or not the unemployed
migrate, will eventually mean a decrease in the purchase of goods and services. When emigration does
occur, as has been the case since 1950, consumer pur-
chases decline still further. This sort of situation
arises when the net income of the total population decreases, and in the farm counties this is less likely
to happen.

3. Most local government funds are derived from
property taxes. There may be some decline in property tax revenue when there is a decline in farm population, but if productivity per farm operator and farm
size both increase, there is likely to be little change
in the farm property total value, again assuming constant prices. This is entirely different from the probable situation in the mining counties. As a consequence of the decreasing demand for coal, the value
of mining properties will decline. As a result of decreased wage income and business income, property
tax delinquency may increase. As a result of the declining population, the demand for housing, and therefore the value, will decrease.

4. Emigration, of course, affects not only tax revenues but also government expenditures. But as stated
before, emigration is not an instantaneous reaction
to unemployment. Realistically speaking, perfect mobility of neither labor nor capital should be assumed.
There is a time lag. But during this time lag there
may be a greater demand for government funds than
during periods of high employment. This is particularly true in the case of demands for welfare funds.
Even after emigration on a large scale has taken place,
the demand for public services may increase the per

capita local tax load, because children of school age
are less than proportionately represented in the mi-
grant group. And as pointed up before, the same is
true of aged persons and the physically handicapped.

This brief survey of some possible effects of emigration on particular counties could be expanded into
a survey of the effects on the state as a whole. But
because Kentucky is currently experiencing unfavorable economic developments in two of the state's most
important industries, it is important that better than
average development take place in other phases of the
economy if the state is to continue the per capita income trends of the past two decades.

COUNTY AND STATE DISTRIBUTIONS
OF INCOME BY SIZE

The trend in the income distributions, unlike the
trend in per capita income, cannot at present be measured, because data are available for one year only. If
adequate statistics for such a measure were at hand
the analysis, to cover the subject, would necessarily
be made in two parts. A change in an income distribution by size may or may not be accompanied by per
capita income changes and may or may not be accompanied by changes in the distribution curve. [19] Suppose, for example, the number of recipients in a particular county remained unchanged but the income of
each was increased uniformly. Per capita income in
such a case would increase, but the income distribution curve (Lorenz curve) would remain unchanged.
But, assuming an increase of 10 per cent in all incomes
below $5,000 and a 5 per cent increase in all other in-
comes, per capita income would again increase but

there would likewise be a shift in the distribution curve
toward the line of equal distribution. The analysis
here, then, pertains to current and historical economic phenomena that may result in possible changes
in income distribution in Kentucky and that may or
may not change the shape of the distribution curves.

References to changes in income distribution sched-
ules or curves are usually made by using such terms
as "a more equitable distribution," "less income inequality," "redistribution of income," and the like.
It is rather easy to read more into these terms than
the author intends; and because of this, it is well to
point out once again that an ideal distribution of income is, for present analytical purposes, nonexistent.

There are three important basic reasons for income inequalities: differences in natural abilities or
aptitudes, differences in environment or opportunity,
and differences in inherited wealth. In order, then,
for a change in any size distribution to take place, a
change that influences one or more of the above factors must occur. Prior to making a brief analysis of
current economic happenings that should be considered, some account will be taken of past events that
have altered the general pattern of income distribution.

Statistics on income distribution, even for the country as a whole, have been relatively scarce until recent years. There is also the difficulty of comparing
published income distribution data because of the conceptual differences in income and recipient. Because
of differences in concept each series of data is presented separately with little attempt to relate them one
to the other except in a general way. Simon Kuznets,
one of the nation's foremost students of income and

income trends, in a study of the upper income groups
said: "The decline in upper group shares from 1939
to 1948, and apparently also to 1950, has no parallel
in our record in either magnitude or duration. . . . The
share of the top 1 per cent. . . declined from a peak of
15. 4 per cent in 1916 to a low of 12. 3 per cent in 1920.
By 1928 it had recovered, temporarily, to 14. 9 per
cent--close to its peak level. . . . It reached a trough
in 1944, 8. 7 per cent, or over a quarter below its 1939
level, 11. 9 per cent; after a temporary recovery to
9. 1 per cent in 1946, it dropped to 8. 5 per cent in
1948. . . . The decline. . . was apparently not due to a
drop in absolute income levels but a much higher rate
of rise of lower incomes during these years when the
countrywide per capita income was rising. "[20] In the
same study it is also shown that the percentage of total income received by the upper 5 per cent of the population[21] declined substantially from 1939 to 1948. No
analysis is made of the income received by other individuals except as a residual group.

In the past few years the Bureau of the Census has
become more and more active in the realm of income
analysis. The data are collected on a sample basis,
however, and are therefore not directly comparable
with adjusted tax return statistics. The trend toward
greater income equality from 1944 to 1948, mentioned
above by Kuznets, is also revealed in the published
statistics of the Bureau of the Census, as shown in
Table 33. For the three years following--1949, 1950,
and 1951--the trend appears to be in the opposite direction. [22]

Not only does there appear to be a tendency for the
upper income classes to receive a smaller percentage
of total income, but there is also some indication that
the lower income receiver groups are also getting a

smaller percentage of total income. The largest increase, percentagewise, has accrued to the receivers in the middle income group.

Table 33
PERCENTAGE OF AGGREGATE MONEY INCOME BEFORE TAXES
RECEIVED BY EACH FIFTH OF INCOME RECIPIENTS RANKED
BY INCOME FOR THE UNITED STATES, 1944 TO 1951

Income Recipients	1944	1945	1947	1948	1949	1950	1951
Lowest fifth	2.6	3.1	3.0	2.9	2.4	2.3	2.5
Second fifth	8.5	9.0	8.9	8.7	8.4	7.9	8.4
Middle fifth	15.6	16.0	16.2	16.6	16.5	16.4	16.7
Next fifth	24.2	24.5	23.4	24.2	25.0	24.3	24.7
Highest fifth	49.1	47.4	48.5	47.6	47.7	49.1	47.7

Source: U.S. Bureau of the Census, Current Population Reports, Consumer Income, Series P-60, No. 11, 9. (1946 data not available)

The Bureau of the Census estimates of the income ranges of each fifth of the income receivers are shown

Table 34
INCOME RANGE FOR EACH FIFTH OF ALL INCOME
RECIPIENTS, 1944 AND 1951

Income Recipients	1944	1951	Percentage Increase in Income Class Limits	
			Minimum	Maximum
Lowest fifth	under $483	under $648	---	34.2
Second fifth	$483--$1,079	$648--$1,662	34.2	54.0
Middle fifth	$1,080--$1,816	$1,663--$2,720	54.0	49.8
Next fifth	$1,817--$2,763	$2,721--$3,859	49.8	39.7
Highest fifth	over $2,763	over $3,859	39.7	---

Source: U.S. Bureau of the Census, Current Population Reports, Consumer Income, Series P-60, No. 11, 9.

in Table 34. The greatest percentage increase in the lower income limits (exclusive of the lowest fifth) from

1944 to 1951 occurred in the middle fifth, where the
minimum income for the group rose from $1,080 to
$1,663--an increase of 54 per cent. It was shown in
Table 33 that this same group received 16.7 per cent
of total income in 1951 as compared to 15.6 per cent
in 1944. The shift away from the highest income receivers pointed up by both Kuznets and the Bureau of
the Census evidently is not resulting in percentage
gains by the recipients in the lowest income classes
but by those in the middle income groups.

By analyzing the factors that have given rise to income distribution changes in the past, perhaps it may
be possible to determine with some degree of accuracy the changes that are currently taking place in the
income distributions of Kentucky and Kentucky counties. Kuznets[23] lists five of "the more obvious and
direct factors" that resulted in the sharp decline in
the shares of the upper income groups from 1939 to
1948.

First, the decline in unemployment is an important factor. Most of those with little or no income in
1939 and who later became employed increased the
proportion of aggregate income received by persons
in the lower or middle income classes.

Second, the rapid growth of farm income greatly
exceeded the growth in total income. Enough has already been said of the relatively low incomes of farmers to indicate that, for the most part, additional farm
income would accrue to the low and middle income
groups.

Third, during the period there was a percentage
increase in service incomes much greater than the percentage increase in property incomes, and service
income is received primarily by low income recipients and property income by high income recipients.

Fourth, there is evidence that among employees the low income receivers secured wage increases greater, percentagewise, than the wage earners in the upper income groups. There was also a reduction in the number of worker groups whose average income was either greatly above or greatly below the national average.

Fifth, the final point is a consideration of the effect of increases in income tax rates. "Take home pay" has become a very important phrase in wage negotiations, and it is quite probable that there have been many wage increases that would have been neither asked for nor granted had income tax liability been left out of the picture. [24]

The same factors that were important in decreasing the share of the upper income groups for the nation as a whole from 1939 to 1948 are, in all probability, active factors in determining present and future changes in the state and the county distributions. During the fiscal year ending June 30, 1953, "unemployment remained fairly high, well above the national average." [25] This statement is in reference to employment conditions for Kentucky as a whole, but the general unemployment in Kentucky that "remained high" already prevailed in 1950. [26] If, then, unemployment in the state decreases, even to the current level of unemployment for the country as a whole, it is probable that the upper income groups would receive relatively less of total income payments in the state than they are now receiving. But even though total unemployment in the state has "remained fairly high" since 1950, different areas of the state have had considerable change in the degree of unemployment. The general trend since 1950 has been for unemployment to decrease in the predominantly manufacturing

areas of the state and to increase in the coal mining
counties. These differences must be considered in
any analysis of changing income distributions on a
small area basis.

The rapid growth in farm income that Kuznets con-
siders important in the decline of upper group income
shares is having its effect in an opposite direction in
the nation as a whole as well as in Kentucky. The increase in total income payments from 1950 to 1952
was greater, percentagewise, than was the increased
income from farm operations. The counties with the
greatest relative number of farm operators are, of
course, the counties where this factor would have the
greatest effect on income distribution.

Relative changes in the amount of total income derived from property, the third factor to be considered
in the Kentucky income distribution trend from 1950
through 1952, indicate a continued decline in the upper
group share of total income. In 1950, property in-
come--rents, dividends, and interest--accounted for
9.4 per cent of total income payments, but in 1952
this percentage had decreased to 7.3.[27] The effect
of changes in this component for the various counties
is difficult to determine. It was pointed up before
that county estimates of this type of income are probably the least reliable of all county allocations.

Point four has to do partly with the changing wage
rates of different income groups. It was shown in
Chapter II that average annual wages in Kentucky have
been increasing relative to the average annual wage
for the nation. There is no reason to assume this
trend will not continue as long as the nation is enjoy-
ing a condition of "full employment," and as long as
average wages in Kentucky are low relative to those
of the nation as a whole. But it would be presuming

too much to say definitely that this trend is resulting
in less income inequality in Kentucky. Whether the
increases in lower wage rates, in higher wage rates,
or in both are resulting in the higher average wage
cannot be accurately determined. But another condition this point suggests is the effect on income equality of underemployment or part time employment. Ac-
companying the rather sharp decline in coal production in some Kentucky counties since 1950 has been a
decline in total employment. But another serious aspect of the decreasing demand for coal, relative to
changes in the size distributions of income, is the fact
that many Kentucky coal miners are working only part
time.

In Chart F, Appendix 2, the income distribution
curves for some of Kentucky's most important coal
producing counties (county groups 10, 15, 24, and 27),
it may be noticed that the county distribution curve
is much nearer the line of equal distribution than
is the distribution curve of the state. Some explanation of this was made previously with emphasis on the
point that, because of the extremely high proportion
of the total work force in these counties employed in
coal mining at, or near, the average wage of all persons employed in this industry, one should expect that
the income distribution curve would be so shaped.
With the decline in coal production from 1950 to 1952
in these same counties, and the resulting unemployment and part time employment in some fields, these
county income curves have probably moved somewhat
farther away from the line of equal distribution. All
of the factors discussed above may be applied to the
coal counties and the same conclusion would be reached.

But in the farming counties, even though total farm
income is declining, it is not possible at this point to

know the consequences. Changes in farm size and
changes in nonagricultural industry are both important.[28]

There are two historically important income distribution determinants which have not been discussed
and which may also be important as distribution determinants in the future. Social security payments
and public assistance payments, as well as other government and private pension plan transfers, have become increasingly important since the nation emerged
from the depression of the 1930's. The net effect of
all such nonwage payments has been to increase tre-
mendously the number of income recipients in the
very low income classes. The merits of these plans
need not be discussed; but the result, as the income
distribution curves for the nation, the states, and the
counties reflect these incomes, would be to move the
curves farther away from the line of equal distribution. The other factor that has no doubt been influen-
tial in the past, and will probably continue to be important, is the role of women in the labor force. One
reason why the income distributions in the coal producing counties approach equality to a greater degree
than the other counties of the state is because of the
lack of women in the labor force. It is rather common knowledge that the average earnings of women are
considerably less than those of men. Greater inequalities in the income distributions are probable when the
number of women in the labor force is relatively large.
But it should not be inferred from this statement that
the employment of women, even though in the first instance it produces income inequalities, is economically undesirable.

The national trend in income distribution, especially noticeable in the upper income groups, points

toward greater equality. This trend is primarily the
result of increasing prosperity, that is, a continuing
state of relatively full employment. It has been shown,
however, that employment conditions in Kentucky are
less favorable from this standpoint than conditions for
the nation as a whole. And for particular counties in
Kentucky unemployment is extremely acute. This condition is alleviated somewhat by migration, but, as
has also been indicated, migration lags behind employment declines. In order to estimate how income
distributions have changed, or may change in the future, one must take account of all factors--those that
tend toward less inequality in income, and those that
tend toward more.

-----

[1] U.S. Department of Labor, Family Budget of City
Workers: October 1950, 2.

[2] See, for example, Kentucky Department of Revenue, "Regional Building Cost Conversion Factors,"
52-54.

[3] Computed from Graham, "State Income Payments
in 1952," 13.

[4] Computed from ibid., 17, and the Consumer
Price Index, prepared by the Bureau of Labor Statistics, U.S. Department of Labor.

[5] This statement, of course, does not hold true for
each county in the state.

[6] See especially Galloway and Beers, Utilization of
Rural Manpower in Eastern Kentucky, 41-51.

[7] Ibid., 51.

[8] The estimated population of Kentucky as of July 1,
1952, was 2,916,000--a net loss of 29,000 since 1950.

During the same period the population of the United
States showed an increase of 3.3 per cent. (U.S. Bureau of the Census, Current Population Reports, Population Estimates, Series P-25, No. 70.)

[9]If the population of Kentucky had gone up in proportion to the population of the nation (3.3 per cent)
it would have been about 120,000 greater than it was
on July 1, 1952.

[10]Bureau of Agricultural Economics, The Farm Income Situation, FIS-199, Table 4.

[11]See also McPherson, "Some Problems and Opportunities Created by Florida's Changing Population."
In this publication of the Bureau of Economic and Business Research of the University of Florida Professor
McPherson comments on the effects of a declining
farm population in relation to both the state and the
national economy.

[12]Kentucky Department of Economic Security, Statistical Journal of Economic Security in Kentucky
(June, 1953), 16. The major employment decreases
have occurred in the counties of eastern Kentucky--
in the underground mines. Employment in the coal
fields of western Kentucky, where strip-mining is extensive and man-day productivity much higher than in
underground mining, has decreased but proportionately much less than in the eastern Kentucky field.

[13]Ibid., (July, 1950), 7.

[14]Ibid.

[15]Ibid., (June, 1953), 17.

[16]Agricultural and Industrial Development Board of
Kentucky, Desk Book of Economic Statistics, Tables

1-4 and 1-5. This estimate is calculated exclusive
of the huge Atomic Energy Commission plant in western Kentucky.

[17]Computed from United States Census of Population: 1950, Vol. II, Part 17, Chap. B, Tables 12 and
43.

[18]Kentucky State Department of Health, "Estimated
Population of Kentucky Counties, as of July 1, 1952."

[19]See Appendix 2 charts.

[20]Shares of Upper Income Groups in Income and
Savings, 40. The numerators of the fractions from
which these ratios are computed include wages and
salaries, business and partnership income, and rents,
royalties, interest, and dividends as reported on the
federal income tax returns of individuals. Excluded
are capital gains and losses and other deductions from
net income with the exception of business and partnership losses.   The denominator is total income received
by individuals, slightly different in concept from income payments to individuals as defined by the Department of Commerce.

[21]The "upper groups" are actually population segments and not groups of income recipients. ". . . . we
estimate the population represented on the returns, "
both those reporting income and the dependents claimed.
Ibid. , p. 3.

[22]"1952 Survey of Consumer Finances, " 976. On the
spending unit basis the trend toward greater income
equality continued up to 1951, at which time the shift
in the opposite direction took place.

[23]Kuznets, Shares of Upper Income Groups in Income and Saving, 41-43.

[24]This is a different expression of the income tax effect than that set forth by Kuznets. The interest of Kuznets is in the fact that during the period 1939 to 1948 income taxes contributed to a decline in the share of disposable income going to the high income recipients to a greater degree, percentagewise, than to the low income recipients.

[25]Kentucky Department of Economic Security, Annual Report: 1952-53, 3.

[26]Ibid. , 6.

[27]Computed from Graham, "State Income Payments in 1952," 15. State income figures for previous years published in this issue, because of revision, are not identical with those published earlier. The revised figures show property income in Kentucky to be 8. 6 per cent of total income payments in 1950, 7. 7 per cent in 1951, and 7. 3 per cent in 1952.

[28]This is not to say changes in farming patterns and techniques and other industrial changes are unimportant in an analysis of the coal counties; but it would appear that they are of minor importance relative to the decline in the major industry--coal production. There may, however, be one important exception. Those persons who derive income from industries with a predominantly local market (primarily the service and trade industries) probably have suffered a substantial income loss because of the decline in coal production.

Income in Kentucky: Allocation to Counties

THE ALLOCATION procedure developed by the Conference on the Measurement of County Income is used extensively in this study. [1] There are, however, some differences, due in part to the availability of other data and to a smaller degree to improved procedures resulting from the experience of the conference. In order to keep the procedure in the simplest possible form it is presented in outline style. In the main it will consist of the income component to be allocated, the allocator and its source, and the county weight, when used.

I. WAGES AND SALARIES
  A. Agriculture. Allocator: Specified farm expenditures, hired labor. Source: Census of Agriculture: 1950, Vol. I, Part 19, County Table 3, line 73.
  B. Mining. Allocator: Annual pay rolls by county. Source: Unpublished UC data, industries 10 to 14. [2]
  C. Manufacturing. Allocator: Annual pay rolls by county. Source: Unpublished UC data, industries 19 to 39.

D. Construction. Allocator: Employment in construction, by county. Source: Census of Population: 1950, Vol. II, Part 17, Chap. B, Table 43. County Weight: Average wage by county computed from unpublished UC data, industries 15 to 17.

E. Public utilities and transportation

1. Railroads. Allocator: Employment in railroads, by county. Source: Census of Population: 1950, Vol. II, Part 17, Chap. B, Table 43.

2. Street railways. Allocator: Annual pay rolls by county. Source: Unpublished UC data, industry 41.

3. Motor and other transportation. Allocator: Annual pay rolls by county. Source: Unpublished UC data, industries 42, 43, and 45.

4. Water transportation. Allocator: Annual pay rolls by county. Source: Unpublished UC data, industry 44.

5. Power and gas. Allocator: Annual pay rolls by county. Source: Unpublished UC data, industries 48 and 49.

6. Communication. Allocator: Annual pay rolls by county. Source: Unpublished UC data, industries 46 and 736.

F. Trade. Allocator: Annual pay rolls by county. Source: Unpublished UC data, industries 50 to 59 and industry 75.

G. Finance. Allocator: Annual pay rolls by county. Source: Unpublished UC data, industries 60 to 67.

H. Service

1. Covered service. Allocator: Annual pay

rolls by county. Source: Unpublished
UC data, industries 70 to 86, less industries 75 (trade), 736 (communication),
80 (hospitals), and 82 (private education).

2. Domestic service. Allocator: Private
household workers, by county. Source:
Census of Population: 1950, Vol. II, Part
17, Chap. B, Table 43. County weight:
Average covered wage in trade and service, unpublished UC data.

3. Hospitals. Allocator: Annual pay rolls
by county. Sources: Unpublished UC data,
industry 80, supplemented by the pay rolls
of nonprofit associations compiled from
Hospitals: Journal American Hospital Association, June, 1951, Part II. (The pay
rolls of a few hospitals, when not reported, were estimated by finding the pay roll
cost per patient in other hospitals in the
same county and applying this cost to the
average daily census of the hospitals that
did not report a pay roll.)

4. Private universities. Allocator: Annual
pay rolls by institution. Source: Unpublished data supplied by the Office of Education, Washington, D.C. The pay rolls
of private colleges and universities that
did not report these data to the Office of
Education were estimated. This was done
by applying the ratio of pay roll to operating costs of the reporting units to the operating costs of the nonreporting units as
estimated by the Department of Commerce.

5. Private elementary and secondary education. Allocator: Number of teachers in

private schools. Source: "Kentucky Public Schools Directory, 1950-51." County
weight: Average earnings of public school
teachers in each county, unpublished data
from Kentucky Department of Education.
6. Religious organizations. Allocator: Number of members in major religious organizations. Source: Census of Religious Bodies: 1936, Vol. I, Table 32, adjusted to
1950 level on basis of 1950 to 1940 population change ratio by county. County weight:
Average covered wage, unpublished UC data.
I. Government
1. Federal government
a. Federal civil executive. Allocator: Number of employees. Source: "Additional
Report of the Joint Committee on Reduction of Nonessential Federal Expenditures," 32-33.[3]
b. Federal legislative. Allocator: Residence of federal legislative personnel.
c. Federal judicial. Allocator: Number
of court personnel in the counties where
the court sits.
d. Federal military. Allocator: Military
population by county. Source: Census
of Population: 1950, Vol. II, Part 17,
Chap. B, Table 43.[4]
2. State government. Allocator: Number of
state employees by county of residence.
Source: The data were furnished by the several departments of the state government.[5]
3. Public education. Allocator: Wages and
salaries paid to teachers and school super-
intendents by county. Source: Unpublished

pay roll data by school district, Kentucky
Department of Education.

4. County, and 5. Municipal. Allocator:
Estimated monthly pay roll. Source: Unpublished data supplied by the Bureau of
the Census. [6]

J. Miscellaneous wages and salaries. Allocat-
or: Total population by county. Source: Census of Population: 1950, Vol. II, Part 17,
Chap. B, Table 43. County weight: Average
wage by county in covered employment, unpublished UC data.

K. Pay roll deductions for social insurance. Allocator: Total wages and salaries exclusive
of agriculture and the noncovered service industries.

II. PROPRIETORS' INCOME
A. Agriculture [7]
1. Income items[8]
a. Livestock and livestock products sold.
Allocator: Livestock and products other than dairy and poultry sold. Source:
Census of Agriculture: 1950, Vol. I,
Part 19, County Table 7, line 57.
b. Dairy products sold. Allocator: Dairy
products sold. Source: Census of
Agriculture: 1950, Vol. I, Part 19,
County Table 4 (part 1), line 33.
c. Poultry and poultry products sold. Allocator: Poultry and poultry products
sold. Source: Census of Agriculture:
1950, Vol. I, Part 19, County Table 4
(part 2), line 3.
d. Vegetables sold. Allocator: Vegetables
sold. Source: Census of Agriculture:

1950, Vol. I, Part 19, County Table 5
(part 5), line 7.

e. Fruits and nuts sold. Allocator: Fruits
    and nuts sold. Source: Census of Agri-
    culture: 1950, Vol. I, Part 19, County
    Table 5 (part 6), line 62.

f. Horticultural specialties sold. Allocat-
    or: Horticultural specialties sold. Source:
    Census of Agriculture: 1950, Vol. I,
    Part 19, County Table 5 (part 7), line 1.

g. All other crops sold. Allocator: Field
    crops other than vegetables and fruits
    and nuts sold. Source: Census of Agri-
    culture: 1950, Vol. I, Part 19, County
    Table 7, line 43.

h. Forest products sold. Allocator: Forest
    products sold. Source: Census of Agri-
    culture: 1950, Vol. I, Part 19, County
    Table 5 (part 7), line 18.

i. Value of home consumption. Allocator:
    Farm products used by farm households
    per farm operator in 1945, by county,
    multiplied by the number of farm oper-
    ators, by county, 1950. Sources: "Farm
    products used by farm households," Cen-
    sus of Agriculture: 1945, Vol. I, Part
    19, County Table 4, line 30; "Farm op-
    erators on farm operated," Census of
    Agriculture: 1945, Vol. I, Part 19, Coun-
    ty Table 1 (part 2), line 10; and "Farm
    operators residing on farm operated,"
    Census of Agriculture: 1950, County
    Table 1, Vol. I, Part 19, line 78.

j. Government payments to owner oper-
    ators. Allocator: Gross payment includ-

ing conservation materials and services.
Source: Kentucky State Committee, Pro-
duction and Marketing Administration,
United States Department of Agriculture,
Kentucky PMA Programs: 1950 Year-
book, Part II, Table 4, Col. 4.

k. Value of inventory changes. Allocator:
Total crops and livestock sold. Source:
Census of Agriculture: 1950, Vol. 1, Part
19, County Table 7, line 39.

2. Expense items

a. Feed purchased. Allocator: Specified
farm expenditures, feed for all livestock
and poultry. Source: Census of Agriculture: 1950, Vol. I, Part 19, County Table 3, line 75.

b. Livestock purchased. Allocator: Specified farm expenditures, livestock and poultry purchased. Source: Census of Agriculture: 1950, Vol. I, Part 19, County
Table 3, line 77.

c. Fertilizer and lime. Allocator: Value of
corn, wheat, tobacco, soybeans, and cotton grown. Source: Kentucky Crop and
Livestock Reporting Service, Bureau of
Agricultural Economics, United States Department of Agriculture, Kentucky Agricultural Statistics: 1950, 77 and 103-32.

d. Cost of operating motor vehicles. Allocator: Specified farm expenditures, sum
of gasoline and other petroleum fuel and
oil, tractor repairs, and other farm machinery repairs. Source: Census of Agriculture: 1950, Vol. I, Part 19, County Table 3, lines 81, 83, and 85.

e. Net rent to landlords. Allocator: Number of acres rented weighted by the average net return per acre, 1947. Sources: "Land rented from others by farm operators," Census of Agriculture: 1950, Vol. I, Part 19, County Table 1, line 6. For net income per acre the "Net Income of Farm Proprietors,"[9] by county, was divided by the "Number of acres in farms," Census of Agriculture: 1950, Vol. 1, Part 19, County Table 1, line 9.

f. Farm mortgage interest. Included in miscellaneous operating expenses.

g. Taxes. Allocator: Assessed value of farms multiplied by the property tax rate, by county. Source: Kentucky Department of Revenue, Kentucky Property Tax Rates: 1950.

h. Depreciation of service buildings. Allocator: Value of land and buildings, average per farm, multiplied by the number of farms. Source: Census of Agriculture: 1950, Vol. I, Part 19, County Table 1, lines 1 and 13.

i. Depreciation of machinery and equipment. Allocator: Specified farm expenditures, other farm machinery repairs. Source: Census of Agriculture: 1950, Vol. 1, Part 19, County Table 3, line 85.

j. Depreciation of motor vehicles. Allocator: Specified facilities and equipment, sum of motor trucks, tractors, and automobiles on farms. Source: Census of Agriculture: 1950, Vol. I, Part 19, County Table 3, lines 26, 30, and 40.

k. Miscellaneous operating expenses. Allocator: Total of all other expenses.
1. Farm wages. Allocator: Specified farm expenditures, hired labor. Source: Census of Agriculture: 1950, Vol. I, Part 19, County Table 3, line 73.

B. Mining. Allocator: Value of coal produced by noncorporate mines. [10] Sources: Estimated noncorporate production by county, Kentucky Department of Mines and Minerals, Annual Report: 1950; average value per ton mined, by county, U.S. Department of Interior, Minerals Yearbook: 1949, 322-23.

C. Manufacturing. Allocator: Gross income of manufacturing proprietors, by county. Source: Unpublished state income tax return statistics for 1950, Kentucky Department of Revenue.

D. Construction. Allocator: Gross income of construction proprietors, by county. Source: Unpublished state income tax return statistics for 1950, Kentucky Department of Revenue.

E. Transportation
1. Water transportation. Allocator: Annual pay rolls by county. Source: Unpublished UC data, industry 44.
2. Other transportation. Allocator: Number of commercial truck registrations by county. Source: Kentucky Department of Revenue, Statistical Appendix to the 1950-51 Annual Report, 26-27.

F. Trade
1. Wholesale. Allocator: Number of proprietors in wholesale trade by county. Source:

Census of Business: 1948, Vol. V, Wholesale Trade, Area Statistics, 16.05-16.07.
County weight: Average covered wage by
county, unpublished UC data.

2. Retail. Allocator: Number of proprietors in retail trade by county. Source:
Census of Business: 1948, Vol. III, Retail Trade Area Statistics, 16.05-16.08.
County weight: Average covered wage by
county, unpublished UC data.

G. Finance. Allocator: Gross income of proprietors of financial institutions. Source: Unpublished state income tax return statistics
for 1950, Kentucky Department of Revenue.

H. Service
1. Hotels. Allocator: Number of hotels and
tourists' courts by county. Source: Census of Business: 1948, Vol. VII, Service
Trades, Area Statistics, 16.14-16.18.
County weight: Average covered wage by
county in trade and service, unpublished
UC data.

2. Amusements. Allocator: Number of proprietors in amusement establishments.
Source: Census of Business: 1948, Vol.
VII, Service Trades, Area Statistics,
16.10-16.13. County weight: Average
wage by county in trade and service, unpublished UC data.

3. Medical and other health services. Allocator: Number of doctors and dentists by
county. Sources: Kentucky State Medical
Association, Kentucky Medical Directory,
1949; "Medical Directory Supplement, No.
3," April 1, 1950; and Directory of Li-

censed Dentists in the State of Kentucky: 1950. County weight: Average covered wage by county, unpublished UC data.

4. Legal services. Allocator: Number of lawyers by county. Source: Martindale-Hubbell Law Directory, Vol. 1(82nd ed.), 587-613. County weight: Average covered wage by county, unpublished UC data.

5. Business services, personal services, miscellaneous repair services, and other services. Allocator: Number of proprietors in these classes. Source: Census of Business: 1948, Vol. VII, Service Trades, Area Statistics, 16.07-16.10.

III. PROPERTY INCOME [11]

A. Dividends, "other" cash interest, and government interest (part). [12] Allocator: Gross dividends and interest received, by county. Source: Unpublished state income tax return statistics for 1950, Kentucky Department of Revenue. [13]

B. Interest income from financial intermediaries, insurance companies, and the balance of government interest. [14] Allocator: The value of intangible personal property and retail sales, weighted equally. Sources: Intangible personal property value from Report of the Department of Revenue: 1951. Statistical Appendix, Tables IV and VII. Retail sales by county from Census of Business: 1948, Vol. III, Retail Trade, Area Statistics, Table 103.

C. Nonfarm cash rent and farm rent paid to nonfarm people. [15] Allocator: Net rent received, by county. Source: Unpublished state income

tax return statistics for 1950, Kentucky Department of Revenue.

D. Agricultural rent received by farm people.
Allocator: Income value of land rented to
others by farm operators. Sources: Average income per acre, by county, computed
from Agricultural Proprietors' Income, 1950,
and "Land Rented to Others by Farm Operators," Census of Agriculture, 1950, Vol. I,
Part 19, County Table 1, line 8.

IV. OTHER INCOME

A. Old-Age and Survivors' Insurance. Allocator:
Dollar amount of monthly benefits in current
status. Source: Bureau of Old-Age and Survivors' Insurance, "Number and amount of
monthly benefits in current payment status as
of February 28, 1951, by type of benefit and
county residence of beneficiary."

B. Railroad retirement benefits, railroad unemployment insurance benefits, and railroad sickness benefits. Allocator: Number of railroad
employees by county. Source: Census of Population: 1950, Vol. II, Part 17, Chap. B, Table 43.

C. State unemployment insurance benefits. Allocator: Estimated unemployment insurance
benefits by county. Source: The Kentucky
Department of Economic Security furnished
the amount of benefits paid out by district, and
these district totals are broken down into county totals proportionate to the covered wages
and salaries paid in each county in the district.

D. Veterans' unemployment allowances and veterans' self-employment allowances. Allo-

cator: Number of claims by county. Sources:
The Kentucky Department of Economic Security furnished data on the number of claims
by district.   These are distributed to the counties in each district on the basis of the Veterans Administration Research Division, "Estimated number of living veterans in Kentucky, by county: June 30, 1951."

E. Public assistance payments. Allocator: Amount
of public assistance payments in May, 1950.
Source: Unpublished data on total monthly
payments by county under all three public
assistance programs, Kentucky Department
of Economic Security.

F. Federal civilian retirement. Allocator: Number of federal civil employees by county.
Source: "Additional Report of the Joint Committee on the Reduction of Nonessential Federal Expenditures," 32-33.   The number of
employees in Veterans Administration and
military establishments are deducted from
the total in each county because of the temporary nature and enormous fluctuations in
this type of employment.

G. Workmen's compensation. Allocator: The
benefits in each industry are distributed to
each county in the same ratio as the wages
and salaries.   Source: "Workmen's Compensation Benefits by Industry," in Kentucky
Department of Industrial Relations, Annual
Report: 1950.

H. Industrial pensions. Allocator: The sum of
wages and salaries in industries where pensions
are most apt to be paid; i.e., mining, manufacturing, and public utilities and transportation.

I. Veterans' subsistance allowances (half). [16]
    Allocator: Number of veterans enrolled in
    the colleges and universities in the state.
    Source: The veteran enrollment was obtained
    from each institution by direct correspond-
    ence.

J. Veterans' subsistance allowances (half), fed-
    eral interest payments on veterans' loans,
    military reserve pay, family allowances and
    allotments of pay to dependents of military
    personnel, mustering-out pay to discharged
    servicemen, enlisted men's cash terminal
    leave payments, state bonuses to veterans,
    National Service Life Insurance special div-
    idend, payments to ex-prisoners-of-war(U.S.)
    by War-Claims Commission, and veterans'
    pensions and compensation (61 per cent). [17]
    Allocator: Estimated number of living vet-
    erans in Kentucky, by county: June 30, 1951.
    Source: Veterans Administration Research
    Division, "Estimated number of living vet-
    erans in Kentucky, by county: June 30, 1951."

K. Veterans' pensions and compensation (39 per
    cent), adjusted service bonds, and military
    retirement. Allocator: Male population 55
    years of age and over. Source: Census of
    Population: 1950, Vol. II, Part 17, Chap. B,
    Table 41.

SITUS ADJUSTMENTS

With the exception of many components of wages
and salaries, the income payments to individuals are
originally allocated to the counties on the basis of resi-

dence of the recipients. The Unemployment Compensation Commission data, which are used as a basis for allocating several types of wage and salary income, are available only on a place of employment basis. The data on commuting, therefore, have value for two important reasons. First, they have value in and of themselves as an important economic phenomenon on which little research has been done, and, second, they have importance as a contributing agent in determining the income of a given county or area.

In computing the income payments to individuals by county for 1950, situs adjustments are made that involve nearly half of Kentucky's counties as well as four adjoining states. These adjustments can be conveniently divided into four categories, each of which will be discussed in turn.

Situs Adjustments in Federal and State Civilian Employment Pay Rolls

Federal civilian employment is distributed rather evenly throughout the state with one important exception. There are four areas where civilians are employed by the armed forces in large numbers. These concentrations of employment are situated, not only in rural areas, but for the most part near county or state borders. It was possible, by correspondence and interview, to determine the residence of these employees and an adjustment is made in the number of federal civil employees by county before this component of income is allocated.

State employees were first calculated on a "county where employed" basis,[18] and situs adjustments made only for those employed in Franklin County. To

determine the residence of the state employees working in this county several of the largest departments
of state government were chosen as a sample and all
Franklin County employees were considered to have
residence by county in the same proportion as those
in the sample departments. Again the adjustments are
made before the pay roll is distributed among the counties.

Situs Adjustments in the Industries Where
Unemployment Compensation Commission
Data on Pay Rolls by County Were
Used as Allocators

It is in this part of the whole employee commuting
analysis (the industries where UC data are used as allocators) where the major pay roll adjustments are
made. UC data are used to distribute the wage and
salary components of income in mining, manufacturing, the "covered" transportation and public utilities
industries, trade, finance, and the "covered" service
industries. The distribution of wage payments by the
use of such data is not in line with the concept of income payments to individuals. It is necessary, therefore, to take a second step in the allocation process
(adjustment for place of residence) in order to make
the data conform in basic concept with the notion of income payments.

Since UC statistics are used to make the original
distribution of these wage and salary components, and
since UC statistics are also the best source of individual firm information on the number of employees and
employee compensation, these data were chosen as the
starting point in the move toward accuracy in the situs

adjustments. The same procedure was followed in
each of the several areas studied, and this procedure, step by step, is as follows.

1. A sample was chosen from the firms listed in
the UC data for each major industry in each county in
the analysis. On this sample would rest, to a great
extent, the accuracy of the whole procedure and for
this reason it was chosen with extreme care. Each
major industry was divided into subgroups. This is
commonly referred to as the two-digit industry breakdown. [19] For example, manufacturing, as a major
industry, has 20 two-digit subgroups, trade has ten,
etc. Among these subgroups in each major industry
there are extreme differences in average plant size
and in average wages. These things were considered
in choosing a representative sample; but another very
important factor not related to the type of industry
which had to be taken into account was plant location,
i. e., was the plant situated so as to be conducive to a
large or small amount of interstate or intercounty commuting?

2. Using this carefully selected sample, the next
step in the procedure was to collect pay roll data by
employee residence. This was done by means of personal interviews with representatives of the chosen
firms. The results were more than satisfying. Whole-
hearted cooperation was received from nearly every
businessman and industrial representative selected
for an interview.

3. The percentage commuting in each of the major industries was obtained by tabulating the data supplied by the sample firms. These percentages, applied to total employment in the county by industry, [20]
gave the approximate number of commuters from each
surrounding county and state to the industrial centers

being studied. Since it was not possible to identify
the commuters with a given wage other than the average for the industry in which they worked, each com-
muter was assumed to have earned this amount. In
each case the average wage for each major industry
was computed for the county in which the commuters
were employed.

4. The gross amount of wages and salaries earned
by all commuters was then added, or deducted, as
the case may be, to the previously calculated gross
wages and salaries in each county from which or to
which employees commuted. The deduction of social
insurance payments, the final step in calculating the
estimated net wages and salaries for each county,
would then be on all taxable earnings received by the
residents of each county.

In order to keep the foregoing procedural discussion in simple terms the problem of interstate commuting was not thoroughly discussed. There were a
few deviations from the indicated procedure in hand-
ling the interstate segment of the situs adjustments.
The samples taken in Kentucky furnished information
on the number of commuters from other states. The
problem, then, was to determine the number of commuters from Kentucky to other states. In two of the
areas studied for possible necessary interstate adjustments there was no concentration of employment in
the adjoining state and, therefore, a counteradjust-
ment in these two instances was not necessary. In one
instance the neighboring state had conducted a commuting study in 1950 and the results of this study were
made available. [21] This was used along with additional information gathered in personal interviews with
employers in the adjoining state.

However, in the area where interstate commuting

is most important--from a Kentucky point of view--
there were no available commuting data with which to
work. A breakdown of total employment and wages
paid in 1950 for the area by major industry group, and
also the two-digit breakdown, was obtained;[22] and
from this source and other sources such as industrial
directories a sample was chosen. Rather careful observation, to make sure the standards set up for the
Kentucky samples were met, seems to indicate a high
degree of reliability in the results obtained.[23] There
was an adjustment in some industries in the percentage of total commuting to this area as a result of a
check on employment statistics from the 1950 census,
but there was no change made in the distribution of all
commuters among the Kentucky counties involved.

Situs Adjustments in Construction
Wages and Salaries

The allocation of construction wages and salaries
presents difficulties that arise in no other instance.
There are changes in the location of construction activity and in the work force that make any available
allocator less reliable than would be desirable. The
best available allocator is probably the number of employees in construction activity by county as reported
by the census.[24] This method of allocation (when employment is weighted by the average wage for the county) makes intercounty situs adjustments unnecessary.
It was discovered, however, in the process of collecting data for the industries where UC data were used
as allocators, that an interstate situs adjustment was
necessary. The amount of this adjustment was determined in a manner similar to other interstate adjust-

ments. There was a net gain to Kentucky as a result
of these computations and this amount was added to
the estimated wages and salaries in construction furnished by the Department of Commerce. The allocation on the basis of employment by county of the total
wage and salary income in construction, therefore,
includes the net interstate adjustment.

Some Further Notes on Employee Commuting

As a result of intensive research on employee commuting many items of interest have come to light.
Some of these merely verify previous assumptions,
while others may have an opposite effect. In no instance should these findings be considered as axioms. [25]

1. The percentage of commuters in manufacturing
is greater than in any other industry, with the possible
exception of construction in areas where activity in
this industry is extremely high.

2. The percentage of commuters is greater in the
firms where employment is large than it is in firms
in the same industry with few employees.

3. Within each major industry the average wage
seems to have very little effect on the amount of commuting.

4. Commuting in a given area increases as level
of employment increases, but at a faster rate.

5. The commuting pattern of female employees is
very similar to the commuting pattern of male employees.

6. In one instance the collective bargaining agreement forbade intercounty commuting.

It should be pointed out here that not all wage and

salary components were taken into account in making the adjustments, nor was there a commuting sample taken in every area of the state where some interstate commuting could occur. The important wage and
salary items not adjusted for were the earnings of railroad employees and the federal civilian employees in
the Louisville area. With the exception of the adjustment for Tennessee, which was made to take into account the earnings of federal civilian employees residing in Tennessee and who are employed at Fort Campbell, Kentucky, the adjustments are all based on earnings in covered employment. It may also be seen in
the following summary of interstate situs adjustments
in wages and salaries for 1950 that the net adjustment for earnings in the construction industry are not
shown separately.

Earned by:	Millions	
Kentucky residents in Ohio . . .	$107.0	
Kentucky residents in Indiana. .	4.5	
Total inflow of income		$111.5
Indiana residents in Kentucky. .	34.5	
Ohio residents in Kentucky . . .	4.6	
Illinois residents in Kentucky . .	0.2	
Tennessee residents in Kentucky	0.6	
Total outflow of income		39.9
Gross inflow of income.		$ 71.6
Estimated social insurance deductions.		1.2
Net inflow of income		$ 70.4

As an indication of the importance of this net in-
flow of wage and salary income into Kentucky it may

be pointed out that $70.4 million in net wages and salaries represents an increase of 4.36 per cent over the Department of Commerce estimate of net wages and salaries received by Kentucky residents.

THE ADVANTAGES AND LIMITATIONS
OF BASIC DATA USED FOR
INCOME ALLOCATORS

One of the most important considerations in county income estimation is the selection of allocators. They will frequently vary in reliability from year to year and from state to state. In most instances allocators should be considered primarily from the standpoint of reliability, but with some emphasis on coverage and the availability of the data from year to year.

Unemployment Compensation
Commission Data

The tax provisions of the national law on unemployment compensation constitute Subchapter C of Chapter IX of the Internal Revenue Code. This law is specific on the minimum coverage a state may have in its own unemployment compensation law, but maximum coverage is for the state to decide.[26] In general, agricultural labor, railroad employees, domestic workers, most members of an employer's family, employees of nonprofit organizations, and several other relatively small groups of workers are not covered. Employees of firms in covered industries that employ fewer than the minimum number of workers are likewise not covered by state unemployment compensation laws. The

Kentucky unemployment compensation law has greater coverage than the specified minimum in the national law. The Kentucky law defines an employer who
is subject to the law as one who employs four or more
persons in covered employment, [27] rather than eight
or more, the specified minimum coverage in the federal law. This extended coverage adds greatly to the
usefulness of wage and salary data collected by the
Kentucky Department of Economic Security in allocating the Department of Commerce state estimates
to the counties.

In Table 35 are shown the percentages that covered
wages and salaries reported in Kentucky for 1950 are
of the Department of Commerce estimates for Kentucky. There are minor differences in definition between the Department of Commerce estimates and the
UC estimates, but for the most part these are few and
adjustments are relatively simple. [28] With the exception of the covered service industries the UC data
in Kentucky are rather complete.

Covered wages and salaries in 1950 accounted for
65 per cent of all wages and salaries in the Department of Commerce estimate of total wage and salary
payments, and about 40 per cent of total state income.
In the same year an average of 391,284 employees
were working in covered employment in Kentucky, and
the firms in covered industry numbered nearly 13,000.[29]

There is another important source of wage and salary allocators, the pay roll statistics compiled by the
Bureau of Old-Age and Survivors' Insurance. [30] It is
quite possible that in some instances these data would
make better allocators than the UC statistics because
all employees in covered industry are insured (this
would add to Kentucky UC data because firms in covered industries with one to three employees would be

included); but since 1949 the detail necessary to work
up good allocators is available only for the manufacturing industries. For county distribution of 1950 income, therefore, the OASI data were of limited value.

Besides the suspension of publication of some of
the desirable OASI statistics, there are other advantages in using Kentucky UC data for purposes of allocation. Some of these advantages are the following.

Table 35
COVERED WAGES AND SALARIES REPORTED BY THE KENTUCKY
DEPARTMENT OF ECONOMIC SECURITY AS A PERCENTAGE
OF THE DEPARTMENT OF COMMERCE ESTIMATES, 1950

Industry	Percentage
Mining	94
Construction	89
Manufacturing	100
Transportation and Public Utilities	92
Trade	86
Finance	80
Covered Service Industries	63

Sources: Computed from unpublished data on income payments to
individuals by source, Office of Business Economics, U.S. Department
of Commerce; and unpublished data on income and average employment,
Kentucky Department of Economic Security.

1. It is possible to obtain detailed data for the entire year, whereas the OASI data in the same detail
are available for the first quarter only.

2. The UC data are in terms of total wages. The
OASI data are in terms of taxable wages only. (Only
the first $3,600 earned in any one year is subject to
the Social Security Tax.)

3. In states where there are more than 100 governmental units with wage and salary data reported by the
Bureau of Old-Age and Survivors' Insurance (in Kentucky there are 120 counties), some of the units must
be combined to hold the total number to 100. There is

then the problem of separating these county groups
for each industry. Where OASI material is used as
the allocator, the county groups may be broken down
by using the UC statistics.

But in using UC data for allocators there are also
some disadvantages and limitations that must be kept
in mind and corrected for.

1. The Kentucky law covers only firms with four
or more employees. As a result the wages paid by
firms with one to three employees are not reported.
This situation is most) serious in the covered trade
and service industries. The small firm data from
OASI tabulations may, if available, be used to fill this
gap.

2. Both the UC and OASI statistics are reported
on the basis of the place of employment rather than on
the basis of the place of residence. The result is the
so-called situs problem that is discussed in some
detail above.

3. Another serious limitation of Kentucky UC data
is that, in the tabulations, firms are not always classified by county, but may be grouped in a "statewide"
category. This is particularly true in cases where
one firm has operations in more than one county, or
where a single operation cannot be identified with a
particular county. An example of the multiple operations type would be a chain of stores in a single company, and the other situation may include covered workers such as insurance company representatives that
work in the whole state or a large portion of it. The
Kentucky Department of Economic Security, however,
has done a particularly fine job of keeping these "statewide" pay rolls at a minimum. In preparing 1950 income allocators some further identification of the firms
listed in the "statewide" category was possible. It

could reasonably be assumed, therefore, that the residual "statewide" pay rolls were distributed among
the counties in the same ratio as the classified pay
rolls.

The advantages and disadvantages listed above can
be expanded to include many other items of some importance, but primarily it must be remembered that
all data have their good qualities as well as their limitations. Occasionally the selection of one series over
another is made on a purely arbitrary basis, but where
this is the case the series that has the better chance
of being continuously available is selected. That procedure is followed throughout this study.

Census Data

The best single source of data that may be used as
allocators for noncovered wages and salaries, agricultural proprietors' income, and some of the "other
income" components may be found in the federal census reports. Census data may also be used as a check
on other allocators or, in some instances, prove to
be the source of the best allocator available.

The most important advantage in using census data
as a source of wage and salary allocators is that the
workers in the different occupations are listed by place
of residence, eliminating the need for situs adjustments. Under "General Methodology" it may be noted
that a number of other uses are made of census materials. The allocation of agricultural proprietors'
income and expense items is accomplished almost
wholly through the use of Census of Agriculture material.

In using census material, as in using other statistics, a knowledge of the limitations of the data is important. Most of the federal census publications have peculiarities that limit, sometimes seriously, their use as a source of income allocators. The most serious drawbacks to the use of census data are these.

1. There is frequently a considerable time lapse between collecting the data and publishing them in enough detail for use in the allocation of income. This is a grave disadvantage if currency is desirable.

2. Census data are available only for certain years.

3. Before census material can be used for the allocation of wages and salaries and some of the other income components, each set of data to be used must be incorporated with a series of county weights.[31]

4. Particularly in the Census of Agriculture, some of the data are collected on a sample basis. This introduces a chance of error that does not characterize some of the other allocators.

5. The self-employed and those persons who work for wages and salaries are grouped together in the employment statistics.

6. Many persons derive income from two or more types of activity. For example, many farm proprietors are also wage and salary earners. The extent of this, and other types of combined activity, cannot be determined from census publications.

Kentucky Income Tax Data

Gross income, as defined for state income tax purposes,[32] received by residents of Kentucky in 1950 was more than twice the amount reported by persons with income tax liability for that year. Because of the differences in concept between taxable income and income

payments to individuals the ratio of reported gross
income to total gross income can only be approximated. [33] This ratio varies from county to county as well
as among occupational groups. There are, however,
some distinct advantages in using these data for allocators in a few instances.

1. In the cases where reported gross income was
used as an allocator there was a dearth of other available data.

2. Kentucky income taxes are reported for 1950
by county of residence.

Reported taxable gross income, on the other hand,
has features that seriously limit its value for county
income allocation.

1. Coverage is far from perfect in most, if not
all, components of income.

2. There is evidence of some underreporting and
noncompliance which is not proportionately the same
in all counties. Reasonably accurate adjustments for
these factors in any single component of income are,
at best, difficult to make.

3. There are conceptual differences between gross
income as defined in the Kentucky law and income payments to individuals as defined by the Department of
Commerce. For example, even though the Department of Commerce estimates interest income from
four major sources, there is no way to determine the
exact amount of taxable interest received by Kentucky
residents.

4. There are likewise conceptual differences in
the definitions of particular industrial or occupational
groups. In this matter the Department of Commerce
follows a well defined pattern, but the Kentucky Department of Revenue cannot, at present, do this. This
is probably not serious in the tax return data used as

allocators in this study, but the extremely large
amount of income in the "unclassified" group (in
some counties this may be as much as 40 per cent)
would indicate that these data should be used only after
careful scrutiny and even then with care.

5. Gross income by county and source from Kentucky income tax returns is not reported annually.

IMPROVEMENTS IN 1939 AND 1947
COUNTY INCOME ESTIMATES

By suggesting that improvements could be made
and have been, in the income estimates prepared by
the Conference on the Measurement of County Income
for the years 1939 and 1947, it is not intended that
these estimates, or that the conference, should be in
any way discredited. The general purposes of the conference were to develop a methodology for estimating
county income and to stimulate research in this area.[34]
The more specific aims were to make county income
estimates for the years 1939 and 1947 and to provide
a tool that would help in understanding the economic
structure of the conference area in greater detail.
Moreover, it would be amiss to say that all revisions
result in improvements in the estimates. Some changes
are merely revisions that have been incorporated on
the basis of data that were provided too late to be used
in the original conference estimates.

The only adjustment made involving the original
1939 income estimates, however, was not in the amount
of income by county but in population data which resulted in a small change in the per capita income of
most counties. This adjustment, which was also made
for 1947, came about as a result of a change in the

method of enumeration by the Bureau of the Census.[35]
In the 1940 Census of Population college students were
reported as residents of their home counties, while
in 1950 they were classified as residents of the county
in which they actually lived while attending college.
County population adjustments were therefore made
to bring the 1939 and 1947 data into conformity with
the 1950 census definition of total population.

Dollarwise, the most important changes made in
the 1947 conference estimates are a result of continued research on the situs problem. The situs adjustments that were made in 1947 are discussed in detail
in one of the conference publications.[36] The revised
figures affect more counties and include intercounty
as well as interstate adjustments.

Manufacturing wages and salaries were redistributed to the counties by means of a different allocator.
The conference estimates for this income segment
were based on an allocator taken from the 1947 Census
of Manufacturers,[37] and the revised estimates are
based on unpublished pay roll data by county (or county groups) furnished by the Bureau of Old-Age and Survivors' Insurance. There are two reasons why this
change was made. First, since it was presumed that
it would be necessary to use either UC data (as for the
1950 estimates) or OASI data in most future estimates,
it seemed desirable to change the 1947 allocator for
the sake of year to year comparability. These two sets
of data have a greater degree of comparability than
either has with the census. Second, there was a strong
indication that in at least two counties the OASI data
were better, and in several counties the Census of
Manufacturers did not reveal the pay roll data because
of the small number of firms.

Further research pertaining to subsistence pay-

ments to veterans disclosed that too little of this segment of income was allocated to the counties where
veterans were attending college. It was revealed that
about 90 per cent, rather than 50 per cent, of all veterans' subsistance payments in Kentucky in 1947 went
to veterans attending college.

A small adjustment was made in agricultural proprietors' income estimates for most counties. A detailed breakdown of the net change in farm inventories
was received too late to be incorporated in the 1947
conference estimates. When adjustments were made
for inventory changes in the separate divisions of livestock and crops, according to the amounts produced
in each county, the result was a small net gain in income to some counties and a small net loss to others.

It was the concensus of many persons with an inti-
mate knowledge of income analysis and familiar with
the economy of the state that, in one county at least,
an error had been made in allocating the wages and
salaries of federal civilian employees. For this reason this component of income was redistributed. The
allocator used in the 1947 revision was the same as
that used in the 1950 allocation which also includes a
situs adjustment for the large military establishments.
The 1947 estimates did not include a situs adjustment
for this component of income.

Wages and salaries paid to railroad employees was
revised somewhat on the basis of data obtained too late
to be used in the 1947 estimates. These data gave the
number of employees for only three counties, but railroad employment in these three counties comprised
38 per cent of the state total. [38]

Finally, these revisions necessitated a change in
the distribution of social insurance deductions because
this component is distributed on the basis of wages

and salaries earned by the residents of each county,
exclusive of farm labor and domestic servants.

COUNTY INCOME DISTRIBUTIONS
IN KENTUCKY

Tables 36 through 43 show the details of income
payments in Kentucky counties. Much of the data presented here has been previously published, [39] and only
that which is new or relevant to this study will be shown.

Table 36 is a distribution of total income payments
received by residents of Kentucky for the years 1939,
1947, and 1950-1952. In this table no account is taken
of the changing value of money; that is, all amounts
are shown in current dollars. It will be noted that
there was a decline in income in a few counties from
1947 to 1952, and only a very small increase in many
others. This is due largely to the decrease in net income from farm operations and decline of employment in coal mining.

The same thing may be said for the county per capita incomes shown in Table 37. From 1947 to 1952
there were five Kentucky counties that showed a decrease in per capita income. Shown in Table 38 are
the per capita incomes in each county for 1939, 1947,
1951, and 1952 relative to the 1950 county per capita
incomes. Adair County per capita income, for example, in 1939 was 33 per cent of the 1950 amount and
in 1952 it was 123 per cent of the 1950 figure.

Table 39 is also a schedule of county per capita incomes for the five years--1939, 1947, and 1950-1952--
but on a constant dollar basis. All amounts are shown
in terms of 1935-39 purchasing power. The county
trends in per capita purchasing power in Table 40 are

based on 1950 as 100. Even though 115 counties had
per capita income increases from 1947 to 1952, only
70 counties showed an increase in per capita purchasing power. As in total income by county, the explanation lies largely in the decrease of net income from
farm operations and the employment decline in coal
mining.

Per capita income in Kentucky in 1952 was 68.9
per cent of the national figure and Kentucky counties
ranged from a low, on the same basis, of 22.0 per
cent to a high of 119.3 per cent. These figures are
shown in Table 41. But, by way of comparison, and
to point up again the value of intrastate income statistics, it could be pointed out that the range in state
per capita incomes for the same year was from 49.9
per cent to 137.9 per cent of the national figure. [40]
Percentagewise, then, the range of per capita incomes
among Kentucky counties is much greater than the
range of per capita incomes among states. (The lowest of the counties is 18.4 per cent of the highest; the
lowest among the states is 36.2 per cent of the highest.) From Table 41 it is also possible to determine
how each county fared, relative to the nation, over the
period from 1939 to 1952. There are many counties
in Kentucky that have not kept pace with the national
rate of growth, and many that have increased more
rapidly.

Table 42 shows the distribution of total income payments in Kentucky counties by type. Wage and salary
payments accounted for 50 per cent or more total income in 41 counties in 1952, and in only nine counties
did the net income from farm operations exceed 50 per
cent of total income payments. Because most sources
of "other income" are determined primarily by things
other than current productive activity, it may be noted

that the percentage derived from this source is high
in the low per capita income counties and low in the
high per capita income counties. It may also be ob-
served from data presented in Table 42 that property
income is usually highest in counties that have been
consistently high on the per capita income scale.

Net income per farm acre is one of the best measures of the local economy in many parts of the state.
These data for 1939, 1947, and 1950-1952 are presented in Table 43. The range for Kentucky counties
in 1952 was from a low of $6 per acre to a high of $44
per acre. These data are presented in chart form in
Chapter III.

---

[1]Copeland, Methods for Estimating Income Payments in Counties.

[2]Social Security Board, Industrial Classification
Code, Description of Industries, Vol. I. This industrial classification code is used by both the Bureau of
Old-Age and Survivors' Insurance and the Bureau of
Employment Security. The relationship between this
code and the Department of Commerce income statistics code can be found in U. S. Department of Commerce, National Income and Product of the United
States: 1929-1950, 61. In Kentucky the Division of Unemployment Insurance is in the Department of Economic Security. The employment and wage data in the
division records are referred to as unemployment compensation commission data, or more frequently by the
initials "UC. "

[3]Sometimes referred to as The Byrd Report. This
lists the employees on a "county where employed" basis. Adjustments were made which had the effect of
listing the employees on a "county of residence" basis

prior to the allocation of this component of income. These adjustments are explained in detail below.

[4]The military population was obtained by deducting civilian labor force from the total labor force. In 1950 this component of income was extremely important in two Kentucky counties; but since the census data are recorded as of April, 1950, the military population data are probably not representative of the whole year. As will be explained later, both the military population and income were deducted from these two counties for purposes of analysis.

[5]The Department of Commerce estimates of state and local government wages and salaries were classified only as public education and nonschool. The total state pay roll for the year was furnished by the Kentucky Personnel Department and this was allocated as explained above. A situs adjustment was also made and is explained below.

[6]This tabulation provided information from which a per capita ratio (pay roll cost per person) could be calculated for cities and counties of various sizes, based on 1950 population and 1947 pay rolls. This ratio was then used to calculate the pay rolls for all counties and cities. Complete data were given for the only county with more than 250,000 population. For the cities, complete data were available for all cities over 25,000 population and for five of the eight cities in the 10,000 to 25,000 population class for 1950 from U.S. Bureau of the Census, "City Employment in 1950," G-GE 50-No. 6, 9, 15, 19, and 29.

[7]The Department of Commerce estimates of agricultural proprietors' income are based on estimates made by the Bureau of Agricultural Economics, U.S. Department of Agriculture, and published each year

in The Farm Income Situation. The published figures
for the income items are in much greater detail than
those furnished by the Department of Commerce. No
detail for expenses has been published since 1945.

[8]The "cash receipts from crops" and "cash receipts from livestock" items in the Department of Commerce estimates are broken down into five and three
groups respectively on the basis of data published in
The Farm Income Situation, (June, 1951), 27-28.

Because of the constantly recurring changes in the
amount of each farm commodity produced, the variance
in price fluctuations between the different farm crops,
and the effect of such other factors as general economic fluctuations and weather conditions which may
cause changes in the relative net return per farm acre
from the many farm crops, it would probably be wise
to re-examine the farm income allocators from year
to year, assuming yearly income estimates are to be
made. It is recommended, for example, that the component "all other crops sold" be broken down into several smaller components if there are data available
to use as allocators. In Kentucky, for example, nearly 80 per cent of gross income from crops sold is derived from the sale of tobacco. The number of acres
grown in each county changes slowly because of the
rigid statutory controls and allocating separately the
income derived from the sale of tobacco may, in some
years, greatly improve the reliability of the county
income estimates. A second point to be made for the
above suggestion may also be illustrated by a normal
Kentucky situation. Most of the cotton grown in Kentucky is grown in a single county. The reliability of
the income estimates in this county may be much greater if the income derived from the production and sale of
cotton were allocated as a separate component of income.

[9]Lancaster, County Income Estimates for Seven Southeastern States, 150-53.

[10]Virtually all proprietary mining activity in the state is in the coal industry.

[11]In the unpublished data on income by source, the Department of Commerce furnished estimates of property income broken down into seven categories: dividends, agricultural and nonagricultural rents, and interest income from financial intermediaries, insurance companies, government, and other cash interest. It will be noticed that for allocation purposes these have been grouped in a somewhat different manner. This is done as a matter of expediency and to avoid unnecessary detail.

[12]This portion of government interest is an approximation of the cash interest in this component. To arrive at this amount the U.S. Savings Bonds, Series E, F, and G held by residents of Kentucky were calculated, and the interest on these assumed to be imputed (not currently received) interest. The amount held by residents of the state was calculated from data in the U.S. Bureau of the Census, Statistical Abstract of the United States: 1951, 342-43.

[13]These Kentucky Department of Revenue data showed interest and dividends in total.

[14]These interest components are all imputed.

[15]Agricultural rent to nonfarm people was calculated as the difference between "net rent to landlords" (an item of agricultural production expense), and "agricultural rent" (a property income component that accrues to farmers only).

[16]From the veteran enrollment and the average in-

come of veteran students, it was estimated that 50 per cent of all veterans' subsistance payments could reasonably be allocated to the counties where the veterans were attending college.

[17]This component is distributed between "all payments as a result of World War II" and "payments as a result of all other wars" on the same basis as for the nation as a whole. U.S. Bureau of the Census, Statistical Abstract of the United States: 1951, 213.

[18]There were a few exceptions to this general rule. In some instances--in the Department of Mines and Minerals, for example--the residence of state employees was obtained.

[19]Social Security Board, Industrial Classification Code, Description of Industries.

[20]Total employment is defined here as total "covered" employment reported in the unpublished UC data, by county, and by industry. No account was taken of the employees of firms that employed fewer than four people because it was found that commuting by the employees of small firms is negligible, and because legal coverage of the Kentucky Unemployment Compensation Act is four or more employees (KRS, 341.050).

[21]"Survey of Indiana Commuting Patterns."

[22]Ohio Bureau of Unemployment Compensation.

[23]A very brief and general summary of worker commuting in the Cincinnati area can be found in: Covington-Kenton County Chamber of Commerce and the Agricultural and Industrial Development Board of Kentucky, Economic and Industrial Survey of Covington, Kentucky, 1-2.

[24]United States Census of Population: 1950, Vol. II, Part 17, Chap. B, Table 43.

[25]Coolsen, Myers, and Martin, Paducah and Western Kentucky Income, Labor, and Retail Trade Patterns, 20-33; and Martin and Myers, Aspects of the
Louisville Area Economy, 20-29.

[26]26 United States Code Annotated 1607.

[27]Kentucky Revised Statutes, 341.050.

[28]The radio broadcasting industry, for example,
is a part of covered service in the UC data and a part
of transportation and other public utilities in the Department of Commerce estimates.

[29]Unpublished data on income and average employment, Kentucky Department of Economic Security.

[30]A description and explanation of the Old-Age and
Survivors' Insurance statistics will be found in U.S.
Department of Commerce, County Business Patterns,
First Quarter, 1948, Part 1. The individual state
reports comprise Part II of the same publication and
similar reports for other years. Tabulations have
been prepared for the first quarter of each year since
1946 giving taxable pay rolls, employees, and units,
by county and industry. The published state bulle-
tins contain summary county statistics for nine industry divisions. The letters OASI will be used when
further reference is made to data from this source.

[31]The average earnings in each industry or in each
profession are different in the different counties. These
variations may be due in part to the extent of urbanization, custom, degree of unionization, etc.

[32]Kentucky Revised Statutes, 141. A more detailed
analysis of the provisions of the Kentucky income tax
law will be found in Chapter IV of this study.

[33]The ratio between reported gross income and total gross income in 1950 was about 48 per cent.

[34]Lancaster, County Income Estimates for Seven Southeastern States, 1.

[35]United States Census of Population: 1950, Vol. II, Part 19, Chap. B, v.

[36]Copeland, Methods for Estimating Income Payments in Counties, 92-95.

[37]United States Census of Manufacturers: 1947, Kentucky, Vol. III, No. MC 116, Table 2. Total salaries and wages of all employees was the allocator used.

[38]Unpublished data on the number of employees of Class I railroads, Bureau of Railway Economics, Washington, D. C.

[39]Myers, Johnson, and Martin, Kentucky Income Payments by Counties: 1939, 1947, 1950, and 1951; and Lancaster, County Income Estimates for Seven Southeastern States. It should be noted, however, that since the 1939 and 1947 estimates were first published by Lancaster refinements on these data have been made, and those not shown in Myers, Johnson, and Martin will be shown here. In these tables it should also be noted that the interstate situs adjustments as well as the intercounty situs adjustments have been incorporated.

[40]Computed from Graham, "State Income Payments in 1950," 17.

Table 36
TOTAL INCOME PAYMENTS TO INDIVIDUALS BY COUNTIES
1939, 1947, 1950, 1951, AND 1952 (thousands of dollars)

	1939	1947	1950	1951	1952
United States	$70,601.0	$185,339.0	$217,672.0	$242,947.0	$255,367.0
Kentucky[a][b]	822.6	2,333.1	2,709.2	3,088.7	3,272.4
Adair	$ 2,728	$ 8,728	$ 7,709	$ 9,344	$ 9,056
Allen	2,826	6,779	6,219	7,349	7,620
Anderson	2,509	7,473	7,623	8,554	8,381
Ballard	2,204	6,553	4,799	9,118	20,862
Barren	6,790	16,613	19,740	22,994	24,441
Bath	2,557	6,770	6,134	7,991	7,624
Bell	8,951	25,709	26,554	27,781	26,680
Boone	3,080	10,676	11,865	12,616	13,097
Bourbon	6,485	17,786	18,477	21,878	22,452
Boyd[a]	20,568	48,406	60,937	67,785	67,619
Boyle[a]	6,258	17,827	19,744	22,610	24,487
Bracken	3,038	5,942	6,738	8,172	7,854
Breathitt	2,704	7,931	8,788	10,676	11,385
Breckinridge	3,382	8,792	8,614	10,753	10,801
Bullitt	1,946	9,075	9,354	10,764	11,426
Butler	1,979	4,888	4,162	4,662	4,723
Caldwell	3,441	8,368	9,218	10,252	10,916
Calloway	4,423	12,280	13,805	15,513	17,233
Campbell	30,717	83,791	95,998	109,264	113,835
Carlisle	1,668	3,782	3,870	5,503	8,662
Carroll	2,624	6,059	7,221	7,654	7,921
Carter	4,494	12,546	11,545	14,657	14,191
Casey	2,633	7,782	7,239	8,694	9,086
Christian[a][b]	8,988	30,556	29,429	33,826	37,765
Clark	6,153	16,957	19,819	22,991	23,485
Clay	2,760	8,173	9,749	10,554	10,674
Clinton	1,056	3,894	4,414	4,682	4,598
Crittenden	2,553	5,914	5,583	6,705	7,609
Cumberland	1,627	4,489	4,262	5,153	5,301
Daviess	16,292	48,069	66,404	77,626	81,094
Edmonson	1,439	3,459	3,922	4,536	4,658
Elliott	945	3,269	3,085	3,904	3,780
Estill	3,098	7,731	8,162	9,439	9,851
Fayette[a]	33,356	113,339	134,748	146,470	154,013
Fleming	3,540	7,434	8,559	10,521	10,626
Floyd	12,075	34,661	40,613	44,120	39,707
Franklin[a]	10,970	29,618	28,592	31,515	35,820
Fulton	4,979	11,514	11,804	12,740	13,775
Gallatin	1,240	2,574	2,468	2,631	2,802

Table 36--continued

	1939	1947	1950	1951	1952
Garrard	$ 3,060	$ 9,160	$ 7,635	$ 8,948	$ 8,695
Grant	2,786	6,383	6,129	7,206	7,227
Graves	8,782	21,620	26,134	29,779	35,654
Grayson	2,856	7,570	8,459	10,106	10,298
Green	2,530	6,291	5,737	7,060	7,639
Greenup	5,086	18,207	16,123	18,514	18,994
Hancock	1,314	3,784	2,635	3,092	3,152
Hardin[b]	5,468	18,916	23,378	28,010	30,347
Harlan	25,988	58,691	69,242	74,959	68,583
Harrison	5,258	12,040	11,748	14,249	14,212
Hart	3,916	10,456	9,081	10,773	10,750
Henderson	8,786	23,376	27,468	30,100	32,272
Henry	3,597	8,421	8,777	10,251	10,787
Hickman	2,171	5,351	4,281	5,004	5,534
Hopkins	8,945	28,592	41,150	45,866	47,370
Jackson	1,861	4,927	5,257	6,245	6,011
Jefferson[a]	209,911	607,177	799,413	899,019	940,051
Jessamine	3,374	9,740	9,628	10,163	9,773
Johnson	4,854	12,159	12,805	13,363	13,519
Kenton	34,067	124,116	147,904	165,682	175,590
Knott	2,309	5,937	6,667	7,230	7,003
Knox	4,806	11,105	11,710	12,726	12,256
LaRue	2,221	6,133	7,204	8,388	8,544
Laurel	3,987	10,512	12,078	13,292	14,095
Lawrence	2,779	6,113	6,266	7,143	7,725
Lee	1,332	3,620	4,085	4,587	5,048
Leslie	1,379	5,223	5,826	6,505	6,686
Letcher	9,522	37,012	26,147	28,554	27,352
Lewis	3,177	6,636	6,535	7,603	7,656
Lincoln	3,900	10,678	10,213	12,047	11,996
Livingston	1,861	4,347	4,260	5,790	7,844
Logan	5,081	13,520	13,661	15,521	15,917
Lyon[a]	1,678	3,146	3,493	4,244	4,128
McCracken	17,518	39,908	55,278	86,303	160,299
McCreary	3,232	6,312	7,629	8,003	7,550
McLean	2,242	5,340	4,849	5,444	5,558
Madison	7,932	24,282	26,200	30,675	29,826
Magoffin	1,700	6,108	4,576	5,228	5,487
Marion	3,584	10,427	12,402	14,478	14,067
Marshall	3,524	7,557	8,488	11,696	20,450
Martin	974	3,839	3,996	4,348	4,107
Mason	7,955	19,508	21,313	24,540	24,986
Meade	1,804	6,089	7,203	8,436	9,878
Menifee	616	1,840	1,802	2,223	2,229

Table 36--continued

	1939	1947	1950	1951	1952
Mercer	$ 4,034	$11,335	$10,947	$12,467	$12,877
Metcalfe	1,827	4,907	5,081	5,989	5,950
Monroe	2,136	6,182	6,117	7,295	7,269
Montgomery	3,478	9,678	10,358	11,969	11,636
Morgan	1,841	5,786	6,529	7,602	7,060
Muhlenberg	6,874	20,459	21,456	23,209	22,909
Nelson	4,866	16,096	14,943	18,034	18,582
Nicholas	2,434	4,799	5,811	7,360	6,757
Ohio	3,860	11,315	11,329	13,250	11,908
Oldham[a]	2,426	7,429	7,728	8,800	9,637
Owen	3,101	7,422	6,659	7,713	7,906
Owsley	1,070	2,341	2,282	2,639	2,582
Pendleton	2,871	6,192	6,734	8,172	7,953
Perry	11,426	35,196	40,449	42,009	37,941
Pike	13,862	48,590	59,787	67,153	63,086
Powell	797	2,313	2,531	3,062	3,219
Pulaski	6,467	19,309	21,837	24,472	24,298
Robertson	978	2,006	2,280	2,872	2,771
Rockcastle	2,154	6,668	6,255	7,557	7,785
Rowan	2,750	6,906	7,678	8,795	8,522
Russell	1,646	7,372	6,059	7,581	7,247
Scott	5,150	12,058	13,554	14,976	14,466
Shelby	6,604	16,060	16,198	19,111	20,028
Simpson	3,320	7,418	7,756	8,893	9,068
Spencer	1,906	4,783	4,698	5,536	5,685
Taylor	2,821	8,354	10,072	11,753	12,061
Todd	2,820	7,530	7,304	8,697	8,670
Trigg	2,344	5,871	5,202	6,067	6,046
Trimble	1,370	3,748	2,733	3,240	3,679
Union[b]	4,393	9,990	10,410	12,322	15,004
Warren	10,061	32,717	36,441	39,641	41,725
Washington	3,148	8,295	9,341	10,696	10,662
Wayne	2,366	6,622	6,318	7,405	7,498
Webster	4,257	8,768	9,718	9,365	9,721
Whitley	6,229	15,755	18,620	19,711	19,804
Wolfe	1,019	2,946	3,195	3,404	3,394
Woodford	5,068	11,465	13,178	14,503	13,903

For explanation, see footnotes to Table 42.

Table 37
PER CAPITA INCOME PAYMENTS TO INDIVIDUALS BY COUNTIES
1939, 1947, 1950, 1951, AND 1952

	1939	1947	1950	1951	1952
United States	$539	$1,293	$1,439	$1,584	$1,639
Kentucky[a][b]	295	849	932	1,071	1,130
Adair	$146	$ 511	$ 438	$ 544	$ 539
Allen	183	498	451	550	560
Anderson	283	875	849	971	974
Ballard	235	780	562	763	1,390
Barren	248	619	694	827	825
Bath	224	663	589	790	762
Bell	206	581	558	590	597
Boone	286	906	912	969	956
Bourbon	365	1,051	1,041	1,259	1,255
Boyd[a]	450	1,054	1,232	1,387	1,366
Boyle[a]	365	1,033	1,037	1,188	1,269
Bracken	325	716	800	999	1,020
Breathitt	113	392	440	555	581
Breckinridge	191	577	555	715	710
Bullitt	205	882	824	949	1,034
Butler	138	419	368	430	462
Caldwell	239	647	698	800	852
Calloway	223	636	685	790	877
Campbell	430	1,174	1,260	1,454	1,476
Carlisle	220	599	624	845	1,096
Carroll	304	744	848	918	990
Carter	177	562	512	671	669
Casey	132	448	415	515	554
Christian[a][b]	266	883	816	941	983
Clark	341	953	1,049	1,236	1,217
Clay	116	368	422	467	511
Clinton	103	389	416	449	451
Crittenden	212	554	516	639	718
Cumberland	137	467	458	577	582
Daviess	313	905	1,160	1,371	1,374
Edmonson	127	364	418	502	548
Elliott	109	453	435	573	548
Estill	174	518	556	668	670
Fayette[a]	428	1,311	1,413	1,524	576
Fleming	267	631	716	907	966
Floyd	229	682	759	841	821
Franklin[a]	483	1,274	1,142	1,271	1,422
Fulton	326	853	864	962	1,044
Gallatin	289	663	622	682	758

Table 37--continued

	1939	1947	1950	1951	1952
Garrard	$259	$ 852	$ 692	$ 834	$ 813
Grant	284	682	625	750	777
Graves	279	721	833	970	1,081
Grayson	163	461	496	606	636
Green	206	570	509	645	694
Greenup	205	768	648	759	815
Hancock	194	636	439	531	573
Hardin[b]	235	613	685	769	867
Harlan	347	847	965	1,071	1,027
Harrison	350	892	855	1,068	1,053
Hart	228	690	593	726	768
Henderson	327	830	894	986	999
Henry	296	760	770	924	914
Hickman	239	687	550	666	748
Hopkins	238	780	1,060	1,202	1,214
Jackson	114	367	401	496	481
Jefferson[a]	548	1,408	1,667	1,865	1,912
Jessamine	269	798	773	830	828
Johnson	190	523	537	576	595
Kenton	368	1,291	1,419	1,602	1,666
Knott	115	308	328	362	371
Knox	155	379	385	428	424
LaRue	232	653	724	857	838
Laurel	155	428	468	525	566
Lawrence	162	420	435	514	568
Lee	123	406	467	546	615
Leslie	92	357	375	426	437
Letcher	236	976	662	739	755
Lewis	203	492	483	577	589
Lincoln	198	590	547	662	667
Livingston	205	588	593	806	1,075
Logan	219	627	612	712	723
Lyon[a]	223	519	607	778	764
McCracken	363	856	1,125	1,348	1,955
McCreary	197	398	458	489	466
McLean	197	537	484	561	561
Madison	264	817	840	995	962
Magoffin	98	430	331	394	439
Marion	212	638	721	857	823
Marshall	214	554	634	900	1,336
Martin	89	352	342	377	360
Mason	420	1,098	1,153	1,359	1,388
Meade	205	691	764	907	1,051
Menifee	109	382	376	480	464

Table 37--continued

	1939	1947	1950	1951	1952
Mercer	$278	$ 814	$ 748	$ 868	$ 888
Metcalfe	169	508	516	626	640
Monroe	153	468	444	542	542
Montgomery	285	794	795	932	888
Morgan	110	417	479	580	504
Muhlenberg	184	632	660	739	763
Nelson	271	884	765	935	934
Nicholas	284	641	772	1,010	965
Ohio	159	542	544	658	637
Oldham[a]	305	881	854	993	1,004
Owen	285	771	683	816	850
Owsley	120	314	312	374	374
Pendleton	278	661	701	874	865
Perry	240	788	869	923	899
Pike	195	652	737	843	847
Powell	104	343	372	464	488
Pulaski	163	522	568	652	675
Robertson	287	692	791	997	1,026
Rockcastle	126	470	449	564	568
Rowan	208	561	604	706	671
Russell	121	566	442	563	594
Scott	355	824	895	1,003	965
Shelby[a]	377	953	912	1,097	1,164
Simpson	284	665	664	777	810
Spencer	283	792	763	926	964
Taylor	207	615	699	828	838
Todd	199	595	567	695	705
Trigg	184	581	537	655	680
Trimble	246	745	531	647	721
Union[b]	254	671	699	857	1,035
Warren	263	820	852	930	994
Washington	244	677	731	855	874
Wayne	138	416	383	461	484
Webster	223	553	625	626	661
Whitley	188	509	583	632	705
Wolfe	102	371	420	467	485
Woodford	432	1,057	1,175	1,327	1,275

For explanation, see footnotes to Table 42.

Table 38
TREND IN PER CAPITA INCOME PAYMENTS TO INDIVIDUALS
BY COUNTIES, 1939, 1947, 1950, 1951, AND 1952 (1950 = 100)

	1939	1947	1950	1951	1952
United States	37	90	100	110	114
Kentucky[a][b]	32	91	100	115	121
Adair	33	117	100	124	123
Allen	41	110	100	122	124
Anderson	33	103	100	114	115
Ballard	42	139	100	136	247
Barren	36	89	100	119	119
Bath	38	113	100	134	129
Bell	37	104	100	106	107
Boone	31	99	100	106	105
Bourbon	35	101	100	121	121
Boyd[a]	37	86	100	113	111
Boyle[a]	35	100	100	115	122
Bracken	41	90	100	125	127
Breathitt	26	89	100	126	132
Breckinridge	34	104	100	129	128
Bullitt	25	107	100	115	125
Butler	38	114	100	117	126
Caldwell	34	93	100	115	122
Calloway	33	93	100	115	128
Campbell	34	93	100	115	117
Carlisle	35	96	100	135	176
Carroll	36	88	100	108	117
Carter	35	110	100	131	131
Casey	32	108	100	124	133
Christian[a][b]	33	108	100	115	120
Clark	33	91	100	118	116
Clay	27	87	100	111	121
Clinton	25	94	100	108	108
Crittenden	41	107	100	124	139
Cumberland	30	102	100	126	127
Daviess	27	78	100	118	118
Edmonson	30	87	100	120	131
Elliott	25	104	100	132	126
Estill	31	93	100	120	121
Fayette[a]	30	93	100	108	112
Fleming	37	88	100	127	135
Floyd	30	90	100	111	108
Franklin[a]	42	111	100	111	125
Fulton	38	99	100	111	121
Gallatin	46	107	100	110	122

Table 38--continued

	1939	1947	1950	1951	1952
Garrard	37	123	100	121	117
Grant	45	109	100	120	124
Graves	33	87	100	116	130
Grayson	33	93	100	122	128
Green	40	112	100	127	136
Greenup	32	119	100	117	126
Hancock	44	145	100	121	131
Hardin[b]	34	89	100	112	127
Harlan	36	88	100	111	106
Harrison	41	104	100	125	123
Hart	38	116	100	122	130
Henderson	37	93	100	110	112
Henry	38	99	100	120	119
Hickman	43	125	100	121	136
Hopkins	22	74	100	113	115
Jackson	28	92	100	124	120
Jefferson[a]	33	84	100	112	115
Jessamine	35	103	100	107	107
Johnson	35	97	100	107	111
Kenton	26	91	100	113	117
Knott	35	94	100	110	113
Knox	40	98	100	111	110
LaRue	32	90	100	118	116
Laurel	33	91	100	112	121
Lawrence	37	97	100	118	131
Lee	26	87	100	117	132
Leslie	25	95	100	114	117
Letcher	36	147	100	112	114
Lewis	42	102	100	119	122
Lincoln	36	108	100	121	122
Livingston	35	99	100	136	181
Logan	36	102	100	116	118
Lyon[a]	37	86	100	128	126
McCracken	32	76	100	120	174
McCreary	43	87	100	107	102
McLean	41	111	100	116	116
Madison	31	97	100	118	115
Magoffin	30	130	100	119	133
Marion	29	88	100	119	114
Marshall	34	87	100	142	211
Martin	26	103	100	110	105
Mason	36	95	100	118	120
Meade	27	90	100	119	138
Menifee	29	102	100	128	123

Table 38--continued

	1939	1947	1950	1951	1952
Mercer	37	109	100	116	119
Metcalfe	33	98	100	121	124
Monroe	34	105	100	122	122
Montgomery	36	100	100	117	112
Morgan	23	87	100	121	105
Muhlenberg	28	96	100	112	116
Nelson	35	116	100	122	122
Nicholas	37	83	100	131	125
Ohio	29	100	100	121	117
Oldham[a]	36	103	100	116	118
Owen	42	113	100	119	124
Owsley	38	101	100	120	120
Pendleton	40	94	100	125	123
Perry	28	91	100	106	103
Pike	26	88	100	114	115
Powell	28	92	100	125	131
Pulaski	29	92	100	115	119
Robertson	36	87	100	126	130
Rockcastle	28	105	100	126	127
Rowan	34	93	100	117	111
Russell	27	128	100	127	134
Scott	40	92	100	112	108
Shelby[a]	41	104	100	120	128
Simpson	43	100	100	117	122
Spencer	37	104	100	121	126
Taylor	30	88	100	118	120
Todd	35	105	100	123	124
Trigg	34	108	100	122	127
Trimble	46	140	100	122	136
Union[b]	36	96	100	123	148
Warren	31	96	100	109	117
Washington	33	93	100	117	120
Wayne	36	109	100	120	126
Webster	36	88	100	100	106
Whitley	32	87	100	108	121
Wolfe	24	88	100	111	115
Woodford	37	90	100	113	109

For explanation, see footnotes to Table 42.

Table 39
PER CAPITA INCOME PAYMENTS TO INDIVIDUALS BY COUNTIES
IN DOLLARS OF 1935-1939 VALUE, [c] 1939, 1947, 1950, 1951,
AND 1952

	1939	1947	1950	1951	1952
United States	$542	$810	$837	$853	$864
Kentucky[ab]	298	533	550	577	595
Adair	$147	$321	$256	$293	$284
Allen	184	313	263	296	295
Anderson	285	550	496	523	513
Ballard	236	490	328	411	732
Barren	249	389	405	446	435
Bath	225	416	344	426	401
Bell	207	365	326	318	315
Boone	288	569	533	522	504
Bourbon	367	660	608	678	661
Boyd[a]	453	662	720	747	720
Boyle[a]	367	649	606	640	669
Bracken	327	450	467	538	537
Breathitt	114	246	257	299	306
Breckinridge	192	362	324	385	374
Bullitt	206	554	481	511	545
Butler	139	263	215	232	243
Caldwell	240	406	408	431	449
Calloway	224	399	400	426	462
Campbell	433	737	736	783	778
Carlisle	221	376	364	455	577
Carroll	305	467	495	495	522
Carter	178	353	299	362	352
Casey	133	281	242	277	292
Christian[ab]	268	555	477	507	518
Clark	343	599	613	666	641
Clay	117	231	246	252	269
Clinton	104	244	243	242	238
Crittenden	213	348	301	344	378
Cumberland	138	293	268	311	307
Daviess	315	568	678	739	724
Edmonson	128	229	244	270	289
Elliott	110	285	254	309	289
Estill	175	325	325	360	353
Fayette[a]	431	823	825	821	830
Fleming	269	396	418	489	509
Floyd	230	428	443	453	433
Franklin[a]	486	800	667	685	749
Fulton	328	536	505	518	550
Gallatin	291	416	363	367	399

Table 39--continued

	1939	1947	1950	1951	1952
Garrard	$261	$535	$404	$449	$428
Grant	286	428	365	404	409
Graves	281	453	487	523	570
Grayson	164	290	290	327	335
Green	207	358	297	348	366
Greenup	206	482	379	409	429
Hancock	195	399	256	286	302
Hardin[b]	236	385	400	414	457
Harlan	349	532	564	577	541
Harrison.	352	560	499	575	555
Hart	229	433	346	391	405
Henderson	329	521	522	531	526
Henry	298	477	450	498	482
Hickman	240	432	321	359	394
Hopkins	239	490	619	648	640
Jackson	115	231	234	267	253
Jefferson[a]	551	884	974	1,005	1,007
Jessamine	271	501	452	447	436
Johnson	191	329	314	310	313
Kenton	370	811	829	863	878
Knott	116	193	192	195	195
Knox	156	238	225	231	223
LaRue	233	410	423	462	442
Laurel	156	269	273	283	298
Lawrence	163	264	254	277	299
Lee	124	255	273	294	324
Leslie	93	224	219	230	230
Letcher	237	613	387	398	398
Lewis	204	309	282	311	310
Lincoln	199	371	320	357	351
Livingston	206	369	346	434	566
Logan	220	394	357	384	381
Lyon[a]	224	326	355	419	403
McCracken	365	538	657	726	1,030
McCreary	198	250	268	263	246
McLean	198	337	283	302	296
Madison	266	513	491	536	507
Magoffin	99	270	193	212	231
Marion	213	401	421	462	434
Marshall	215	348	370	485	704
Martin	90	221	200	203	190
Mason	423	690	673	732	731
Meade	206	434	446	489	554
Menifee	110	240	220	259	244

Table 39--continued

	1939	1947	1950	1951	1952
Mercer	$280	$511	$437	$468	$468
Metcalfe	170	319	301	337	337
Monroe	154	294	259	292	286
Montgomery	287	499	464	502	468
Morgan	111	262	280	313	266
Muhlenberg	185	397	386	398	402
Nelson	273	555	447	504	492
Nicholas	286	403	451	544	508
Ohio	160	340	318	355	336
Oldham[a]	307	553	499	535	529
Owen	287	484	399	440	448
Owsley	121	197	182	202	197
Pendleton	280	415	409	471	456
Perry	241	495	508	497	474
Pike	196	410	430	454	446
Powell	105	215	217	250	257
Pulaski	164	328	332	351	356
Robertson	289	435	462	537	541
Rockcastle	127	295	262	304	299
Rowan	209	352	353	380	354
Russell	122	356	258	303	313
Scott	357	518	523	540	508
Shelby[a]	379	599	533	591	613
Simpson	286	418	388	419	427
Spencer	285	497	446	499	508
Taylor	208	386	408	446	442
Todd	200	374	331	374	371
Trigg	185	365	314	353	358
Trimble	248	468	310	349	380
Union[b]	256	421	408	462	545
Warren	265	515	498	501	524
Washington	246	425	427	461	460
Wayne	139	261	224	248	255
Webster	224	347	365	337	348
Whitley	189	320	341	341	371
Wolfe	103	233	245	252	256
Woodford	435	664	686	715	672

For explanation, see footnotes to Table 42.

Table 40
TREND IN PER CAPITA INCOME PAYMENTS TO INDIVIDUALS
BY COUNTIES IN DOLLARS OF 1935-1939 VALUE,[c] 1939-
1952 (1950 = 100)

	1939	1947	1950	1951	1952
United States	65	97	100	102	103
Kentucky[a b]	54	97	100	105	108
Adair	57	125	100	114	111
Allen	70	119	100	113	112
Anderson	57	111	100	105	103
Ballard	72	149	100	125	223
Barren	61	96	100	110	107
Bath	65	121	100	124	117
Bell	63	112	100	98	97
Boone	54	107	100	98	95
Bourbon	60	109	100	112	109
Boyd[a]	63	92	100	104	100
Boyle[a]	61	107	100	106	110
Bracken	70	96	100	115	115
Breathitt	44	96	100	116	119
Breckinridge	59	112	100	119	115
Bullitt	43	115	100	106	113
Butler	65	122	100	108	113
Caldwell	59	100	100	106	110
Calloway	56	100	100	107	116
Campbell	59	100	100	106	106
Carlisle	61	103	100	125	159
Carroll	62	94	100	100	105
Carter	60	118	100	121	118
Casey	55	116	100	114	121
Christian[a b]	56	116	100	106	109
Clark	56	98	100	109	105
Clay	48	94	100	102	109
Clinton	43	100	100	100	98
Crittenden	71	116	100	114	126
Cumberland	51	109	100	116	115
Daviess	46	84	100	109	107
Edmonson	52	94	100	111	118
Elliott	43	112	100	122	114
Estill	54	100	100	111	109
Fayette[a]	52	100	100	100	101
Fleming	64	95	100	117	122
Floyd	52	97	100	102	98
Franklin[a]	73	120	100	103	112
Fulton	65	106	100	103	109
Gallatin	80	115	100	101	110

Table 40--continued

	1939	1947	1950	1951	1952
Garrard	65	132	100	111	106
Grant	78	117	100	111	112
Graves	58	93	100	107	117
Grayson	57	100	100	113	116
Green	70	121	100	117	123
Greenup	54	127	100	108	113
Hancock	76	156	100	112	118
Hardin[b]	59	96	100	104	114
Harlan	62	94	100	102	96
Harrison	71	112	100	115	111
Hart	66	125	100	113	117
Henderson	63	100	100	102	101
Henry	66	106	100	111	107
Hickman	75	135	100	112	123
Hopkins	39	79	100	105	103
Jackson	49	99	100	114	108
Jefferson[a]	57	91	100	103	103
Jessamine	60	111	100	99	96
Johnson	61	105	100	99	100
Kenton	45	98	100	104	106
Knott	60	100	100	102	102
Knox	69	106	100	103	99
LaRue	55	97	100	109	104
Laurel	57	99	100	104	109
Lawrence	64	104	100	109	118
Lee	45	93	100	108	119
Leslie	42	102	100	105	105
Letcher	61	158	100	103	103
Lewis	72	110	100	110	110
Lincoln	62	116	100	112	110
Livingston	60	107	100	125	164
Logan	62	110	100	108	107
Lyon[a]	63	92	100	118	114
McCracken	56	82	100	111	157
McCreary	74	93	100	98	92
McLean	70	119	100	107	105
Madison	54	104	100	109	103
Magoffin	51	140	100	110	120
Marion	51	95	100	110	103
Marshall	58	94	100	131	190
Martin	45	111	100	102	95
Mason	63	103	100	109	109
Meade	46	97	100	110	124
Menifee	50	109	100	118	111

Table 40--continued

	1939	1947	1950	1951	1952
Mercer	64	117	100	107	107
Metcalfe	56	106	100	112	112
Monroe	59	114	100	113	110
Montgomery	62	108	100	108	101
Morgan	40	94	100	112	95
Muhlenberg	48	103	100	103	104
Nelson	61	124	100	113	110
Nicholas	63	89	100	121	113
Ohio	50	107	100	112	106
Oldham[a]	62	111	100	107	106
Owen	72	121	100	110	112
Owsley	66	108	100	111	108
Pendleton	68	101	100	115	111
Perry	47	97	100	98	93
Pike	46	95	100	106	104
Powell	48	99	100	115	118
Pulaski	49	99	100	106	107
Robertson	63	94	100	116	117
Rockcastle	48	113	100	116	114
Rowan	59	100	100	108	100
Russell	47	138	100	117	121
Scott	68	99	100	103	97
Shelby[a]	71	112	100	111	115
Simpson	74	108	100	108	110
Spencer	64	111	100	112	114
Taylor	51	95	100	109	108
Todd	60	113	100	113	112
Trigg	59	116	100	112	114
Trimble	80	151	100	113	123
Union[b]	63	103	100	113	134
Warren	53	103	100	101	105
Washington	58	100	100	108	108
Wayne	62	117	100	111	114
Webster	61	95	100	92	95
Whitley	55	94	100	100	109
Wolfe	42	95	100	103	104
Woodford	63	97	100	104	98

For explanation, see footnotes to Table 42.

Table 41
PER CAPITA INCOME PAYMENTS TO INDIVIDUALS BY COUNTIES
AS A PERCENTAGE OF UNITED STATES AVERAGE, 1939,
1947, 1950, 1951, AND 1952

	1939	1947	1950	1951	1952
United States	100.0	100.0	100.0	100.0	100.0
Kentucky[a][b]	54.7	65.7	64.8	67.6	68.9
Adair	27.1	39.5	30.4	34.3	32.9
Allen	34.0	38.5	31.3	34.7	34.2
Anderson	52.5	67.7	59.0	61.3	59.4
Ballard	43.6	60.3	39.1	48.2	84.8
Barren	46.0	47.9	48.2	52.2	50.3
Bath	41.6	51.3	40.9	49.9	46.5
Bell	38.2	44.9	38.8	37.2	36.4
Boone	53.1	70.1	63.4	61.1	58.3
Bourbon	67.7	81.3	72.3	79.5	76.6
Boyd[a]	83.5	81.5	85.8	87.6	83.3
Boyle[a]	67.7	79.9	72.3	75.0	77.4
Bracken	60.3	55.4	55.6	63.1	62.2
Breathitt	21.0	30.3	30.6	35.0	35.4
Breckinridge	35.4	44.6	38.6	45.1	43.3
Bullitt	38.0	68.2	57.3	59.9	63.1
Butler	25.6	32.4	25.6	27.1	28.2
Caldwell	44.3	50.0	48.5	50.5	52.0
Calloway	41.4	49.2	47.6	49.9	53.5
Campbell	79.8	90.8	87.6	91.8	90.1
Carlisle	40.8	46.3	43.4	53.3	66.9
Carroll	56.4	57.5	58.9	58.0	60.4
Carter	32.8	43.5	35.6	42.4	40.8
Casey	24.5	34.6	28.8	32.5	33.8
Christian[a][b]	49.4	68.3	56.9	59.4	60.0
Clark	63.3	73.7	72.9	78.0	74.3
Clay	21.5	28.5	29.3	29.5	31.2
Clinton	19.1	30.1	28.9	28.3	27.5
Crittenden	39.3	42.8	35.9	40.3	43.8
Cumberland	25.4	36.1	31.8	36.4	35.5
Daviess	58.1	70.0	80.6	86.6	83.8
Edmonson	23.6	28.2	29.0	31.7	33.4
Elliott	20.2	35.0	30.2	36.2	33.4
Estill	32.3	40.1	38.6	42.2	40.9
Fayette[a]	79.4	101.4	98.1	96.2	96.2
Fleming	49.5	48.8	49.8	57.3	58.9
Floyd	42.5	52.7	52.7	53.1	50.1
Franklin[a]	89.6	98.5	79.4	80.2	86.8
Fulton	60.5	66.0	60.0	60.7	63.7
Gallatin	53.6	51.3	43.2	43.1	46.2

Table 41--continued

	1939	1947	1950	1951	1952
Garrard	48.1	65.9	48.1	52.7	49.6
Grant	52.7	52.7	43.4	47.3	47.4
Graves	51.8	55.8	57.9	61.2	66.0
Grayson	30.2	35.7	34.5	38.3	38.8
Green	38.2	44.1	35.4	40.7	42.3
Greenup	38.0	59.4	45.0	47.9	49.7
Hancock	36.0	49.2	30.5	33.5	35.0
Hardin[b]	43.6	47.4	47.6	48.5	52.9
Harlan	64.4	65.5	67.1	67.6	62.7
Harrison	64.9	69.0	59.4	67.4	64.2
Hart	42.3	53.4	41.2	45.8	46.9
Henderson	60.7	64.2	62.1	62.2	61.0
Henry	54.9	58.8	53.5	58.3	55.8
Hickman	44.3	53.1	38.2	42.0	45.6
Hopkins	44.2	60.3	73.7	75.9	74.1
Jackson	21.2	28.4	27.9	31.3	29.3
Jefferson[a]	101.7	108.9	115.6	117.7	116.7
Jessamine	49.9	61.7	53.7	52.4	50.5
Johnson	35.3	40.4	37.3	36.4	36.3
Kenton	68.3	99.8	98.6	101.1	101.6
Knott	21.3	23.8	22.8	22.9	22.6
Knox	28.8	29.3	26.8	27.0	25.9
LaRue	43.0	50.5	50.3	54.1	51.1
Laurel	28.8	33.1	32.5	33.1	34.5
Lawrence	30.1	32.5	30.2	32.4	34.7
Lee	22.8	31.4	32.5	34.5	37.5
Leslie	17.1	27.6	26.1	26.9	26.7
Letcher	43.8	75.5	46.0	46.7	46.1
Lewis	37.7	38.1	33.6	36.4	35.9
Lincoln	36.7	45.6	38.0	41.8	40.7
Livingston	38.0	45.5	41.2	50.9	65.6
Logan	40.6	48.5	42.5	44.9	44.1
Lyon[a]	41.4	40.1	42.5	49.1	46.6
McCracken	67.3	66.2	78.2	85.1	119.3
McCreary	36.5	30.8	31.8	30.9	28.4
McLean	36.5	41.5	33.6	35.4	34.2
Madison	49.0	63.2	58.4	62.8	58.7
Magoffin	18.2	33.3	23.0	24.9	26.8
Marion	39.3	49.3	50.1	54.1	50.2
Marshall	39.7	42.8	44.1	56.8	81.5
Martin	16.5	27.2	23.8	23.8	22.0
Mason	77.9	84.9	80.1	85.8	84.7
Meade	38.0	53.4	53.1	57.3	64.1
Menifee	20.2	29.5	26.1	30.3	28.3

Table 41--continued

	1939	1947	1950	1951	1952
Mercer	51.6	63.0	52.0	54.8	54.2
Metcalfe	31.4	39.3	35.9	39.5	39.0
Monroe	28.4	36.2	30.9	34.2	33.1
Montgomery	52.9	61.4	55.2	58.8	54.2
Morgan	20.4	32.3	33.3	36.6	30.8
Muhlenberg	34.1	48.9	45.9	46.7	46.6
Nelson	50.3	68.4	53.2	59.0	57.0
Nicholas	52.7	49.6	53.6	63.8	58.9
Ohio	29.5	41.9	37.8	41.5	38.9
Oldham[a]	56.6	68.1	59.5	62.7	61.3
Owen	52.9	59.6	47.5	51.5	51.9
Owsley	22.3	24.3	21.7	23.6	22.8
Pendleton	51.6	51.1	48.7	55.2	52.8
Perry	44.5	60.9	60.4	58.3	54.9
Pike	36.2	50.4	51.2	53.2	51.7
Powell	19.3	26.5	25.9	29.3	29.8
Pulaski	30.2	40.4	39.5	41.2	41.2
Robertson	53.2	53.5	55.0	62.9	62.6
Rockcastle	23.4	36.3	31.2	35.6	34.7
Rowan	38.6	43.4	42.0	44.6	40.9
Russell	22.4	43.8	30.7	35.5	36.2
Scott	65.9	63.7	62.2	63.3	58.9
Shelby[a]	69.9	73.7	63.2	69.3	71.0
Simpson	52.7	51.4	46.1	49.1	49.4
Spencer	52.5	61.3	53.0	58.5	58.8
Taylor	38.4	47.6	48.6	52.3	51.1
Todd	36.9	46.0	39.4	43.9	43.0
Trigg	34.1	44.9	37.3	41.4	41.5
Trimble	45.6	57.6	36.9	40.8	44.0
Union[b]	47.1	51.9	49.6	54.1	63.1
Warren	48.8	63.4	59.2	58.7	60.6
Washington	45.3	52.4	50.8	54.0	53.3
Wayne	25.6	32.2	26.6	29.1	29.5
Webster	41.4	42.8	43.4	39.5	40.3
Whitley	34.9	39.4	40.5	39.9	43.0
Wolfe	18.9	28.7	29.2	29.5	29.6
Woodford	80.1	81.7	81.7	83.8	77.8

For explanation, see footnotes to Table 42.

Table 42

PERCENTAGE DISTRIBUTION OF INCOME PAYMENTS TO
INDIVIDUALS BY TYPE, BY COUNTIES, 1952

State and County	Net Wages and Salaries	Net Proprietors' Income		Property Income	Other Income
		Farm	Nonfarm		
United States	68.5	5.4	9.8	10.5	5.8
Kentucky[a][b]	63.6	10.5	10.7	7.4	7.8
Adair	21.0	49.0	12.0	6.2	11.8
Allen	34.7	34.9	11.7	5.3	13.3
Anderson	40.1	31.1	11.6	8.4	8.7
Ballard	79.4	8.3	8.4	1.2	2.7
Barren	40.4	35.0	10.1	6.2	8.3
Bath	19.9	56.4	7.4	5.3	11.0
Bell	62.4	1.5	15.6	6.2	14.2
Boone	58.7	15.9	10.2	7.3	7.9
Bourbon	44.5	29.3	8.5	11.3	6.4
Boyd[a]	73.3	0.6	12.0	7.5	6.6
Boyle[a]	60.0	15.4	9.3	8.6	6.7
Bracken	22.1	47.7	11.8	6.5	11.9
Breathitt	47.5	17.5	17.1	4.3	13.6
Breckinridge	32.8	40.6	10.4	4.6	11.6
Bullitt	62.6	15.8	10.8	3.9	7.0
Butler	27.0	37.3	14.5	3.3	17.9
Caldwell	47.4	19.5	14.1	6.0	13.1
Calloway	56.1	15.6	12.9	5.0	10.3
Campbell	77.1	2.2	9.0	5.3	6.3
Carlisle	64.5	20.6	6.7	2.5	5.6
Carroll	44.2	23.9	11.6	10.7	9.6
Carter	57.0	13.5	12.3	3.5	13.7
Casey	16.3	48.9	18.5	5.1	11.2
Christian[a][b]	60.0	12.5	13.4	6.7	7.3
Clark	43.9	28.8	11.2	9.0	7.1
Clay	49.0	19.8	11.7	3.1	16.4
Clinton	34.3	33.8	12.6	3.3	16.0
Crittenden	48.1	21.7	14.4	5.4	10.4
Cumberland	23.7	44.2	14.5	4.9	12.7
Daviess	68.8	5.6	11.8	7.8	6.1
Edmonson	32.3	34.3	12.0	4.7	16.7
Elliott	32.1	40.6	8.3	1.5	17.4
Estill	63.2	9.1	11.8	3.5	12.3
Fayette[a]	65.3	4.6	11.0	12.4	6.7
Fleming	21.2	53.3	10.5	6.0	9.0
Floyd	67.7	2.5	14.3	3.0	12.4
Franklin[a]	67.0	6.5	11.0	9.0	6.6
Fulton	53.5	13.9	14.1	8.9	9.6

Table 42--continued

State and County	Net Wages and Salaries	Net Proprietors' Income		Property Income	Other Income
		Farm	Nonfarm		
Gallatin	32. 6	36. 7	10. 7	9. 8	10. 2
Garrard	30. 6	44. 0	9. 9	7. 5	8. 0
Grant	25. 7	48. 5	9. 0	7. 2	9. 7
Graves	67. 5	11. 0	9. 1	5. 9	6. 5
Grayson	32. 7	38. 1	13. 3	4. 3	11. 6
Green	24. 5	45. 6	14. 7	6. 3	8. 9
Greenup	64. 9	8. 4	10. 6	2. 5	13. 6
Hancock	29. 0	36. 6	14. 7	5. 7	14. 1
Hardin[b]	60. 3	15. 8	10. 7	6. 7	6. 4
Harlan	75. 3	0. 4	8. 9	6. 1	9. 3
Harrison	36. 1	38. 4	9. 4	8. 3	7. 8
Hart	29. 1	44. 2	11. 5	6. 3	8. 8
Henderson	60. 1	9. 5	13. 0	9. 5	7. 8
Henry	27. 1	48. 3	10. 6	6. 6	7. 5
Hickman	39. 2	36. 1	11. 5	4. 9	8. 3
Hopkins	68. 0	3. 3	13. 0	8. 1	7. 6
Jackson	35. 3	33. 7	15. 5	2. 1	13. 5
Jefferson[a]	74. 7	0. 6	9. 2	9. 9	5. 6
Jessamine	41. 5	30. 5	10. 0	8. 9	9. 1
Johnson	49. 3	8. 8	14. 3	8. 4	19. 2
Kenton	79. 9	0. 8	8. 5	5. 0	5. 8
Knott	42. 3	10. 0	21. 3	1. 8	24. 7
Knox	48. 2	14. 7	13. 6	4. 3	19. 2
LaRue	32. 0	42. 7	11. 9	5. 3	8. 0
Laurel	44. 1	21. 4	16. 3	3. 6	14. 7
Lawrence	46. 5	21. 6	10. 1	4. 3	17. 4
Lee	49. 8	14. 8	17. 0	2. 9	15. 5
Leslie	46. 5	8. 8	19. 9	4. 6	20. 2
Letcher	68. 6	2. 5	13. 6	3. 3	12. 0
Lewis	33. 7	40. 7	8. 9	3. 5	13. 2
Lincoln	31. 5	42. 0	10. 6	5. 3	10. 5
Livingston	55. 7	21. 3	12. 8	2. 6	7. 6
Logan	40. 3	31. 3	12. 4	7. 4	8. 6
Lyon[a]	41. 6	31. 9	10. 5	5. 1	11. 0
McCracken	82. 7	0. 8	9. 5	3. 7	3. 3
McCreary	54. 9	5. 9	17. 0	3. 4	18. 7
McLean	34. 6	29. 5	13. 3	7. 1	15. 5
Madison	50. 0	22. 5	10. 6	8. 2	8. 6
Magoffin	39. 1	25. 4	16. 8	2. 2	16. 5
Marion	42. 1	30. 7	11. 0	6. 9	9. 3
Marshall	73. 5	4. 8	13. 7	1. 5	6. 4
Martin	42. 7	10. 0	24. 9	2. 7	19. 7

INCOME IN KENTUCKY

Table 42--continued

State and County	Net Wages and Salaries	Net Proprietors' Income		Property Income	Other Income
		Farm	Nonfarm		
Mason	50.1	23.1	10.3	11.0	5.4
Meade	62.5	23.0	5.8	3.0	5.8
Menifee	26.4	44.5	10.6	1.8	16.6
Mercer	38.9	33.1	11.8	8.4	7.9
Metcalfe	13.5	62.9	9.5	6.4	7.8
Monroe	23.7	44.8	12.3	5.6	13.5
Montgomery	40.4	27.0	11.7	12.8	8.1
Morgan	37.5	35.2	10.8	2.9	13.6
Muhlenberg	59.6	5.8	15.5	6.2	13.0
Nelson	45.9	25.7	14.3	6.4	7.7
Nicholas	28.4	50.9	5.8	6.3	8.6
Ohio	48.1	20.5	11.6	4.9	15.0
Oldham[a]	52.1	21.7	11.0	8.0	7.2
Owen	22.2	56.7	8.8	5.2	7.3
Owsley	23.3	43.5	10.3	2.4	20.6
Pendleton	23.5	53.6	8.0	7.0	8.0
Perry	69.9	2.2	11.7	4.1	12.1
Pike	68.4	2.7	13.7	3.8	11.5
Powell	30.8	26.2	20.8	2.6	19.5
Pulaski	48.5	21.5	12.4	4.8	12.8
Robertson	12.6	63.1	9.5	5.8	8.9
Rockcastle	39.6	27.0	14.7	2.9	15.8
Rowan	53.8	17.0	13.2	4.6	11.4
Russell	30.1	37.2	14.8	3.9	14.0
Scott	38.9	33.3	10.1	10.3	7.4
Shelby[a]	36.7	38.7	9.4	9.7	5.5
Simpson	36.0	36.1	9.8	8.2	9.9
Spencer	25.5	55.5	7.7	5.8	5.5
Taylor	42.2	31.4	13.2	5.4	7.8
Todd	37.4	36.4	10.7	4.9	10.5
Trigg	44.1	26.5	11.6	7.7	10.0
Trimble	16.0	66.6	4.2	5.6	7.6
Union[b]	61.9	10.5	13.0	6.9	7.7
Warren	54.1	17.0	12.1	8.2	8.6
Washington	23.7	52.8	8.7	7.2	7.6
Wayne	32.4	32.7	16.3	3.9	14.7
Webster	45.1	16.9	14.4	9.4	14.2
Whitley	55.9	7.2	12.5	8.2	16.3
Wolfe	29.9	30.1	22.9	2.0	15.1
Woodford	44.7	24.9	11.5	13.3	5.6

Table 42--continued

Note: Because of rounding, the figures for each county may not add
to 100 per cent.

[a]Such institutional population as inmates of homes for delinquent or
dependent children, homes and schools for the mentally or physically
handicapped, places providing specialized medical care, homes for the
aged, and federal and state prisons are excluded. As these inmates in
the state prisons in Lyon and Oldham counties received certain wages,
these payments are excluded.

[b]The military pay roll and population have not been included in the
designated counties for the years shown. Military pay roll data are not
readily obtainable. Military population data are confidential since the
Korean conflict began. For many purposes comparability between counties is better maintained through exclusion of the pay roll of military
personnel living in military camps. The figures for Kentucky are likewise computed exclusive of the military income and population in those
counties and inclusive of interstate situs adjustments.

[c]Adjustments effected by use of Consumer Price Index, U.S. Department of Labor, Bureau of Labor Statistics.

Table 43

NET INCOME PAYMENTS FROM FARM OPERATIONS PER ACRE
IN FARMS, 1939, 1947, 1950, 1951, AND 1952

	1939	1947	1950	1951	1952
United States	$ 4	$13	$11	$13	$12
Kentucky	6	18	15	19	18
Adair	$ 6	$20	$16	$21	$19
Allen	6	15	10	13	13
Anderson	7	19	17	21	21
Ballard	7	23	11	11	12
Barren	10	24	21	27	28
Bath	8	23	22	32	30
Bell	6	14	7	8	9
Boone	6	19	13	14	15
Bourbon	10	31	27	39	37
Boyd	3	8	3	5	7
Boyle	11	31	27	36	34
Bracken	10	20	23	32	30
Breathitt	4	14	9	10	10
Breckinridge	4	13	11	16	14
Bullitt	4	16	10	14	15
Butler	4	10	6	8	8
Caldwell	3	12	11	14	13
Calloway	7	17	12	14	13
Campbell	6	20	22	25	35
Carlisle	6	15	15	17	17
Carroll	10	24	19	22	24
Carter	4	12	8	11	10
Casey	7	19	16	21	19
Christian	4	16	10	13	13
Clark	9	33	37	47	44
Clay	4	12	10	12	10
Clinton	4	16	13	16	15
Crittenden	3	8	7	9	8
Cumberland	4	14	11	14	14
Daviess	7	24	14	16	18
Edmonson	5	11	10	13	13
Elliott	4	14	11	15	13
Estill	4	10	6	8	7
Fayette	5	30	30	42	44
Fleming	8	17	21	29	29
Floyd	6	9	6	7	7
Franklin	9	24	16	19	18
Fulton	10	29	14	14	17
Gallatin	8	18	15	15	18

Table 43--continued

	1939	1947	1950	1951	1952
Garrard	$11	$39	$23	$30	$27
Grant	7	19	17	22	22
Graves	7	17	12	14	12
Grayson	4	15	11	15	14
Green	8	24	16	21	21
Greenup	4	7	8	9	10
Hancock	5	21	11	14	12
Hardin	4	17	14	18	17
Harlan	5	18	4	5	6
Harrison	10	26	21	29	28
Hart	8	24	15	20	20
Henderson	6	15	9	10	12
Henry	10	23	23	29	31
Hickman	7	17	12	13	14
Hopkins	3	8	5	5	6
Jackson	6	17	13	18	16
Jefferson	- 2	21	13	17	35
Jessamine	10	37	28	33	29
Johnson	5	13	11	13	11
Kenton	5	11	13	16	21
Knott	4	10	6	7	7
Knox	4	11	10	11	12
LaRue	6	21	20	25	24
Laurel	6	18	14	16	18
Lawrence	4	9	7	8	8
Lee	4	14	10	12	11
Leslie	4	6	5	6	6
Letcher	7	16	7	7	8
Lewis	4	12	10	14	14
Lincoln	7	27	22	28	26
Livingston	3	10	8	10	10
Logan	6	18	13	17	15
Lyon	5	14	12	14	12
McCracken	5	14	9	9	11
McCreary	7	14	8	9	10
McLean	6	18	9	11	11
Madison	9	26	24	30	26
Magoffin	4	11	9	12	11
Marion	6	20	19	24	22
Marshall	5	11	7	7	6
Martin	3	7	5	5	6
Mason	13	32	28	38	39
Meade	4	14	13	16	15
Menifee	3	12	11	16	14

Table 43--continued

	1939	1947	1950	1951	1952
Mercer	$ 9	$33	$22	$27	$27
Metcalfe	7	19	17	22	22
Monroe	6	17	12	16	16
Montgomery	8	28	22	30	28
Morgan	4	12	13	18	14
Muhlenberg	3	10	6	7	7
Nelson	7	26	14	19	20
Nicholas	9	21	23	34	28
Ohio	4	12	7	9	9
Oldham	5	19	11	16	19
Owen	9	21	17	21	22
Owsley	6	12	10	12	12
Pendleton	8	18	22	28	26
Perry	8	11	7	8	9
Pike	5	11	7	7	8
Powell	3	11	10	14	12
Pulaski	5	18	15	19	18
Robertson	10	19	24	35	32
Rockcastle	5	17	13	17	16
Rowan	3	12	11	15	13
Russell	5	16	17	22	22
Scott	11	22	26	30	28
Shelby	10	27	21	30	33
Simpson	9	22	18	22	23
Spencer	9	24	20	25	26
Taylor	6	29	16	23	23
Todd	5	15	12	15	14
Trigg	4	14	7	9	8
Trimble	9	29	18	22	27
Union	5	16	6	8	9
Warren	7	20	17	22	22
Washington	9	27	25	31	30
Wayne	4	13	9	12	12
Webster	5	13	8	9	9
Whitley	3	11	8	9	10
Wolfe	3	14	8	11	10
Woodford	13	31	25	27	32

Sources: Computed from the net income from farm operations and United States Census of Agriculture: 1950, Vol. I, Part 19, State Table 1 and County Table 1; ibid., Vol. II, Chap. 1, Table 10; and United States Census of Agriculture: 1945, Vol. I, Part 19, County Table 1 (part 1).

Income in Kentucky: Distribution by Size

THE PROCEDURE followed in the distribution of 1950 incomes by size is necessarily divided into two major parts--determining the total number of recipients for each county or group of counties, and determining the distribution of these recipients according to income size.

ESTIMATING THE TOTAL NUMBER OF INCOME RECIPIENTS[1]

The term income recipient may be rather confusing. A better way of saying it may be "the total number of incomes," with the further qualification that many small incomes will be considered as part of a larger income. Suppose, for example, the wife of an employed man has income from an estate or trust. If this supplemental income is small there is, for all practical purposes, only a single income and therefore a single income recipient. Or suppose the spouse of a person receiving Old-Age and Survivors' Insurance benefits is also eligible for benefits and receives a spouse's share. This, again, is considered a single income and a single income recipient.

The total civilian labor force in Kentucky as reported in the 1950 Census of Population, less unpaid family workers, was 954,866. [2] This figure is used as an estimate of the total number of persons employed at some time during the year and implies that those who were unemployed at the time the census was taken did have income from employment sometime in 1950.

There is necessarily a constant turnover in the labor force--that is, new workers are entering the labor force and others are leaving at all times. Since the Department of Commerce estimates of income payments includes the incomes of those who, because they are just entering or leaving the labor force, work only part of the year, it seemed quite proper to make allowances for this factor in estimating the number of recipients. The annual turnover rate for male workers was assumed to be 2.5 per cent and for female workers 10 per cent--an average of 40 years and 10 years respectively spent in the labor force. This is probably an underestimate, but no adequate source of information is available. If the turnover rates are 2.5 and 10.0 per cent, the number of new workers who entered the labor force in 1950 was about 39,500. [3]

Another element to be considered is the number of persons--housewives, retired persons, and others-- who entered the labor force in 1950 because of expanded opportunity for employment. There was an increase in covered employment in the state during 1950 in spite of the fact that there was no increase in population. This increase, based on the average for the first three months of the year to the average for the last three months [4] after allowing for the absorption into the labor force of all unemployed persons reported by the census, amounts to about 20,300. This figure

includes the labor force increases in both covered
and noncovered employment.

There are many persons who have incomes from
various sources and who are not a part of the labor
force, such as retired persons, persons receiving public assistance in various forms, and persons who receive only income from property. There is no way
of determining how many individuals receive income
from property only--rents, royalties, dividends, and
interest--but of those who filed state income tax returns on 1950 incomes there were about 4,400. Probably there are many more, but as stated before, if
the earnings of the principal income recipient of a
family are supplemented by a small property income
of another member of the family there is, for all practical purposes, but one income and one recipient.

In 1951 the Kentucky Department of Economic Security made a study to determine how many recipients of public assistance payments also received income from some other source. [5] It is possible, from
this study, to reduce the possible error resulting
from counting some recipients twice, e.g., as wage
recipients and as recipients of public assistance. The
number of recipients and their incomes under the public assistance and Old-Age and Survivors' Insurance
programs are also available by county. [6] The number
of recipients in other retirement and welfare programs
is more difficult to estimate, and for this reason may
be less reliable. [7] These recipients, however, are
a very small part of the estimated 162,900 recipients
whose income in 1950 was not supplemented by either
wage or proprietary earnings.

The number of income recipients in each county
was determined by following the procedure outlined
above. It will be noted later in this Appendix that

some relatively minor adjustments involving only a
few counties are necessary. The following is a re-
capitulation of the number of income recipients for
the state as a whole as estimated by this method.

Total civilian labor force less
unpaid family workers.   954,900

Added adjustment for annual
turnover factor   39,500

Added adjustment for increased
employment opportunity   20,300

Recipients of property income
only   4,400

Recipients of transfer payments
only, after major adjustments
for the double counting of
recipients   162,900

Total number of income
recipients 1,182,000

ALLOCATING THE TOTAL INCOME AND
THE TOTAL NUMBER OF RECIPIENTS
TO THE INCOME SIZE GROUPS

The allocation of incomes and recipients to income
size groups is accomplished in three major steps. Income data taken from Kentucky individual income tax
returns is first adjusted to a point where the incomes
are conceptually comparable to the census definition.[8]
Census materials are then employed to distribute the
balance of "cash" income to the size groups below
$3,000, and the final phase has to do with bringing the
incomes into conformity with the income payments
concept.

Actually the entire procedure is devoted to the ultimate inclusion in the size distribution of all the elements included in income payments to individuals and the exclusion of the income received by persons not within the scope of this concept.

Allocate All Income Reported to the Kentucky Department of Revenue on State Income Tax Pay Returns for 1950--Returns on Which There Was a Tax Liability

Nearly a quarter of a million Kentucky residents paid an income tax to the commonwealth on their 1950 incomes.[9] As a first step these taxpayers and their incomes are distributed to the proper income size groups. As a matter of course only a part of all income payments to Kentucky residents is accounted for in this first allocation. But this fraction of total income is not small. Nearly half of all taxable income received by residents of the state is now accounted for and allocated.

Deduct Net Capital Gains

Capital gains, as such, are not a part of income payments to individuals. But since they are, in part, taxable as income in Kentucky, the net capital gains reported under the tax law in each income size group are deducted. Deducting net capital gains from the income groups makes necessary an adjustment in the number of individuals in each income group also. In most counties there were only a few persons who reported capital gains and usually not more than one or two for any income size group. In the larger counties

where several persons in a single size group may
have reported net capital gains the adjustments are
made assuming each had reported the same amount
of income from this source. On occasion there is a
net capital loss reported in a particular size group of
a county, and adjustment for this is made by adding
in the amount of capital loss reported and moving the
recipient, or recipients, to the proper group. Less
than 1 per cent of all income taxed is in the form of
net capital gains and in most counties the necessary
adjustments are extremely small.

Allocate All Income and Income Receivers From No-Pay Tax Returns

Besides the 234,000 pay returns for 1950 there were
about 90,000 income tax returns on which there was
no tax liability. As explained earlier, the pay returns
were completely tabulated; but the no-pay returns were
not. In counties where there were 50 returns or less
of this type all returns were tabulated; in counties where
there were over 50 and less than 1,000 no-pay returns
a random sample of 50 was taken; and in counties where
there were over 1,000 a 5 per cent random sample was
taken. From these samples the total number of recipients and income for each size group are calculated on a
county basis, and added to the pay return data.

Allocate the Income and Income Recipients from 1950 Income Tax Returns Filed in 1952

There are always those who, even though they have
knowledge of the law, try to avoid paying the state in-

come tax. And there are many persons entering the labor force each year who may not realize they have a tax liability. Along with these there are persons that may have been in the labor force for many years without ever incurring a tax liability, but who because of increased earnings may have incurred a liability for a particular year. The Kentucky Department of Revenue is at all times trying to keep compliance with the income tax law at a maximum, and it is through these efforts that many potential taxpayers who do not file returns are detected. In 1952 there were about 10,000 persons filing pay returns on 1950 incomes as a result of these compliance checks or for other reasons. A tabulation of these returns, by county, was furnished by the Kentucky Department of Revenue. From this tabulation the amount of taxable income received by these recipients cannot be determined. Late returns, however, according to officials in the Income Tax Division, were filed primarily by wage earners. The noncompliance was discovered when the pay roll data supplied by Kentucky employers was checked against the returns filed. The income size distributions by county of wage and salary earners who did comply with the law voluntarily and on time, then, provided a basis for allocating the incomes of recipients who filed late. The determined amount of income and the number of recipients who filed late returns are here allocated to the proper size groups.

Adjust for Noncompliance and Underreporting

The corrections for noncompliance and underreporting are made to account for respectively the incomes of those persons who were legally required to

file returns but failed to do so or who, if they did
file returns, reported less income than the taxable
amount they received. In making these adjustments
there is very little factual material to work with, and
the problem is magnified because there are sound
reasons for believing that the situation differs from
county to county. It is a situation, however, that cannot be ignored. Because in spite of the limited knowledge as to the extent, there is definite knowledge that
some underreporting and noncompliance did, and still
does, exist. [10] Four adjustments aimed at correcting
for noncompliance and underreporting are made--two
that relate to particular counties and two that relate
to all counties.

From the data as to county income by source previously estimated it was a relatively simple operation
to estimate the amount of taxable income received by
the residents of each county. From the income tax
statistics furnished by the Kentucky Department of
Revenue and taxable income received the ratio of reported taxable income to total taxable income was computed for each county. These ratios verified the hy-
potheses of executives in the Income Tax Division of
the Department of Revenue and of other students in
the field that compliance is poor in Kenton and Campbell Counties relative to other counties in the same
per capita income range. It is pointed up in Appendix
1 that thousands of persons living in these two counties are employed in Ohio. Because so many residents of these two counties are employed outside the
state, and because one of the important compliance
checks of the Kentucky income tax law--a legal provision that out-of-state employers may disregard--
is a provision that employers file with the Kentucky
Department of Revenue a record of employee earn-

ings, there is a greater opportunity for some of the residents of this area to evade the law than exists in other areas of the state. Adjustments are made, therefore, that have the effect of bringing Campbell and Kenton Counties into line with the unweighted mean of the ratios (taxable income reported to taxable income received) for the other three counties which together with these two comprise the five highest on a per capita income basis. Of the other three counties in this group of five, one on a population basis is smaller; another about the same size; and the third larger than either of the two counties for which the adjustments are made. The unweighted average of the percentage of taxable income reported by the residents of these three counties is assumed to be the percentage that should have been reported by the residents of Kenton and Campbell Counties in 1950 assuming comparable compliance with the law. These two counties are here brought up to this level, but no change is made in the percentage distribution of income and recipients among the income size groups.

A second adjustment for noncompliance and under-reporting is made in four counties for altogether different reasons. These four counties are large producers of coal but there is very little opportunity for industrial employment outside the mines. As a consequence the number of women in the labor force is extremely low, percentagewise, relative to other counties with similar per capita incomes. A careful analysis of the relationships between income tax data and labor force data by sex seems to indicate that one of the results of high female employment is a high percentage of wages and salaries reported for income tax purposes. In order to get a view of this phenomenon that would be both clear and measurable a least-squares

regression line was fitted to the ratios of wages and
salaries reported for state income tax purposes to
total wages and salaries earned. The counties and
county groups were spaced on the horizontal axis according to per capita income and the ratio scale was
represented by the vertical axis. The ratios of the
four counties previously mentioned fell considerably
below the regression line and were proportionately
lower than any of the other county or county group ratios. The percentage of wages and salaries that would
have been reported had their ratio points fallen on the
regression line is assumed to be the amount that would
have been reported had the residents of these counties
complied with the law as did the residents of other
counties with comparable per capita incomes. It must
be understood that these adjustments differ from those
made for Kenton and Campbell Counties in several important respects. First, the adjustments made for
the coal-producing counties are made for wage and
salary compliance only, but as before no change is
made in the percentage distributions of the type of income affected. Second, it should not be inferred that
excessive evasion of tax liability is common in these
four counties. The assumption on which these adjustments rest is that there are far fewer families with
more than one wage earner as indicated by the census
labor force data previously referred to; and this fact,
coupled with the fact that the average family size in
the coal counties is greater than that of the state, indicates a larger allowance for dependents in computing tax liability. In counties that one may refer to
as single industry counties, such as the four coal counties under consideration here, there is quite reasonably an unusual concentration of incomes within a small
range clustered around the average income for work-

ers in the important industry. (See Table 40.) Taking into account these average earnings, family size, and low female employment it would seem methodologically sound to make the adjustments outlined above.

The preceding paragraphs deal only with specific counties, and the adjustments outlined are made for the purpose of bringing all counties and county groups into a state of relative comparability insofar as compliance with the provisions of the income tax law is concerned. It is rather common knowledge, however, that there are some persons in every county who fail to file returns when, under the statutory requirements, they should do so. Failure to file returns is, in most instances, a result of lack of knowledge of the law or of its provisions. Only in a minority of cases is there any indication of willful violation. On the basis of information supplied by persons in charge of income tax administration in the state the majority of these cases of noncompliance are in the low income classes. Accurate information on the amount of noncompliance is, of course, unavailable. Estimates, based on the best information available, of a 15 per cent understatement as a result of noncompliance in the $3,000--$3,999 group, a 5 per cent understatement in the $4,000--$4,999 group, and a 1 per cent understatement in the $5,000--$6,999 income size group were made. The amount of income and the number of recipients in these three size groups are increased by the above percentages in all counties except Franklin. [11] These noncompliance adjustments are made after the adjustments for individual counties are added in.

The fourth, and last, adjustment of the taxable income reported is made for underreporting--reporting less than the total amount of taxable income received. Unlike noncompliance, this amount was as-

sumed to be uniform throughout the income size groups.
But, as in the case of noncompliance, it is more often
than not the result of error and not of intent to evade
tax liability. All available evidence seems to indicate underreporting of about 3 per cent in all income
size groups. [12] The amount of income and the number of recipients in each size group, after all other
adjustments have been made, are adjusted upward by
this assumed amount of underreporting.

Assume All Income of a Taxable Nature
in the Size Groups $3,000-$3,999
and Above Accounted For

The different concepts of income used by the National Income Division of the Department of Commerce, the Bureau of the Census, and the Kentucky
Department of Revenue have been discussed earlier.
In working with data from all three of these sources
a great deal of care must be exercised when convert-
ing from one concept to another. The procedure, as
outlined up to this point, has to do only with income
as defined by law for Kentucky income tax purposes.
And at this point it must be assumed that the distribution as it stands is a theoretically complete picture of
the distribution of all taxable incomes and income recipients for the size groups above $3,000. Because
the distribution of recipients for the size groups below $3,000 will be made on the basis of data provided
by the Bureau of the Census the incomes represented
in the upper classes should be brought into conformity with this concept. In order to do this the nontaxable cash income received by persons with taxable incomes above $3,000 must be allocated.

Some of the important cash income items not taxable in Kentucky are unemployment compensation, various types of payments to veterans, and some dividends and interest.

A Method of Estimating Changes in the Number
of Recipients and the Amount of Income by
Size Groups as Nontaxable Types of
Income Are Allocated

After determining the number of recipients and the amount of income in each size group from state income tax returns for 1950, plus adjusting for those who have tax liability and do not file returns and for those who understate their taxable income, it is necessary to devise a method for allocating the nontaxable types of income. All adjustments, with one exception, have the net effect of moving some of the recipients and their incomes into a higher size group. Because of the hundreds of calculations that have to be made, a simplified formula for finding the number of recipients and the amount of income they receive, moving from one group to another, is employed. At the outset certain assumptions were made that may seem to violate the laws of sound statistical procedure, and probably do to some extent; but it would also appear in retrospect that the errors committed by these known violations are not quantitatively serious. Following the procedural outline a discussion of these possible errors will be in order.

From the adjusted income tax data an average income in each size group above $3,000 is calculated. Given any one of these average figures and the class limits a median figure can be approximated. This ap-

proximation is made by finding the difference between
the average income of the groups (arithmetic mean)
and the midpoint of the class (class mark), and then
assuming the median (the income value that will divide all recipients in the group into two equal parts)
to be twice this difference from the class mark, and
in the same direction from the class mark as is the
mean. Next, it is assumed that between the class
median and the class limits each half of the recipients would be evenly distributed. [13]

With these assumptions and a known number of recipients in each class who received a particular type
of income and the average amounts received (how
these values are determined and the processes used
will be explained in each instance), it is then possible to determine the number of recipients to move into a higher income size group when a particular component of income is added to that already allocated.
Furthermore, it is possible to determine the total income of these persons, which must also be moved to
a higher group, by multiplying the number of recipients to be moved by their average income. Their average income is calculated as follows. Suppose an adjustment is being made from the $3,000--$3,999 size
group to the $4,000--$4,999 size group, and the amount
of income being added to the incomes of all persons
receiving the type being allocated is $40. Then those
persons with incomes of $3,960 or more in the lower
size group to whom an additional $40 is being allo-
cated would be moved into the higher income class
and the mean income of those persons would be $3,980
before being moved and $4,020 after being moved.
Assigning letters to each of the values used in the
computations the process may be written as a formula.

a = the amount of additional income for each
recipient of the type for which the adjustment is being made

b = the upper class limit

c = the class median as previously determined

d = the number of recipients in the income
class with the type of income for which
the adjustment is being made

Then,

$(\frac{a}{b-c})(\frac{d}{2})$ = the number of recipients to be
moved into the next higher size
group. (Let this value = x)

Then,

$x(b - \frac{a}{2})$ = the dollar amount of income received by those recipients moving
to the higher group. This amount,
using the illustration above, would
be deducted from the $3,000--
$3,999 group and added to the
$4,000--$4,999 group.

After completing the above adjustments a new number of recipients in each size group with the type of
income being allocated is determined, and this number multiplied by the average amount of income received of the type being allocated is then added to each
size group to complete the process.

But there is still a single place in each allocation
where the formula will not apply. Because these computations, in the process of allocating nontaxable cash
income, are based on gross income as reported on
state income tax returns (with adjustments for noncompliance and underreporting) for persons with taxable incomes of $3,000 and above, the adjustments of

income and income receivers from the $2,000--$2,999
group into the $3,000--$3,999 group cannot be made
by using the process described. In this one instance
a similar procedure is used. It is assumed that those
recipients (again going back to the original illustration) receiving $3,000--$3,040, who as a consequence
of the adjustments, will move higher in the $3,000--
$3,999 income class will be replaced by the same
number of persons from the $2,000--$2,999 income
size group and the average income of these recipients would be $2,980. The formula for calculating
the number of income recipients who move into the
$3,000--$3,999 income class reads as follows:

$$x = \left(\frac{a}{c - 3,000}\right)\left(\frac{d}{2}\right)$$

After working through the entire procedure to com-
pletion using the formula discussed it was discovered
that an error of major importance had been made in
estimating the number of persons and income that
move from group $2,000--$2,999 to group $3,000--
$3,999. From a careful examination of the data it
was found necessary to go through the process of allocation another time, and in the new allocation both
the number of persons and their income in this adjustment are increased by one-third. [14] Under different
conditions, or in using different basic data, this adjustment may vary somewhat in one direction or the
other.

Allocate Nontaxable Cash Income That Accrues
Exclusively to Wage and Salary Recipients

Several components of income payments, exclusive of direct payment of wages and salaries, are re-

ceived almost entirely by persons who work for others for pay. These income items include railroad sickness benefits, railroad unemployment compensation benefits, state unemployment compensation benefits, workmen's compensation, veterans' subsistence allowances (noncollege), and veterans' unemployment compensation. It may be argued that the latter two of the components listed above do not accrue entirely to wage earners; but there is no way to ascertain how much of either type is received by persons who do not work for wages. For this reason and because these two components of income represent such a very small percentage of the total, it is assumed that all benefits of this type are received by wage earners.

Obviously it is impossible to know how many wage and salary workers are recipients of one or more of these components of income or in what income size groups these recipients may be. One alternative, which was the one selected, would be to assume that all wage and salary workers with an income of less than $7,000 in 1950 would benefit equally, and that those earning more than $7,000 would receive no income from these components. Obviously, again, this is not reality. But close observation will reveal the scheme to be more practical than it at first appears. Far and away the most important of the income components listed are unemployment benefits (exclusive of veterans' unemployment benefits) and workmen's compensation. The amount of benefits received by an eligible worker under these programs is dependent to a considerable degree on his average earnings and length of employment. Persons with high income, if they become eligible, would no doubt receive more in benefits than persons with small incomes. And even

though persons who had small incomes in 1950, if they
are eligible, may have received benefits over a longer period of time, there are many wage earners in
the lower income classes who may never become eligible for any of the benefits listed. Notable among
these persons are domestic servants and farm laborers. The number of wage earners in each of the three
size groups from $3,000--$6,999 is determined from
the state income tax return data for 1950. The percentage wage earners are of all recipients in each size
group, calculated from the pay and no-pay returns,
is multiplied by the total number of recipients in the
corresponding size groups as determined at this point
in the procedure. The average income from these
components to each wage earner is found by dividing
the total of the components by the number of private
wage and salary workers reported by the census. [15]

Allocate the Government Payments to Veterans of World War II That Are Not Based on Income or Employment Status

Several types of payments made to veterans by the
federal or state governments bear no relation to the
income or employment status of the recipients. The
components of income that fall within this group are
state bonuses to veterans; National Service Life Insurance special dividends; veterans' pensions and com-
pensations (World War II only); federal interest payments on veterans' loans; military reserve pay (this
component, of course, is not all received by veterans,
but division between veterans and nonveterans is impossible and the total amount is rather small); mus-
tering-out-pay; enlisted men's cash terminal leave

payments; and payments to former prisoners-of-war
(United States) by the War Claims Commission.

The number of World War II veterans living in Kentucky on June 30, 1951, was 255,000.[16] The average
income to each veteran from these components of income in 1950 was $429, nearly half of which was in
the form of National Service Life Insurance special
dividends. No series of data is available that shows
how the veteran population is distributed among the
several income classes. In the absence of a more
desirable series the veterans are distributed among
the income size groups on the basis of "age of head
of spending unit" as given in the "1951 Survey of Consumer Finances."[17] It is assumed that veterans are
distributed among the income groups in the same ratio
as are the heads of spending units between 24 and 54
years of age. Even though the Kentucky income tax
data does include some statistics relative to the age
of the recipients they are considered inferior to the
"Survey of Consumer Finances" material for use here.

At this point in the allocation procedure 18.7 per
cent of all income recipients have been previously allocated to the income size groups above $3,000. The
number of veterans in these size groups, however, is
more than 18.7 per cent of all veterans because the
number of persons between the ages of 24 and 54 who
are heads of spending units are 67 per cent of all heads
of spending units in the size groups above $3,000, where-
as in all spending units these same persons comprise
only 62 per cent of the total. Because of this disproportionate number of heads of spending units aged 24
to 54 in the upper income groups, a disproportionate
number of veterans would also be found in these income groups. Continuing with the assumption that veterans should follow the same distribution pattern as

persons between 24 and 54, the number of veterans
in the income size groups above $3,000 is estimated
to be 20.2 per cent of all veterans rather than 18.7
per cent. [18]

After determining the total number of veterans in
the income groups above $3,000 there remains the
problem of apportioning this total to the separate size
groups. A distribution of persons between the ages
of 24 and 54 years by income class is first calculated
and from this distribution the estimated 51,400 veterans with incomes of more than $3,000 are allocated.
The distribution of persons in this age group is made
from the percentage distribution taken from the "Survey of Consumer Finances."[19] Because the income
classes in this series are not comparable to the income classes used here, the total number of persons
with incomes of over $5,000, and between the ages of
24 and 54, are distributed to the size groups in exact
proportion to the number of recipients previously allocated to these groups.

Allocate the Government Payments to
Veterans of All Other Wars

Most of the payments to veterans of other wars are
in the form of pensions and compensation or adjusted
service bonds. The latter is less than 1 per cent of
the total. Very simply, this allocation is made in the
same way as World War II veterans' payments, using
material from the same sources. The age distribution used to allocate the veterans among the size groups
is based on the heads of spending units 55 years old
and over. The estimated number of veterans in this
series, with incomes of $3,000 and over, is 9,400,

and the average amount per veteran is $416.[20] Un-
like the veterans of World War II there are proportionately fewer in the income groups above $3,000
than there are in all income classes. The ratio here
is 28 per cent (heads of spending units 55 years old
and over in all income groups) to 24 per cent (the
heads of spending units 55 years old and over in the
income classes above $3,000).

Allocate Nontaxable Cash Interest and Dividends

Kentucky income tax is not paid on the interest received from government securities (all levels of government with the exception of foreign obligations and
state and local government securities of other states),
nor is it paid on dividends received on bank stock or
on the stock of savings and loan companies. The total
income to Kentucky residents from these sources in
1950 amounted to over $22 million.[21] In order to dis-
tribute this amount to the proper size groups it is first
assumed that income of this type would accrue to persons who reported dividends and interest on their 1950
income tax returns and that the amount received by
persons in each size group would be in direct proportion to the average amount of taxable dividends and
interest reported. There is one exception to this rule.
Data from tax returns are not a reliable measure of
income received in the income size groups below $3,000.
It is assumed here that the same amount of dividends
and interest reported by recipients in the $3,000--
$3,999 group is the amount received by persons in the
0--$999, $1,000--$1,999, and $2,000--$2,999 size
groups. The average income from this source ranged

from $188 in the $3,000--$3,999 group to $47,240
for those who reported incomes of $200,000 or more;
and the number of persons reporting dividend and interest income. on 1950 state income tax returns ranged
from 10.6 per cent in the $3,000--$3,999 group to
100 per cent for those with incomes above $200,000.
There are, of course, variations from these state averages from county to county.

Assume Conceptual Comparability Between the Income Now Allocated to Size Groups $3,000--$3,999 and Above and Income As Defined by the Bureau of the Census

The four adjustments in cash income and in the
number of recipients by size groups for all income
classes greater than $3,000 that are made after all
taxable income in these classes is accounted for presumably brings the income of these groups into the
range of comparability with income as defined by the
Bureau of the Census. A comprehensive discussion
of the different concepts of income is previously giv-
en. From this discussion it will be remembered that,
in general, the census definition of income is synonymous with cash income. And all cash income, taxable and nontaxable, received by persons with incomes
of $3,000 or more has been allocated. [22]

Distribute the Income Recipients and Their Cash Income to the Size Groups Below $3,000

The total number of income recipients for the state
and the counties was estimated prior to the allocation

of nontaxable cash income because this information
was necessary in making some of those allocations.
These same estimates are likewise necessary in this
phase of the procedure; but, as will be shown later,
they are also subject to slight revision (see Table 38).
The number of recipients already allocated to the income size groups above $3,000 deducted from the es-
timated number of recipients for any county or group
of counties would provide an estimate of the number
of recipients to be allocated to the size groups below
$3,000. The amount of cash income to be allocated
to these groups could likewise be determined. These
estimates of the number of recipients and the amount
of cash income they received coupled with the county
distributions of families and unrelated individuals by
income class, as reported in the 1950 Census of Population,[23] provide the basic data for making the allocation of cash income and the recipients to the 0--$999,
$1,000--$1,999, and $2,000--$2,999 income classes.

Prior to going into the distribution process, as related to the income classes below $3,000, some of the
stumbling blocks in the basic data that should be overcome will be mentioned. The nature of these obsta-
cles render some of them more important than others.
But in order for the procedure to be at all clear a brief
summary of these impediments appears to be essen-
tial.

1. The definition of income recipient used by the
Bureau of the Census, as explained earlier, is different from that used in this study.

2. The census concept of income is somewhat different from the income payments concept, but more
important is the fact that the incomes reported in the
1950 Census of Population are 1949 incomes--not 1950--
and the income size breakdowns as presented here are

based on the income received in the latter year. If
there had been only slight changes in the amounts of
income received from different sources, and if the
incomes of all persons had fluctuated uniformly, this
problem would be less serious. But such is far from
being the case. The total amount of income derived
from farm operations declined, from 1949 to 1950,
by 17.6 per cent. The average monthly income of
workers covered by the unemployment compensation
law increased in all but two counties, varying greatly
by location and type of industry.

    3. The changing residence of persons likewise
created problems. In estimating the amount of income received by the residents of each county only
incidentally, as a rule, did a change of residence from
one county to another enter into the picture. And the
nature of the statistics used to allocate wages and salaries, which in most counties is the largest component of income received, is not at all conducive to allocating all of a particular wage earner's income to
his county of residence as of December 31, 1950, or
as of any other date if he changed his residence during the year. This is as it should be, of course, for
an income by source distribution by county. But the
census data report this same wage earner in a particular income class and as a resident of the county
where he lived when enumerated although a part, or
all, of his income for the preceding year may have
been earned in another county or another state.

    But this problem of residence has another impor-
tant facet. State income taxes are payable on or before April 15 of the year following the year in which
the income was received. And again, residence as of
April 15, 1951, or as of the date the return was filed,
is not evidence of the fact that the reported income
was earned in the county of current residence.

There is also another residence factor that may, or may not, be of some significance. The depth of the 1949 recession was reached in early 1950, just prior to the census enumeration dates. There could have been, at that time, many persons who had previously migrated to other states and other counties who had not become permanent residents in their new locations and, because of the recession, had returned "home." These persons, then, could have been enumerated as residents of a county where they had no intention of staying--and did not stay--when the recession ended.

4. Distributing recipients and their income to the three lower income classes is further complicated by the fact that complete accuracy in the estimates of total cash income for counties would be the exception rather than the rule. This is just as true of the estimates of total income recipients and of all other statistical series used in the allocation procedure, particularly the adjustments for noncompliance and underreporting.

It would be possible, of course, to go into all of the points in much greater detail, but enough has been said to indicate the nature of the problem and to indicate also that there is no easy way out of the dilemma-- no single allocation formula that would be applicable in all instances. With the foregoing as a background, then, the method of allocating cash income received and income recipients to the size groups below $3,000 will be explained.

Using the census distribution of incomes by county for families and unrelated individuals an average income for the $1,000--$1,999 and the $2,000--$2,999 size groups for each county or county group is determined, rather than assuming the average for these groups to be identical to the class mark. The distri-

bution of recipients in the census is by $500 inter-
vals for incomes up to $5,000. In order to find the
approximate average income of the recipients in the
$1,000--$1,499 census group for a particular county
it is first assumed that the recipients in this group are
distributed along a straight line determined by the number of recipients in the next lower and next higher
group. If, for example, with the income scale on the
horizontal axis and the recipient scale on the vertical
axis, a straight line is drawn from a point determined
by the class mark and the number of recipients in the
$500--$999 census group to a point determined by the
class mark and the number of recipients in the $1,500--
$1,999 census group, the slope of the line is an indi-
cation of how the recipients in the $1,000--$1,499 group
are distributed and an average income for the group
can be approximated. [24] Similarly, an approximation
of the average income for the recipients in the census
size group $1,500--$1,999 can be estimated. From
these two estimates and the number of recipients in
the size groups $1,000--$1,499 and $1,500--$1,999
a weighted average income for the two groups is computed, and is assumed to be the average income of all
recipients in the $1,000--$1,999 income class. By
this procedure average incomes in the $1,000--$1,999
and $2,000--$2,999 size groups are determined for
all counties and county groups.

The distribution of recipients among the three size
groups below $3,000 is first made by distributing the
estimated total number for these groups in the same
proportion as reported by the census. By multiplying the number of recipients so allocated to each of the
two size groups--$1,000--$1,999 and $2,000--$2,999--
by the estimated average income in these groups a total amount of cash income received in each is esti-

mated. The income allocated to these two groups deducted from the total to be allocated to all groups under $3,000 necessarily leaves a residual amount for
the recipients in the 0--$999 size group. This resid-
ual divided by the estimated number of recipients receiving it is the average received by each. By this
method the accumulated errors or discrepancies, that
could not be entirely avoided because of the reasons
outlined, are concentrated in the 0--$999 income class
and the result is an unreasonably high, or low, average income in this class for many of the counties or
county groups. The problem, then, is to correct for
any error on the basis of the best available information and to distribute whatever error there may be
among all three of the lower income groups.

Before making any attempt to correct or adjust the
data for influencing factors not taken account of in the
procedure, a careful analysis was made of the several
counties and county groups where the above procedure
seemed to be applicable. The first observation to be
made here was that per capita income is not a determining factor as to the appropriateness of the procedure. There are counties and county groups in all per
capita income ranges where the procedure is particularly suitable. The procedure is not suitable if, in
a particular county, violent economic changes occurred
during 1950; or if the minor economic changes that
would have a tendency to change the distribution pattern were not accompanied by other economic changes
that would have a balancing effect. In some counties,
for example, there were changes in the average earnings of covered workers (and presumably approximately the same change in earnings for all wage and salary workers) that came very close to balancing out
the drop in average incomes caused by decreased farm

proprietors' incomes; in other cases the change in average wages fell short or was more than enough. It depended, of course, on the relative number of wage earners to farmers and the amount of change in the average income of each. Another important factor is the amount of industrial expansion during the year (1950). Where industrial expansion was greatest--all other things considered--the procedure worked least well. Applicability of the procedure varied also with the time of year when industrial expansion took place. The last but, in the mind of the writer, not the least important adjustment factor considered is the percentage of women in the total work force. From the lowest to highest per capita income counties there is an increasing number of women in the work force relative to the number of men. As it was pointed up before, this factor is important in determining why county per capita incomes are different. A deviation from this general pattern creates procedural difficulties for this reason: In two counties with similar per capita incomes, with one county having a high and the other a low relative number of women in the labor force, the average income per recipient is much higher in the latter, in other words, the one with few working women. It is not, then, a high or low number of female workers as such that creates the difficulty, but a marked deviation from the tendency for higher income counties to have a larger number of women in the labor force, percentagewise, than the low income counties.

In order to visualize in the clearest possible manner the influence of each of these factors on income distribution by size, a summary sheet in tabular form was set up to show the numerical value of each factor for each county or county group. Particular notice

was then given the counties and county groups where
the procedure seemed to provide a proper distribution of income and income recipients, and how, in
these several aspects under consideration, the other
counties or county groups differed. The necessary
adjustments are made, then, based on observation.
As a general rule these adjustments are rather small.
In one county group, for example, where average covered wages increased $156 per year (8 per cent) from
1949 to 1950 and the decrease in average farm income
was 17.6 per cent (the state average), and the distribution of income by type showed wage earners and
farmers received approximately equal shares of the
total income, an adjustment in the census distribution
of recipient units was made. The census distribution
of families and unrelated individuals in this instance
for the size groups 0--$999, $1,000--$1,999 and $2,000--
$2,999 is in the proportion of 1.00, 0.57, and 0.33
respectively. The adjusted ratio is 1.00, 0.55, and
0.30. In this instance no changes were made in the
average incomes for recipients in the $1,000--$1,999
or the $2,000--$2,999 size groups--$1,440 and $2,418
respectively--and the average income of recipients
receiving less than $1,000 in this instance was esti-
mated to be $420.

    In all but a few counties and county groups the var-
iations in procedure are also minor, and in most of
these instances also the determined number of income
recipients fails to match exactly the number of recipients previously estimated. There are cases, however, where such is not the case; and to hold to the
procedure and to keep the number of recipients at or
near the estimated total other adjustments are made.
In a few instances these adjustments are in average
incomes. In four cases an adjustment of 5 per cent

is made in the estimate of total cash income--three
are additions and the other a subtraction.

Allocate All Imputed Income That Accrues to
Farm Proprietors Only--the Value of Food
and Fuel Produced and Consumed on the
Farm--and Government Payments to
Owner-Operators

The imputed income to Kentucky farmers in 1950
is the largest of all imputed income items. In 1950
over a third of the net income of farm operators from
farm operations was derived from home consumption
and a much smaller amount from government payments. The latter is not an imputed item but is included here for the sake of convenience. The average
income[25] per farm operator from these sources was
$432 for the state but varied slightly from county to
county. Of the 218,476 farm operators in Kentucky
in 1950,[26] less than 5 per cent filed state income tax
returns on which there was a tax liability. The exact
number is not known because the Kentucky Department
of Revenue classified only those persons who received
more than half of their taxable income from farm operations as farmers. It cannot be presumed from this
that compliance with the law is any worse or any better
for farmers as a group than for all income recipients.
But with so few farmers in the state who report taxable incomes and with practically no farm returns
from some of the counties it is impracticable to use
tax return data to allocate imputed farm income to the
size classes in the counties and county groups. The
best available series of data are the county income
statistics in the 1950 Census of Population.[27] From

the census data a tabulation was made showing the incomes of the farm population for the counties and county groups. In this tabulation the census size groups
were used. Because of the decrease of 17.6 per cent
in net income from farm operations to the farmers of
Kentucky from 1949 to 1950 there was a general downward adjustment of these series. [28] The recipients
in the census income groups were then combined to
match the size groups in this study. With this distribution of recipients and an average income per farm
operator by county from these sources, it is possible,
by use of the adjustment procedure previously explained, to make the adjustments for imputed farm
income.

Allocate Imputed Interest--
"Insurance Companies"

In the concept of income payments to individuals,
the net income of individuals from life insurance companies is not the amount paid out by the insurance com-
panies--the accumulated "property income (monetary
and imputed interest, dividends, and net rents) received by life insurance carriers is regarded as being
withheld to the account of policyholders and is treated
as though it were actually disbursed. "[29] This component of income, therefore, accrues to all persons
holding life insurance policies and, it is assumed, in
proportion to the amount of premiums paid. Data on
these two requirements to the allocation of imputed interest from this source are taken from the "Survey of
Consumer Finances. "[30] From this source is is possible to determine the percentage of insured income
recipients in each size group and the average premium

paid--also by size group. By weighting the calculated number of recipients of imputed interest from
insurance companies by the average premium paid a
series is obtained that makes possible the distribution of this component among the income classes, and
the average income from this component to the recipients in each class. By using the adjustment formulas the number of recipients and the amount of income
to be moved from one income class to the next are determined.

Allocate All Other Imputed Interest

The combined amount of imputed interest items received by residents of the state other than from insurance companies totaled about $35 million. This
component consists partly of imputed interest paid by
financial intermediaries--commercial banks, savings
and loan associations, credit unions, etc.--and is
made up of "the excess of property income received
over property income actually returned in monetary
form to owners of the funds entrusted to the interme-
diary."[31] "For all financial intermediaries except
commercial banks the flows of imputed interest paid
by intermediaries are treated as going entirely to persons."[32] The imputed interest income paid by commercial banks is divided into several parts, one of
which is imputed interest income to individuals.

Other interest payments in this component are, in
the strict sense of the word, not imputed but cash. This
is the estimated interest income to persons from small
denomination federal bonds (savings bonds). Interest
on these bonds is not realized in most instances until
the bonds are redeemed, and in the concept of income

used by the Bureau of the Census the money received
from the sale of property was not to be included as
income. The logical assumption, therefore, is that
the interest earned on these bonds, and collected when
the bonds are redeemed, would likewise not be included. Another factor which received consideration
in making this decision is that these bonds are held
by persons with lower incomes than are other securities yielding nontaxable interest, [33] indicating that if
this type of payment were to be allocated to the income
classes as cash income the allocation should not be
made with other nontaxable interest and dividends. It
is in line, then, with the notion that adjustments should
be kept at a minimum without undue loss of accuracy
that this component of income be classified as imputed and distributed among the size groups as is the
imputed interest on other liquid assets.

The percentage of all spending units by income class
holding liquid assets in 1950 is used as a basis for determining the number of recipients, with "other imputed interest" income. The "Survey of Consumer
Finances" is again used as a source of information.[34]
In order, again, to make the necessary adjustments
of income and recipients from one group to the next
it is assumed that all recipients of income from this
source in a particular income class receive an equal
amount. The estimated amount received in each instance is further assumed to be in direct proportion
to the amount of dividends and interest reported on
state tax returns. The big difference in the distribution of imputed interest and nontaxable cash interest
is in the number of recipients in the various size
groups. In this distribution there are relatively, as
well as absolutely, larger numbers of recipients in the
lower income classes.

It must be remembered that the total amount of each income component for which an adjustment is necessary is taken from the detailed source breakdown by county derived from the procedure outlined in Appendix 1.

Allocate Imputed Subsistence Payments to Veterans Attending College Under Public Laws 16 and 346

It is true that in a few instances veterans in college are the recipients of income from wages or from some other source. But it seemed advisable, for purposes of allocating this rather small component of income, to assume 75 per cent of the veterans on the G. I. Bill had an average cash income of $750 and that 25 per cent had cash incomes over $1,000. It is also assumed that all veterans in the 0--$999 size group move into the $1,000--$1,999 group when their imputed income is added and that those already in this income class do not move up. Both the income amount and the number of recipients are relatively small and no effort is made to determine how many actually do have incomes that put them in a higher income class. The total veteran enrollment receiving government subsistence was obtained by direct correspondence with the colleges of the state, [35] and it is assumed that all veterans receiving this type of benefit in 1950 received an equal amount.

Allocate the Imputed Wages of Farm Laborers and Domestic Servants

This income component is estimated to be about $10 million--15 per cent of all wages and salaries received by these two groups. [36] This is a small component of income, but it accrues almost entirely to persons with low incomes. The average wage for domestic servants, as computed from the number employed[37] and their total income[38] (for Kentucky only) was nearly $1,500. No way could be found for statistically allocating domestic workers to particular size groups, but it is quite probable that not all domestic workers earn between $1,000 and $1,999 annually. A purely arbitrary distribution was set up for these persons based on a rather comprehensive knowledge of the economy of the state. In this distribution the 0--$999, $1,000--$1,999, $2,000--$2,999, and the $3,000--$3,999 size groups were assumed to include 25 per cent, 50 per cent, 20 per cent, and 5 per cent of the domestic workers respectively.

In allocating farm laborers to particular income groups an entirely different problem arose. There is a seasonal factor in the demand for farm labor that is practically nonexistent in domestic work. It is a well known fact, however, that the yearly earnings of most farm laborers is small even though a part of the year may be spent at other occupations or as unemployed. Of the 44,137 hired workers on Kentucky farms in 1950, 2,800 farms reported that workers were paid on a monthly basis, 2,500 on a weekly basis, and 18,300 on a daily basis. [39] The pay scales in these instances were predominately (the modal wage) $50--$84 per month, $12--$19 per week, and $2--$4 per day respectively. In all instances the predominant yearly wage, then, was well under $1,000. In many instances, however, average wages of over $2,000 per year were reported. The distribution of all workers employed in agriculture for each county and county group is presumed to follow the census distribution by size of income for hired farm labor in the state.

The final allocation of this component, using, of
course, the allocation formulas previously outlined,
is based on the combined distributions of domestic
workers and hired farm workers--assuming each recipient in both these categories received the average
imputed amount which varied somewhat from the state
average of $144 for the different counties and county
groups.

Allocate Deductions for Social Insurance

Income, as defined by both the Bureau of the Census and the state income tax law, includes the social
insurance premiums (pay roll taxes) paid by employees. These, however, are not included as a part of
income payments to individuals. A final adjustment
is therefore necessary that has the effect of deducting these payments from the total income as allocated
and of moving some recipients and their incomes into
lower size groups. The same procedure as outlined
in the discussions on adjustment formulas is used. But
in computing the adjustments to be made the formula
has to be

$$(\frac{a}{c - \text{lower class limit}})(\frac{d}{2}) = x \text{ rather than}$$

$$(\frac{a}{b - c})(\frac{d}{2}) = x \text{ because the recipients and in-}$$

come are being moved into lower size groups.

The number of wage earners in each income size
group is determined as follows: For the size groups
0--$3,000 by the percentage of wage earners in each
class as reported in the "Survey of Consumer Finances,"[40] and for the size groups above $3,000 from

the percentage wage earners are of all persons who
reported taxable incomes for 1950 to the Kentucky Department of Revenue. From this distribution the number of hired farm workers and domestic servants is
deducted, and this distribution of wage earners is used
as an allocator.

The average amount paid by insured workers varies among groups up to $3,000 and above. Only the
first $3,000 earned by a person covered by Old-Age
and Survivors' Insurance was taxable during the calendar year 1950, and this is far and away the most important program of social insurance in terms of total tax paid and total coverage. There are social insurance programs, however, where the amount paid
by the employees is a larger percentage of wages and
salaries earned, and for this reason the average payment is slightly in excess of the 1.5 per cent tax on
wages under the Old-Age and Survivors' Insurance
program. In the adjustment calculations it is assumed
that in each of the size groups above $3,000 each wage
earner paid the same amount of tax, and that for the
size groups below $3,000 the average tax for wage earn-
ers in each group became proportionately smaller.
All adjustments are based on the assumption that each
covered wage earner in a particular income class paid
the same amount of tax.

AN EVALUATION OF BASIC DATA

Data from four major sources, as well as from
numerous minor sources, are used in making the income distributions by size. The most important, and
probably the most accurate, source of statistical information is a tabulation of 1950 state income tax re-

turns furnished by the Kentucky Department of Revenue. The most comprehensive survey ever undertaken, as far as is known by the author, of any income tax return data was made by this agency from the 1950 individual tax returns. Of the resident returns that showed a tax liability--the pay returns--a complete tabulation of those reported in 1951 was made. It furnished taxable income data for all counties--by size group, occupation, age of the recipient, and source of income. No-pay returns--returns on which there was no apparent tax liability--were also tabulated in the same way but only on a sample basis. Pay and no-pay returns filed in 1952 on 1950 incomes (late returns) were tabulated for each county, but only by number of returns filed and the amount of tax liability. Incomes reported on the pay and no-pay returns were broken down into 21 size groups ranging from 0--$999 to $200,000 and over. Some of the groups are combined in working up the county distributions in this study.

Most basic of all the data used in making the size distributions are the estimates of total income payments for the state and the counties. These estimates are not only the source of total income received by the residents of the state and of the counties; they are also the source of estimates of particular income components. For example, payments to veterans, nontaxable interest and dividends, unemployment compensation, etc., have all been allocated to counties, and the totals for these components determine the total amount of each adjustment in the county distributions.

The third source of basic data are the United States. Bureau of the Census publications. Both the 1950 Census of Population and the 1950 Census of Agriculture are used as sources of statistical information. In us-

ing data from these sources it should be remembered
that some series are far more reliable than others,
and an analysis of each series used would be necessary if a complete evaluation were given.   At this
time only a few observations on the income data will
be made.   Simply, income as defined by the census
is synonymous with cash income.   But cash income
here is somewhat different than the cash segment of
income payments, because included in the census concept are "contributions for support received from persons not residing in the same household. "[41] No known
series of data are available that could be used to bring
these two concepts of cash income into conformity,
and for this reason, since outside support is largely
in the form of alimony and kindred payments, it is assumed that these amounts were proportionately distributed throughout the income groups and therefore
not a disturbing factor. It is quite probable, also, that
the distributions of income as published by the Bureau
of the Census are not all that could be desired because
of the method used in making the survey.   There is a
strong indication that the enumerators did not follow
instructions to the letter.   But even if they had, there
would still be considerable room for error because to
different people income has a different meaning. This
is especially true in the case of self-employed persons.   And there is always the fraudulent reply or re-
fusal to reply to the enumerator's questions that must
be considered.   "It seems unlikely that a full report
of family income can be obtained by interviews without going into detail to an impracticable extent. Moreover, the unascertained income is fairly sure to be
chiefly in the higher brackets. "[42] It is not the intention of the author, by the preceding criticism, to dis-
credit the area income statistics as published by the

Bureau of the Census. A preliminary report[43] ap-
praising the reliability of census income data has been
published, and comparisons with other income statistics indicate that for many uses the data will prove
to be extremely valuable.

Since 1947 an analysis of consumer incomes and
expenditures in the United States entitled "Survey of
Consumer Finances" has been available.[44] Some use
is made of data from this source when information on
the amount of a particular type of income going to recipients in various income classes is needed. These
data, however, are not for individual recipients but
for spending units. A further shortcoming stems from
the fact that all data are for the country as a whole
and no state breakdowns are provided. It is believed,
nevertheless, that information from this source is the
best available for this limited purpose.

The population data for World War II veterans referred to in the section on methodology were compiled by the Veterans Administration and based on
the county of residence as reported on applications
for National Service Life Insurance special dividends.

Some data from annual reports of various departments of the state government other than the Kentucky
Department of Revenue are accepted at face value
and used in the allocation procedure.

FREQUENCY DISTRIBUTIONS OF INCOME
RECIPIENTS BY INCOME CLASS

The distribution of income and recipients by county group are shown in Table 44. The counties in each
group are the same as shown in Table 32. There is
a general tendency, as would be expected, for the per-

centage of recipients in the income size groups below $2,000 to decrease and in the other size groups
to increase as per capita income increases. Deviations from these general tendencies, however, are
frequent and important. These deviations are, for
the most part, a result of the different economic struc-
tures of the counties or county considered, but they
are also the result of the racial composition of county populations and other factors. An example of each
of these points is Perry and Fayette Counties (groups
24 and 38). In Perry County there is a definite tendency for incomes to cluster around the average wage
in the coal mining industry and at the same time there
are relatively few incomes in the high or low size
groups. The incomes in Fayette County, where 17.3
per cent of the population is Negro as compared to
3.3 per cent in Perry, show a great deal more dis-
persion throughout the income classes. There is, however, little difference in the average income per recipient between the two counties. There are many other factors, of course, that should be taken into account if a detailed comparison of the income distributions in these two counties were to be thoroughly analyzed; for example, the predominant industries in Fayette County and the composition of the population of
both counties by age and sex.

The only series in both the recipient distributions
or in the income distributions that seems to show no
trend (increase or decrease) from the low to the high
per capita income counties is the percentage of income
received in the $2,000 to $2,999 income size group.
Approximately the same percentage of total income
goes to recipients in this bracket whether the county
group has a high or low per capita income.

The following tables and charts also present in cu-

mulative form the size group data for the county groups.
The charts are all in the form of Lorenz curves, and
each chart shows the income distribution of the state
and one county group. It is not suggested that the state
distribution of income by size is ideal or that the distribution of income in any county or county group is
ideal. The charts are presented for purposes of comparison only. The cumulative percentage of income
is shown on the vertical axis and the cumulative percentage of recipients on the horizontal axis. Neither
per capita nor per recipient income can be determined
from a Lorenz curve. Identical per capita or per recipient incomes may result in different Lorenz curves,
or two county groups may have identical Lorenz curves
and different per capita and per recipient incomes. In
county group 1, for example, 80. 6 per cent of all income recipients received incomes of less than $2,000
and received 54 per cent of total income payments. In
county group 23 the same percentage of recipients
(80. 6) had incomes of less than $3, 000 and also re-
ceived 54 per cent of the income received by all recipients in the group. These two county groups have
different per capita and per recipient incomes, but at
one point, at least, the distribution curves coincide.

The diagonals on the charts represent lines of equal
income distribution. If each recipient received the
same amount of income, the distribution would be represented by a diagonal irrespective of the income level.
For this reason it is the inclination of many observ-
ers to measure income inequalities by noting the deviation of the distribution curve from the diagonal. Once
again it should be pointed out that there are many income recipients who voluntarily work only part of the
year, who are voluntarily retired, or who, for other
voluntary reasons, have different income amounts.

The diagonal, then, should not be construed as an ideal of income distributions, but only as a point of reference. [45]

Probably the most interesting and relevant fact disclosed in Table 45 and in the Lorenz curves is that there seems to be little correlation between income equality by county and level of per capita income. In comparing the cumulative distributions for each of the county groups with the distribution for the state, there are noticeable differences in income equality, but the county groups that have an income distribution with less inequality than that of the state cannot be tagged as either high or low on the per capita income scale--they may be either. In part, and to varying degrees, income inequalities seem to be a function of the type of prevailing industry. There is greater equality of incomes in the major mining counties than in the state as a whole, for example; and slightly more equality in Jefferson County than in the state which may result from the high employment in manufacturing. These are observations only and not conclusions. The causes of income inequality are many and are for the most part beyond the scope of this study.

---

[1]See Welch, "Estimating the Number of Earners for Income Size Distribution Analysis," in Studies in Income and Wealth, Vol. XIII, 560-71.

[2]United States Census of Population: 1950, Vol. II, Part 17, Chap. B, Table 43. Both military population and income are deleted from the size distributions because no adequate statistics on these amounts are available in time of national emergency, and further because many uses of distribution data imply that such should be the procedure to follow.

[3]According to the Bureau of the Census estimate
there was very little change in the total population of
the state from 1950 to 1951 and adjustment for this
factor was not necessary.

[4]Unpublished data on total wages and average employment, Kentucky Department of Economic Security.
See also U. S. Bureau of the Census, Current Population Reports: Labor Force, Series P-50, No. 31, 15.

[5]Unpublished statistical study, Kentucky Department of Economic Security. This study covered the
state as a whole and was based on a 2 per cent sample of old-age assistance recipients and a 5 per cent
sample of the recipients of aid to dependent children.
These persons were asked to state the amount and
source of any supplemental income they received. A
tabular summary of this survey showed, for each of
these two classes of public assistance recipients, the
percentage who received income from each of the following sources: Old-Age and Survivors' Insurance,
other pensions, employment, farm produce, rental
property, alimony, responsible relatives, and other.

[6]Public assistance payments and the number of re-
cipients by county for all programs, unpublished data,
Kentucky Department of Economic Security; and pay-
ments and number of recipients by county receiving
Old-Age and Survivors' Insurance, unpublished data,
Bureau of Old-Age and Survivors' Insurance, Federal
Security Agency.

[7]Teacher retirement information by county, unpublished data, Kentucky Department of Education. Railroad retirement based on average retirement pay, U. S.
Bureau of the Census, Statistical Abstract of the United
States: 1951, 228, and distributed to counties propor-

tionate to railroad employment. Federal civilian retirement based on average retirement pay, ibid., and
distributed to counties on the basis of federal civilian
employment outside the military establishments. Al-
lotments to dependents of military personnel distributed to counties on the basis of veteran population,
Veterans Administration Research Division, "Veteran Population Survey," June 30, 1951 (mimeographed), and average monthly allotment, U.S. Department of Defense.

[8]In this part of the procedure only those size groups
$3,000--$3,999 and over are considered because of
the extreme unreliability of tax data in the lower income classes.

[9]Unpublished data taken from state income tax return statistics, Kentucky Department of Revenue.

[10]Farioletti, "Some Results from the First Year's
Audit Control Program of the Bureau of Internal Revenue," 65-78.

[11]The state capital is located in Franklin County
and the ratio of taxable income to income reported on
individual income tax returns indicated nearly perfect compliance for this county.

[12]The assumption that underreporting, as a percentage of income, was uniform throughout the size
groups and that the amount was about 3 per cent was
based on information obtained from a detailed audit
by the Kentucky Department of Revenue of a sample
number of returns over a two-month period.

[13]This procedure was followed in all except two relatively infrequent cases. The first case has to do with
the smaller income size groups--those with $1,000
intervals. If, in these groups, the mean income hap-

pened to be more than $100 less or more than $100
greater than the class mark, the median was assumed
to be $100 further from the class mark than was the
mean and in the same direction. For example, if,
for a particular county, the mean income in the 0--
$999 class was $650 the median was assumed to be
$750. The second type deviation from the procedure
as outlined was made in any instance where, in the upper income classes--those above $5,000--the average
income for a particular size group was such as to make
the standard procedure impracticable. In these cases
a freehand curve was drawn approximating the distribution for the group and the next lower and next higher size group, and from this curve the approximate
number of income recipients that changed groups, because of an added amount of nontaxable income, was
determined.

[14]After working through the procedure the first time
the derived size group distributions were plotted. On
the same distribution curves the "adjustment lines"
(these are actually a series of steps, two for each income class) were plotted and from these it was clearly indicated that the adjustments from the $2,000--
$2,999 to the $3,000--$3,999 size group had been too
small. An accurate estimation was, of course, impossible to make, but all signs pointed to an understatement of one-third as the best approximation that
could be made.

[15]United States Census of Population: 1950, Vol. II,
Part 17, Chap. B, Tables 29 and 43.

[16]Veterans Administration Research Division, "Estimated number of living veterans in Kentucky by county: June 30, 1951." This document gives the estimated veteran population by county for "World War II,"
and "veterans of all other wars."

[17]"1951 Survey of Consumer Finances, " 936.

[18]It was determined from these calculations that 51,400 veterans were included in the income size groups $3,000--$3,999 and higher.

[19]"1951 Survey of Consumer Finances, " 936.

[20]This figure may appear high as an average payment per veteran, but it is high because much of this income is paid to dependents of deceased veterans. There are, in other words, many recipients of this type of income who are not accounted for in computing the average payment. A similar circumstance, only of much less significance, exists in the case of World War II veterans' payments.

[21]Cash interest on government securities: See note of how this component was calculated in conjunction with the distribution of income by source in Appendix 1. Dividends on bank stock: Amount of cash dividends on this type of stock, by county, from unpublished tabulations, Kentucky Department of Revenue. Dividends on the stock of savings and loan companies: The rate of return on bank stock was computed on the assessed value from Kentucky Department of Revenue, Statistical Appendix to the 1949-1950 Annual Report, 10, and this rate applied to the assessed value of the capital stock of building and loan associations, ibid.

[22]As explained earlier there are a few minor exceptions which will not be worked into the procedure, but which are of very small importance relative to total income payments. Probably they would have little or no effect on the distribution of income among the different income classes.

[23]United States Census of Population: 1950, Vol.

II, Part 17, Chap. B, Tables 45 and 46.

[24] The slope of the line in one instance, for example indicated there were 42 per cent more recipients
with a $1,500 income in 1949 (census income data are
for 1949) than with incomes of $2,000. In this cen-
sus income group there were 3,410 recipient units.
The interval of $500 between the class limits is first
divided into ten subgroups of $50 each; and the class
mark of each subgroup is assumed to be the arithmetic mean of incomes received by recipient units in
this income range. Each of the $50 subgroups from
the $1,500--$1,549 class to the $1,950--$1,999 class
has proportionately fewer recipient units as indicated
by the slope of the distribution line. The arithmetic
mean of the 3,410 recipient units in this example is
calculated to be $1,735--$15 below the class mark.
By this method average incomes for the recipient units
in the "less than $500" census groups cannot be de-
termined and are therefore estimated.

[25] The value of food and fuel produced and consumed
on farms by farm families is measured in terms of
prices received by farmers for the type of product
consumed. U.S. Department of Commerce, National
Income and Product of the United States: 1929-1950,
40. Government payments to owner operators are partly in cash and partly in goods and services. In 1950
gross soil conservation payments in Kentucky amounted to $7,795,000 and of this amount $2,419,000 was
in the form of materials and services. (Kentucky State
Committee, Production and Marketing Administration,
U.S. Department of Agriculture, Kentucky PMA Programs: 1950 Yearbook, Part II, Table 4, Cols. 4 and
6.) The value of home-produced food and fuel produced and consumed on Kentucky farms in 1950 was

nearly $90 million; and net government payments to owner-operators about $6 million.

[26] United States Census of Agriculture: 1950, Vol. I, Part 19, State Table 1 and County Table 1.

[27] United States Census of Population: 1950, Vol. II, Part 17, Chap. B, Tables 32, 45, and 46.

[28] It should also be pointed out that these data do not have the same meaning as the farm proprietor data in the Census of Agriculture, but for use here this difference is not significant.

[29] U.S. Department of Commerce, National Income and Product of the United States: 1929-1950, 94.

[30] "1951 Survey of Consumer Finances," 1526.

[31] U.S. Department of Commerce, National Income and Product of the United States: 1929-1950, 93.

[32] Ibid., 95.

[33] "1951 Survey of Consumer Finances," 643. Data from this source were compared with data from the state income tax returns. See also Kimmel, Share Ownership in the United States, 116.

[34] "1951 Survey of Consumer Finances," 642.

[35] See the section on the type distribution of this component, Appendix 1.

[36] U.S. Department of Commerce, National Income and Product of the United States: 1929-1950, 65.

[37] United States Census of Population: 1950, Vol. II, Part 17, Chap. B, Tables 30 and 43.

[38] Unpublished data on income payments to individuals by source, U.S. Department of Commerce.

[39] United States Census of Agriculture: 1950, Vol.

I, Part 19, State Table 19 and County Table 3.

[40]"1951 Survey of Consumer Finances," 931.

[41]United States Census of Population: 1950, Vol. II, Part 17, Chap. B, xiv.

[42]Noyer and Hilgard, "Estimated Income Distribution in Three Surveys of Consumer Requirements," in Studies in Income and Wealth, Vol. VIII, 270.

[43]Miller, "An Appraisal of the 1950 Census Income Data," 28-43.

[44]Published annually in the Federal Reserve Bulletin.

[45]See also Garvy, "Inequality of Income: Causes and Measurement," in Studies in Income and Wealth, Vol. XV, 25-74.

Table 44
DISTRIBUTION OF TOTAL INCOME PAYMENTS AND RECIPIENTS
IN KENTUCKY BY COUNTY GROUP, 1950

Group 1--Butler, Knott, Knox, Leslie,
Magoffin, Martin, Menifee,
Owsley, Powell, Wayne   39,539 recipients

Income Size Group	Percentage Distribution	
	Recipients	Income
less than $ 1,000	48.51	18.35
$ 1,000 - 1,999	32.07	35.48
2,000 - 2,999	13.14	24.18
3,000 - 3,999	3.44	8.92
4,000 - 4,999	1.57	5.26
5,000 - 6,999	0.80	3.44
7,000 - 9,999	0.27	1.68
10,000 - 14,999	0.11	1.02
15,000 and over	0.09	1.68

Group 2--Adair, Casey, Clay, Clinton,
Edmonson, Elliott, Hancock,
Jackson, Lawrence, Wolfe   39,063 recipients

Income Size Group	Percentage Distribution	
	Recipients	Income
less than $ 1,000	44.61	18.13
$ 1,000 - 1,999	36.13	38.17
2,000 - 2,999	13.37	23.47
3,000 - 3,999	3.37	8.36
4,000 - 4,999	1.33	4.29
5,000 - 6,999	0.70	2.89
7,000 - 9,999	0.26	1.50
10,000 - 14,999	0.14	1.24
15,000 and over	0.10	1.94

Table 44--continued

Group 3--Allen, Breathitt, Cumberland,
        Laurel, Lee, McCreary, Monroe,
        Morgan, Rockcastle, Russell   46,680 recipients

Income Size Group	Percentage Distribution	
	Recipients	Income
less than $ 1,000	42.26	17.22
$ 1,000 - 1,999	35.47	34.50
2,000 - 2,999	15.12	25.00
3,000 - 3,999	4.02	9.38
4,000 - 4,999	1.65	5.00
5,000 - 6,999	0.85	3.34
7,000 - 9,999	0.33	1.86
10,000 - 14,999	0.17	1.38
15,000 and over	0.14	2.33

Group 4--Carter, Crittenden, Grayson,
        Green, Johnson, Lewis, McLean,
        Metcalfe, Trigg, Trimble   44,092 recipients

Income Size Group	Percentage Distribution	
	Recipients	Income
less than $ 1,000	42.00	14.37
$ 1,000 - 1,999	30.99	29.08
2,000 - 2,999	17.21	26.86
3,000 - 3,999	5.58	12.23
4,000 - 4,999	2.21	6.25
5,000 - 6,999	1.18	4.38
7,000 - 9,999	0.40	2.06
10,000 - 14,999	0.27	2.07
15,000 and over	0.16	2.68

Table 44--continued

Group 5--Breckinridge, Estill, Hickman,
          Lincoln, Ohio   26,932 recipients

Income Size Group	Percentage Distribution	
	Recipients	Income
less than $ 1,000	42.36	13.99
$ 1,000 - 1,999	28.95	26.63
2,000 - 2,999	17.26	26.48
3,000 - 3,999	6.43	13.90
4,000 - 4,999	2.56	7.20
5,000 - 6,999	1.61	5.84
7,000 - 9,999	0.50	2.51
10,000 - 14,999	0.19	1.42
15,000 and over	0.13	2.02

Group 6--Bell   14,813 recipients

Income Size Group	Percentage Distribution	
	Recipients	Income
less than $ 1,000	34.21	10.15
$ 1,000 - 1,999	34.62	29.14
2,000 - 2,999	20.81	28.12
3,000 - 3,999	4.85	9.22
4,000 - 4,999	2.56	6.30
5,000 - 6,999	1.45	4.57
7,000 - 9,999	0.67	3.08
10,000 - 14,999	0.42	2.82
15,000 - 24,999	0.26	2.72
25,000 and over	0.17	3.87

Table 44--continued

Group 7--Ballard, Pulaski, Todd,
· Whitley   30, 382 recipients

Income Size Group	Percentage Distribution	
	Recipients	Income
less than $ 1,000	37. 14	12. 41
$ 1,000 - 1,999	32. 73	27. 39
2,000 - 2,999	17. 37	24. 49
3,000 - 3,999	7. 19	14. 15
4,000 - 4,999	2. 60	6. 77
5,000 - 6,999	1. 83	6. 03
7,000 - 9,999	0. 60	2. 83
10,000 - 14,999	0. 29	2. 09
15,000 - 24,999	0. 15	1. 60
25,000 and over	0. 10	2. 24

Group 8--Bath, Hart, Livingston,
Lyon, Rowan   18, 925 recipients

Income Size Group	Percentage Distribution	
	Recipients	Income
less than $ 1,000	36. 59	13. 02
$ 1,000 - 1,999	36. 11	32. 88
2,000 - 2,999	18. 40	27. 50
3,000 - 3,999	4. 66	9. 81
4,000 - 4,999	1. 93	5. 32
5,000 - 6,999	1. 31	4. 50
7,000 - 9,999	0. 57	2. 73
10,000 - 14,999	0. 23	1. 75
15,000 and over	0. 19	2. 50

Table 44--continued

Group 9--Carlisle, Gallatin, Grant,
        Logan, Webster   20,507 recipients

| Income Size Group | Percentage Distribution | |
	Recipients	Income
less than $ 1,000	38.80	12.65
$ 1,000 - 1,999	29.65	24.88
2,000 - 2,999	18.50	25.81
3,000 - 3,999	6.56	12.81
4,000 - 4,999	3.00	7.60
5,000 - 6,999	2.16	7.11
7,000 - 9,999	0.75	3.47
10,000 - 14,999	0.33	2.16
15,000 and over	0.26	3.50

Group 10--Letcher, Muhlenberg   24,404 recipients

| Income Size Group | Percentage Distribution | |
	Recipients	Income
less than $ 1,000	32.71	12.09
$ 1,000 - 1,999	30.91	23.62
2,000 - 2,999	22.08	27.59
3,000 - 3,999	7.32	12.72
4,000 - 4,999	3.14	7.15
5,000 - 6,999	2.40	7.10
7,000 - 9,999	0.80	3.25
10,000 - 14,999	0.29	1.77
15,000 - 24,999	0.23	2.21
25,000 and over	0.12	2.48

Table 44--continued

Group 11--Greenup, Hardin, Marshall,
      Simpson   27,401 recipients

Income Size Group	Percentage Distribution Recipients	Income
less than $ 1,000	32.81	8.90
$ 1,000 - 1,999	27.20	19.83
2,000 - 2,999	17.35	20.78
3,000 - 3,999	12.82	21.73
4,000 - 4,999	5.66	12.25
5,000 - 6,999	2.78	7.78
7,000 - 9,999	0.74	2.93
10,000 - 14,999	0.32	1.91
15,000 - 24,999	0.19	1.73
25,000 and over	0.12	2.16

Group 12--Barren, Calloway, Garrard,
      Owen   26,143 recipients

Income Size Group	Percentage Distribution Recipients	Income
less than $ 1,000	31.75	10.36
$ 1,000 - 1,999	35.19	28.28
2,000 - 2,999	20.38	27.18
3,000 - 3,999	6.98	13.01
4,000 - 4,999	2.87	6.90
5,000 - 6,999	1.47	4.67
7,000 - 9,999	0.70	3.10
10,000 - 14,999	0.31	1.90
15,000 - 24,999	0.23	2.44
25,000 and over	0.11	2.15

Table 44--continued

Group 13--Caldwell, Fleming, Pendleton, Taylor, Union	24,308 recipients	
Income Size Group	Percentage Distribution	
	Recipients	Income
less than $ 1,000	37.16	11.48
$ 1,000 - 1,999	28.27	22.42
2,000 - 2,999	19.69	25.89
3,000 - 3,999	7.55	13.92
4,000 - 4,999	3.53	8.45
5,000 - 6,999	2.25	6.94
7,000 - 9,999	0.77	3.39
10,000 - 14,999	0.46	2.96
15,000 - 24,999	0.23	2.34
25,000 and over	0.10	2.22

Group 14--LaRue, Marion, Mercer, Washington	20,990 recipients	
Income Size Group	Percentage Distribution	
	Recipients	Income
less than $ 1,000	30.10	9.61
$ 1,000 - 1,999	35.06	27.01
2,000 - 2,999	21.17	27.27
3,000 - 3,999	7.35	13.19
4,000 - 4,999	2.90	6.77
5,000 - 6,999	1.83	5.57
7,000 - 9,999	0.79	3.39
10,000 - 14,999	0.46	2.86
15,000 - 24,999	0.25	2.57
25,000 and over	0.09	1.75

Table 44--continued

Group 15--Floyd, Pike   43,470 recipients

Income Size Group	Percentage Distribution Recipients	Income
less than $ 1,000	21.54	7.43
$ 1,000 - 1,999	26.66	17.57
2,000 - 2,999	30.75	33.09
3,000 - 3,999	11.36	16.80
4,000 - 4,999	5.29	10.13
5,000 - 6,999	3.03	7.52
7,000 - 9,999	0.80	2.73
10,000 - 14,999	0.30	1.53
15,000 - 24,999	0.16	1.31
25,000 and over	0.11	1.89

Group 16--Henry, Meade, Nelson,
          Spencer   17,842 recipients

Income Size Group	Percentage Distribution Recipients	Income
less than $ 1,000	32.69	10.15
$ 1,000 - 1,999	30.69	23.99
2,000 - 2,999	22.54	28.80
3,000 - 3,999	6.73	12.07
4,000 - 4,999	3.72	8.56
5,000 - 6,999	2.08	6.24
7,000 - 9,999	0.78	3.30
10,000 - 14,999	0.41	2.56
15,000 - 24,999	0.21	2.17
25,000 and over	0.14	2.77

Table 44--continued

Group 17--Bracken, Jessamine, Montgomery,
       Nicholas, Robertson   18,219 recipients

| Income Size | Percentage Distribution | |
Group	Recipients	Income
less than $ 1,000	28.90	9.22
$ 1,000 - 1,999	35.70	27.54
2,000 - 2,999	21.97	28.05
3,000 - 3,999	6.87	12.24
4,000 - 4,999	3.07	7.11
5,000 - 6,999	1.89	5.73
7,000 - 9,999	0.95	3.92
10,000 - 14,999	0.34	2.14
15,000 - 24,999	0.21	2.09
25,000 and over	0.11	1.96

Group 18--Christian   14,396 recipients

| Income Size | Percentage Distribution | |
Group	Recipients	Income
less than $ 1,000	30.46	8.60
$ 1,000 - 1,999	31.80	22.90
2,000 - 2,999	21.80	25.87
3,000 - 3,999	8.11	13.42
4,000 - 4,999	3.31	7.16
5,000 - 6,999	2.28	6.42
7,000 - 9,999	0.92	3.61
10,000 - 14,999	0.70	4.15
15,000 - 24,999	0.41	3.82
25,000 and over	0.22	4.05

Table 44--continued

Group 19--Graves   8,099 recipients

Income Size Group	Percentage Distribution	
	Recipients	Income
less than $ 1,000	27.34	7.90
$ 1,000 - 1,999	30.42	22.07
2,000 - 2,999	24.48	29.37
3,000 - 3,999	9.95	16.67
4,000 - 4,999	4.21	9.11
5,000 - 6,999	2.25	6.22
7,000 - 9,999	0.68	2.65
10,000 - 14,999	0.33	1.99
15,000 - 24,999	0.23	2.20
25,000 and over	0.10	1.81

Group 20--Bullitt, Carroll   13,126 recipients

Income Size Group	Percentage Distribution	
	Recipients	Income
less than $ 1,000	30.73	9.04
$ 1,000 - 1,999	30.06	22.32
2,000 - 2,999	23.14	28.33
3,000 - 3,999	9.68	16.42
4,000 - 4,999	3.18	7.05
5,000 - 6,999	1.55	4.45
7,000 - 9,999	0.70	2.84
10,000 - 14,999	0.47	2.91
15,000 - 24,999	0.31	2.99
25,000 and over	0.18	3.66

Table 44--continued

Group 21--Madison	13,574 recipients	
Income Size Group	Percentage Distribution	
	Recipients	Income
less than $ 1,000	35.21	9.56
$ 1,000 - 1,999	30.15	23.88
2,000 - 2,999	18.83	23.65
3,000 - 3,999	7.12	12.74
4,000 - 4,999	4.06	9.38
5,000 - 6,999	2.67	7.96
7,000 - 9,999	1.11	4.64
10,000 - 14,999	0.53	3.29
15,000 - 24,999	0.21	2.01
25,000 and over	0.11	2.88

Group 22--Warren	17,583 recipients	
Income Size Group	Percentage Distribution	
	Recipients	Income
less than $ 1,000	25.06	6.98
$ 1,000 - 1,999	32.45	21.21
2,000 - 2,999	23.01	25.25
3,000 - 3,999	9.95	15.41
4,000 - 4,999	4.64	9.28
5,000 - 6,999	2.56	6.65
7,000 - 9,999	1.15	4.25
10,000 - 14,999	0.61	3.30
15,000 - 24,999	0.36	3.16
25,000 and over	0.21	4.22

Table 44--continued

Group 23--Anderson, Fulton, Harrison, Oldham	19,463 recipients	
Income Size Group	Percentage Distribution Recipients	Income
less than $ 1,000	33.87	10.92
$ 1,000 - 1,999	37.31	29.19
2,000 - 2,999	15.71	20.47
3,000 - 3,999	6.05	11.11
4,000 - 4,999	3.08	7.33
5,000 - 6,999	2.00	6.05
7,000 - 9,999	0.94	4.19
10,000 - 14,999	0.53	3.44
15,000 - 24,999	0.34	3.26
25,000 and over	0.17	4.05

Group 24--Perry	14,901 recipients	
Income Size Group	Percentage Distribution Recipients	Income
less than $ 1,000	16.22	5.13
$ 1,000 - 1,999	22.34	13.28
2,000 - 2,999	31.44	30.43
3,000 - 3,999	18.86	24.57
4,000 - 4,999	6.36	10.91
5,000 - 6,999	3.11	6.77
7,000 - 9,999	0.87	2.70
10,000 - 14,999	0.38	1.78
15,000 - 24,999	0.22	1.62
25,000 and over	0.19	2.80

Table 44--continued

Group 25--Henderson	12,392 recipients	
Income Size Group	**Percentage Distribution**	
	Recipients	Income
less than $ 1,000	29.14	6.99
$ 1,000 - 1,999	26.98	18.36
2,000 - 2,999	24.25	26.75
3,000 - 3,999	9.03	13.93
4,000 - 4,999	5.25	10.50
5,000 - 6,999	2.76	7.12
7,000 - 9,999	1.11	4.04
10,000 - 14,999	0.85	4.52
15,000 - 24,999	0.40	3.38
25,000 and over	0.23	4.41

Group 26--Boone, Scott, Shelby	19,005 recipients	
Income Size Group	**Percentage Distribution**	
	Recipients	Income
less than $ 1,000	25.70	7.24
$ 1,000 - 1,999	31.41	21.02
2,000 - 2,999	22.73	25.44
3,000 - 3,999	9.91	15.37
4,000 - 4,999	5.28	10.61
5,000 - 6,999	2.93	7.67
7,000 - 9,999	1.02	3.76
10,000 - 14,999	0.52	2.88
15,000 - 24,999	0.36	3.11
25,000 and over	0.15	2.91

Table 44--continued

Group 27--Harlan	26,258 recipients	
Income Size Group	Percentage Distribution	
	Recipients	Income
less than $ 1,000	16.09	4.56
$ 1,000 - 1,999	23.05	13.80
2,000 - 2,999	31.67	30.52
3,000 - 3,999	17.35	22.06
4,000 - 4,999	5.46	9.19
5,000 - 6,999	4.47	9.67
7,000 - 9,999	1.02	3.06
10,000 - 14,999	0.43	1.98
15,000 - 24,999	0.26	1.86
25,000 and over	0.20	3.31

Group 28--Boyle	8,710 recipients	
Income Size Group	Percentage Distribution	
	Recipients	Income
less than $ 1,000	25.55	7.02
$ 1,000 - 1,999	32.76	20.88
2,000 - 2,999	21.49	23.28
3,000 - 3,999	9.35	14.03
4,000 - 4,999	4.89	9.61
5,000 - 6,999	3.30	8.31
7,000 - 9,999	1.22	4.34
10,000 - 14,999	0.73	3.90
15,000 - 24,999	0.49	4.37
25,000 and over	0.23	4.25

Table 44--continued

Group 29--Bourbon	8,210 recipients	
Income Size Group	Percentage Distribution	
	Recipients	Income
less than $ 1,000	26.85	7.73
$ 1,000 - 1,999	31.21	20.64
2,000 - 2,999	24.18	26.37
3,000 - 3,999	8.77	13.30
4,000 - 4,999	3.50	6.94
5,000 - 6,999	2.81	7.21
7,000 - 9,999	1.28	4.65
10,000 - 14,999	0.73	3.81
15,000 - 24,999	0.43	3.64
25,000 and over	0.26	5.71

Group 30--Clark	8,427 recipients	
Income Size Group	Percentage Distribution	
	Recipients	Income
less than $ 1,000	27.09	7.68
$ 1,000 - 1,999	29.76	18.50
2,000 - 2,999	21.88	22.89
3,000 - 3,999	9.79	14.14
4,000 - 4,999	4.59	8.73
5,000 - 6,999	3.60	8.71
7,000 - 9,999	1.50	5.22
10,000 - 14,999	0.93	4.78
15,000 - 24,999	0.52	4.20
25,000 and over	0.34	5.15

Table 44--continued

Group 31--Hopkins	16,944 recipients	
Income Size Group	Percentage Distribution	
	Recipients	Income
less than $ 1,000	31.23	8.31
$ 1,000 - 1,999	25.35	15.75
2,000 - 2,999	19.60	19.70
3,000 - 3,999	8.40	11.97
4,000 - 4,999	6.56	12.03
5,000 - 6,999	5.56	13.35
7,000 - 9,999	1.94	6.29
10,000 - 14,999	0.64	3.05
15,000 - 24,999	0.35	2.87
25,000 - 49,999	0.27	3.56
50,000 and over	0.10	3.13

Group 32--McCracken	21,640 recipients	
Income Size Group	Percentage Distribution	
	Recipients	Income
less than $ 1,000	24.81	6.53
$ 1,000 - 1,999	25.26	14.91
2,000 - 2,999	21.56	20.97
3,000 - 3,999	15.27	20.54
4,000 - 4,999	6.39	11.06
5,000 - 6,999	3.92	8.77
7,000 - 9,999	1.43	4.56
10,000 - 14,999	0.66	3.11
15,000 - 24,999	0.39	2.89
25,000 - 49,999	0.23	3.18
50,000 and over	0.09	3.48

Table 44--continued

Group 33--Franklin, Woodford	18,417 recipients	
Income Size Group	Percentage Distribution	
	Recipients	Income
less than $ 1,000	27.37	5.90
$ 1,000 - 1,999	26.80	17.17
2,000 - 2,999	22.46	23.61
3,000 - 3,999	11.76	17.18
4,000 - 4,999	5.29	10.02
5,000 - 6,999	3.57	8.76
7,000 - 9,999	1.30	4.49
10,000 - 14,999	0.81	4.05
15,000 - 24,999	0.39	3.13
25,000 - 49,999	0.18	2.80
50,000 and over	0.07	2.90

Group 34--Mason	9,945 recipients	
Income Size Group	Percentage Distribution	
	Recipients	Income
less than $ 1,000	31.48	8.55
$ 1,000 - 1,999	27.73	19.06
2,000 - 2,999	22.76	26.27
3,000 - 3,999	10.27	16.32
4,000 - 4,999	3.45	7.13
5,000 - 6,999	2.22	5.90
7,000 - 9,999	0.83	3.15
10,000 - 14,999	0.57	3.26
15,000 - 24,999	0.39	3.50
25,000 - 49,999	0.21	3.18
50,000 and over	0.08	3.69

Table 44--continued

Group 35--Daviess		29,758 recipients

| Income Size Group | Percentage Distribution | |
	Recipients	Income
less than $ 1,000	27.70	7.27
$ 1,000 - 1,999	25.72	16.25
2,000 - 2,999	22.18	23.01
3,000 - 3,999	13.79	20.52
4,000 - 4,999	5.23	9.88
5,000 - 6,999	3.12	7.63
7,000 - 9,999	1.05	3.64
10,000 - 14,999	0.51	2.62
15,000 - 24,999	0.41	3.28
25,000 - 49,999	0.21	3.16
50,000 and over	0.08	2.75

Group 36--Boyd		21,830 recipients

| Income Size Group | Percentage Distribution | |
	Recipients	Income
less than $ 1,000	20.67	5.30
$ 1,000 - 1,999	19.75	10.43
2,000 - 2,999	24.91	22.47
3,000 - 3,999	15.52	19.26
4,000 - 4,999	10.72	17.05
5,000 - 6,999	5.53	11.19
7,000 - 9,999	1.54	4.45
10,000 - 14,999	0.73	3.13
15,000 - 24,999	0.36	2.45
25,000 - 49,999	0.21	2.55
50,000 and over	0.05	1.71

Table 44--continued

Group 37--Campbell		35,599 recipients
Income Size Group	Percentage Distribution	
	Recipients	Income
less than $ 1,000	22.91	6.20
$ 1,000 - 1,999	18.53	10.47
2,000 - 2,999	26.48	24.71
3,000 - 3,999	15.69	20.01
4,000 - 4,999	8.51	13.99
5,000 - 6,999	4.99	10.54
7,000 - 9,999	1.60	4.86
10,000 - 14,999	0.63	2.69
15,000 - 24,999	0.41	2.82
25,000 - 49,999	0.22	2.82
50,000 and over	0.03	0.88

Group 38--Fayette		48,263 recipients
Income Size Group	Percentage Distribution	
	Recipients	Income
less than $ 1,000	20.68	5.17
$ 1,000 - 1,999	30.58	16.86
2,000 - 2,999	21.34	18.92
3,000 - 3,999	12.25	15.10
4,000 - 4,999	6.41	10.19
5,000 - 6,999	4.44	9.13
7,000 - 9,999	1.95	5.72
10,000 - 14,999	1.09	4.66
15,000 - 24,999	0.68	4.63
25,000 - 49,999	0.47	5.51
50,000 and over	0.11	4.10

Table 44--continued

Group 39--Kenton		54,546 recipients
Income Size Group	Percentage Distribution	
	Recipients	Income
less than $ 1,000	19.38	5.20
$ 1,000 - 1,999	20.11	11.35
2,000 - 2,999	28.73	26.83
3,000 - 3,999	15.67	19.84
4,000 - 4,999	8.68	14.21
5,000 - 6,999	4.98	10.42
7,000 - 9,999	1.34	4.01
10,000 - 14,999	0.57	2.52
15,000 - 24,999	0.35	2.45
25,000 - 49,999	0.16	1.95
50,000 and over	0.04	1.22

Group 40--Jefferson		276,938 recipients
Income Size Group	Percentage Distribution	
	Recipients	Income
less than $ 1,000	20.19	5.14
$ 1,000 - 1,999	22.22	11.76
2,000 - 2,999	26.17	22.88
3,000 - 3,999	14.98	17.86
4,000 - 4,999	7.63	11.77
5,000 - 6,999	4.94	9.87
7,000 - 9,999	1.88	5.33
10,000 - 14,999	0.93	3.93
15,000 - 24,999	0.60	3.95
25,000 - 49,999	0.34	3.95
50,000 and over	0.12	3.55

Note: Because of rounding the figures may not add to 100 per cent.

Table 45
CUMULATIVE PERCENTAGE DISTRIBUTION OF INCOME AND
INCOME RECIPIENTS IN KENTUCKY, 1950

Income Size Group	State		County Group			
			1		2	
	Recip- ients	In- come	Recip- ients	In- come	Recip- ients	In- come
Under $ 1,000	28.5	8	48.5	18	44.6	18
$ 1,000 - 1,999	56.2	26	80.6	54	80.7	56
2,000 - 2,999	78.6	51	93.7	78	94.1	80
3,000 - 3,999	89.3	67	97.1	87	97.5	88
4,000 - 4,999	94.4	77	98.7	92	98.8	92
5,000 - 6,999	97.6	85	99.5	95	99.5	95
7,000 - 9,999	98.7	89	99.8	97	99.8	97
10,000 - 14,999	99.3	92	99.9	98	99.9	98
$15,000 and over	100.0	100	100.0	100	100.0	100

Income Size Group	County Group					
	3		4		5	
	Recip- ients	In- come	Recip- ients	In- come	Recip- ients	In- come
Under $ 1,000	42.3	17	42.0	15	42.4	14
$ 1,000 - 1,999	77.8	52	73.0	44	71.3	41
2,000 - 2,999	92.9	77	90.2	71	88.6	67
3,000 - 3,999	96.9	87	95.8	83	95.0	81
4,000 - 4,999	98.5	92	98.0	89	97.6	88
5,000 - 6,999	99.4	95	99.2	93	99.2	94
7,000 - 9,999	99.7	97	99.6	95	99.7	97
10,000 - 14,999	99.9	98	99.8	97	99.9	98
15,000 and over	100.0	100	100.0	100	100.0	100

Table 45--continued

Income Size Group	County Group					
	6		7		8	
	Recip-ients	In-come	Recip-ients	In-come	Recip-ients	In-come
Under $ 1,000	34.2	10	37.1	12	36.6	13
$ 1,000 - 1,999	68.8	39	69.8	39	72.7	46
2,000 - 2,999	89.6	67	87.2	64	91.1	73
3,000 - 3,999	94.4	76	94.4	78	95.8	83
4,000 - 4,999	97.0	82	97.7	85	97.7	88
5,000 - 6,999	98.4	87	98.8	91	99.0	92
7,000 - 9,999	99.1	90	99.4	94	99.6	95
10,000 - 14,999	99.5	93	99.7	96	99.8	97
15,000 and over	100.0	100	100.0	100	100.0	100

Income Size Group	County Group					
	9		10		11	
	Recip-ients	In-come	Recip-ients	In-come	Recip-ients	In-come
Under $ 1,000	38.8	13	32.7	12	32.8	9
$ 1,000 - 1,999	68.4	38	63.6	36	60.0	29
2,000 - 2,999	86.9	64	85.7	64	77.4	50
3,000 - 3,999	93.5	77	93.0	77	90.2	72
4,000 - 4,999	96.5	85	96.1	84	95.9	84
5,000 - 6,999	98.7	92	98.5	91	98.7	92
7,000 - 9,999	99.4	95	99.3	94	99.4	95
10,000 - 14,999	99.7	97	99.6	96	99.7	97
15,000 and over	100.0	100	100.0	100	100.0	100

Table 45--continued

Income Size Group	County Group					
	12		13		14	
	Recip-ients	In-come	Recip-ients	In-come	Recip-ients	In-come
Under $ 1,000	31.7	10	37.2	12	30.1	10
$ 1,000 - 1,999	66.9	38	65.5	34	65.2	37
2,000 - 2,999	87.3	65	85.2	60	86.4	64
3,000 - 3,999	94.3	78	92.7	74	93.7	77
4,000 - 4,999	97.2	85	96.2	83	96.6	84
5,000 - 6,999	98.7	90	98.4	90	98.4	90
7,000 - 9,999	99.4	93	99.2	93	99.2	93
10,000 - 14,999	99.7	95	99.7	96	99.7	96
15,000 and over	100.0	100	100.0	100	100.0	100

Income Size Group	County Group					
	15		16		17	
	Recip-ients	In-come	Recip-ients	In-come	Recip-ients	In-come
Under $ 1,000	21.5	7	32.7	10	28.9	9
$ 1,000 - 1,999	48.2	25	63.4	33	64.6	37
2,000 - 2,999	78.9	58	85.9	62	86.6	65
3,000 - 3,999	90.3	75	92.6	74	93.5	77
4,000 - 4,999	95.6	85	96.3	83	96.6	84
5,000 - 6,999	98.6	92	98.4	89	98.5	90
7,000 - 9,999	99.4	95	99.2	92	99.4	94
10,000 - 14,999	99.7	97	99.6	95	99.7	96
15,000 and over	100.0	100	100.0	100	100.0	100

Table 45--continued

Income Size Group	County Group					
	18		19		20	
	Recip- ients	In- come	Recip- ients	In- come	Recip- ients	In- come
Under $ 1,000	30.5	9	30.7	9	27.3	8
$ 1,000 - 1,999	62.3	32	60.8	31	57.7	30
2,000 - 2,999	84.1	58	83.9	59	82.2	59
3,000 - 3,999	92.2	71	93.6	75	92.2	76
4,000 - 4,999	95.5	78	96.8	82	96.4	85
5,000 - 6,999	97.8	84	98.3	87	98.7	91
7,000 - 9,999	98.7	88	99.0	90	99.4	94
10,000 - 14,999	99.4	92	99.5	93	99.7	96
15,000 and over	100.0	100	100.0	100	100.0	100

Income Size Group	County Group					
	21		22		23	
	Recip- ients	In- come	Recip- ients	In- come	Recip- ients	In- come
Under $ 1,000	35.2	9	33.9	11	25.1	7
$ 1,000 - 1,999	65.4	33	71.2	40	57.6	28
2,000 - 2,999	82.2	57	86.9	61	80.6	54
3,000 - 3,999	91.3	70	93.0	72	90.5	70
4,000 - 4,999	95.4	79	96.1	79	95.1	79
5,000 - 6,999	98.1	87	98.1	85	97.7	86
7,000 - 9,999	99.2	92	99.0	89	98.8	90
10,000 - 14,999	99.7	95	99.5	93	99.4	93
15,000 and over	100.0	100	100.0	100	100.0	100

Table 45--continued

Income Size Group	County Group					
	24		25		26	
	Recip- ients	In- come	Recip- ients	In- come	Recip- ients	In- come
Under $ 1,000	16.2	5	29.1	7	25.7	7
$ 1,000 - 1,999	38.5	18	56.1	25	57.1	28
2,000 - 2,999	69.9	48	80.4	52	79.8	53
3,000 - 3,999	88.8	73	89.4	66	89.7	68
4,000 - 4,999	95.2	84	94.7	77	95.0	79
5,000 - 6,999	98.3	91	97.5	84	97.9	87
7,000 - 9,999	99.2	94	98.6	88	98.9	91
10,000 - 14,999	99.6	96	99.4	93	99.4	94
15,000 and over	100.0	100	100.0	100	100.0	100

Income Size Group	County Group					
	27		28		29	
	Recip- ients	In- come	Recip- ients	In- come	Recip- ients	In- come
Under $ 1,000	16.1	5	25.6	7	26.8	8
$ 1,000 - 1,999	39.1	19	58.4	28	58.0	29
2,000 - 2,999	70.8	49	79.9	51	82.2	55
3,000 - 3,999	88.1	71	89.2	65	91.0	68
4,000 - 4,999	93.6	80	94.1	75	94.5	75
5,000 - 6,999	98.1	90	97.4	83	97.3	82
7,000 - 9,999	99.1	93	98.6	87	98.6	86
10,000 - 14,999	99.5	95	99.3	92	99.3	90
15,000 and over	100.0	100	100.0	100	100.0	100

Table 45--continued

Income Size Group	County Group					
	30		31		32	
	Recip-ients	In-come	Recip-ients	In-come	Recip-ients	In-come
Under $ 1,000	27.1	8	31.2	8	24.8	7
$ 1,000 - 1,999	56.9	26	56.5	24	50.1	22
2,000 - 2,999	78.8	49	76.1	44	71.7	43
3,000 - 3,999	88.6	63	84.5	56	87.0	63
4,000 - 4,999	93.2	72	91.1	68	93.4	74
5,000 - 6,999	96.6	81	96.7	81	97.3	83
7,000 - 9,999	98.3	86	98.6	87	98.7	88
10,000 - 14,999	99.2	91	99.2	90	99.4	91
15,000 and over	100.0	100	100.0	100	100.0	100

Income Size Group	County Group					
	33		34		35	
	Recip-ients	In-come	Recip-ients	In-come	Recip-ients	In-come
Under $ 1,000	27.4	6	31.5	9	27.7	7
$ 1,000 - 1,999	54.2	23	59.2	28	53.4	23
2,000 - 2,999	76.7	47	82.0	54	75.6	46
3,000 - 3,999	88.5	64	92.3	70	89.4	66
4,000 - 4,999	93.8	74	95.7	77	94.6	76
5,000 - 6,999	97.4	83	97.9	83	97.7	84
7,000 - 9,999	98.7	87	98.7	86	98.8	88
10,000 - 14,999	99.5	91	99.3	89	99.3	91
15,000 and over	100.0	100	100.0	100	100.0	100

Table 45--continued

Income Size Group	County Group					
	36		37		38	
	Recip-ients	In-come	Recip-ients	In-come	Recip-ients	In-come
Under $ 1,000	20.7	5	22.9	6	20.7	5
$ 1,000 - 1,999	40.5	15	41.4	16	51.3	22
2,000 - 2,999	65.4	38	67.9	41	72.6	41
3,000 - 3,999	80.9	57	83.6	61	84.9	56
4,000 - 4,999	91.6	74	92.1	75	91.3	66
5,000 - 6,999	97.1	85	97.1	85	95.7	75
7,000 - 9,999	98.6	89	98.7	90	97.6	81
10,000 - 14,999	99.3	92	99.3	93	98.8	86
15,000 and over	100.0	100	100.0	100	100.0	100

Income Size Group	County Group			
	39		40	
	Recip-ients	In-come	Recip-ients	In-come
Under $ 1,000	19.4	5	20.2	5
$ 1,000 - 1,999	39.5	16	42.4	17
2,000 - 2,999	68.2	43	68.6	40
3,000 - 3,999	83.9	63	83.6	58
4,000 - 4,999	92.6	77	91.2	70
5,000 - 6,999	97.6	88	96.1	80
7,000 - 9,999	98.9	92	98.0	85
10,000 - 14,999	99.5	95	98.9	89
15,000 and over	100.0	100	100.0	100

Chart F
LORENZ CURVES FOR THE DISTRIBUTION OF INCOME PAYMENTS
IN KENTUCKY AND KENTUCKY COUNTIES, 1950

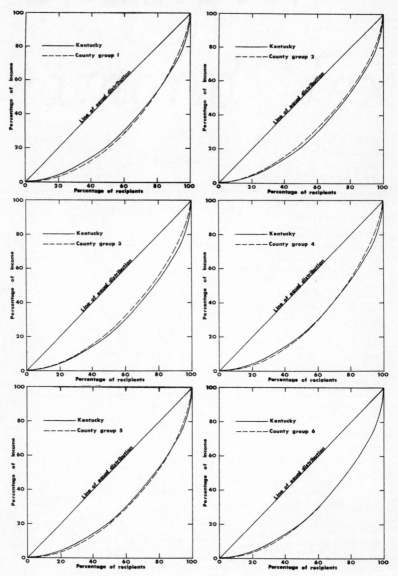

Chart F--continued

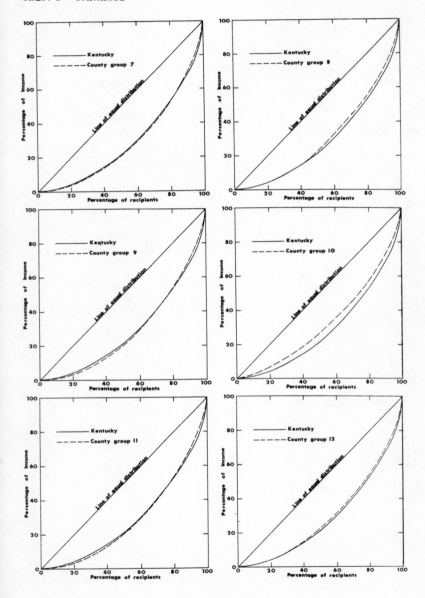

Chart F--continued

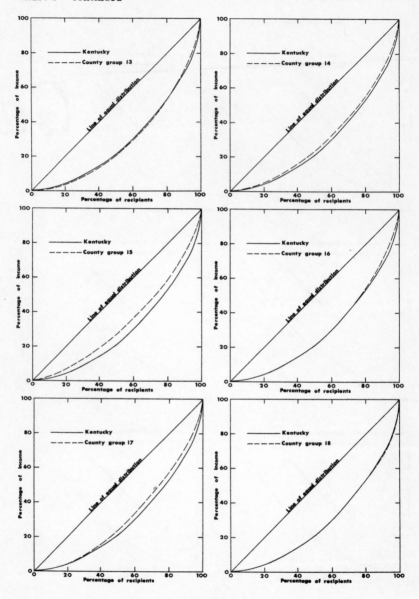

Chart **F--con**tinued

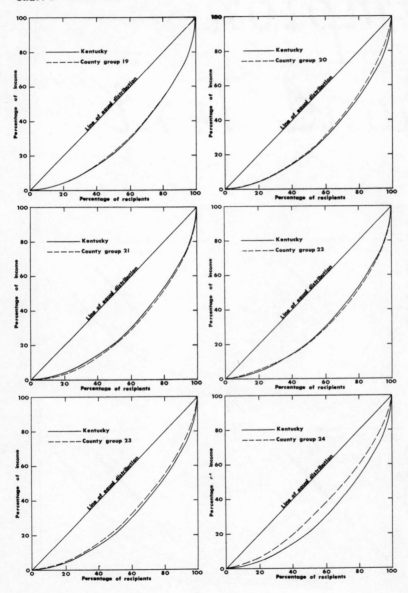

Chart F--continued

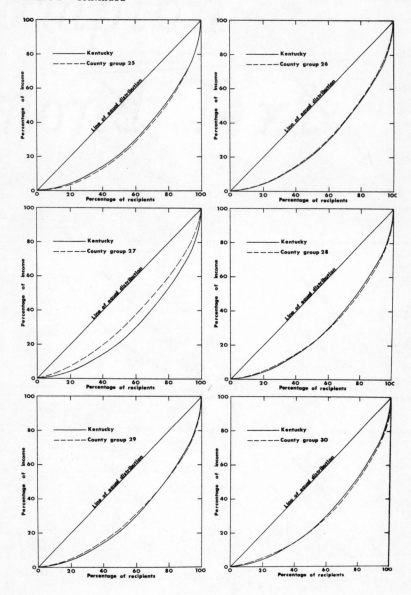

Chart F--continued

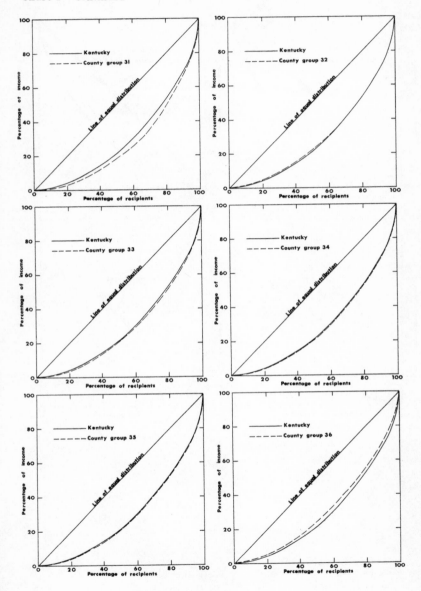

Chart F--continued

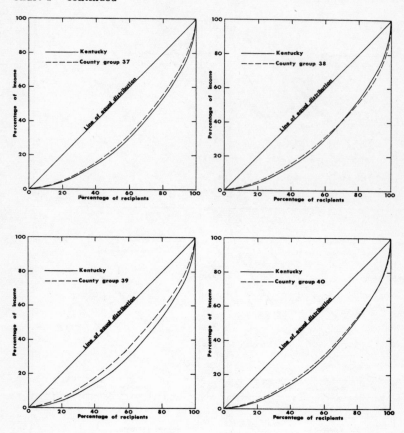

Source: Table 45

APPENDIX 3

Evaluation of Procedures

IN THIS study two distinct types of individual income distribution in Kentucky are presented--by county and by size. The reliability of these data can best be approximated by a close examination of the methods employed in deriving the final estimates.

AN EVALUATION OF THE METHODOLOGY EMPLOYED IN DERIVING TOTAL AND PER CAPITA INCOME PAYMENTS BY COUNTY

In the method of estimating county income payments employed in this study primary emphasis--from the standpoint of reliability--is put on the selection of allocators. In Appendix 1 the advantages and disadvantages of using county allocators from each of the major sources--UC statistics, census data, etc.--are presented. Some allocators, of course, are more reliable than others, usually depending upon whether they are directly or indirectly related to the component of income with which they are used. In most instances where an indirectly related allocator is used the component of income to be allocated is rather small, and in only 16 out of 77 separate allocations is an indirect allocator resorted to.

Nearly 60 per cent of all income payments received by the residents of Kentucky in 1950 were in
the form of net wages and salaries. A total of 27 different allocations are used to distribute this type of
income to the counties; but in only one instance--in
the allocation of miscellaneous wages and salaries--
is an indirectly related allocator used. Wage and salary allocators are taken from two major sources--
employment statistics published by the Bureau of the
Census and total wage payments by industry in covered employment as reported to the Kentucky Department of Economic Security. Because data from both
of these sources are extremely reliable the allocation of wage and salary payments to the counties, with
one important exception, is also assumed to be reasonably accurate. The exception referred to comes
about as a result of using the covered wage (UC) allocators. Wages earned by persons in covered employment are reported on a place of employment basis. In
keeping with the income payments concept--a measure of income by place of residence--adjustments are
necessary in instances where the residents of one
county work and receive income in another county.
This problem is especially acute in areas of high or
rapidly expanding employment and in areas where the
center of employment is near a county or state bor-
der. As explained in Appendix 1 several studies of
employee commuting in the state were made. The results of these studies make necessary an adjustment
in net wages and salaries in nearly half of the state's
counties, and also for the commuting of wage earners
between Kentucky and four adjoining states. In all
probability there is some employee commuting between counties in almost every area of the state; but,
as sample investigations indicate, the net employee

commuting in areas other than those for which adjustments are made is not important.

Some of the wage and salary components of income
fluctuate considerably from year to year, but because
current data are used in allocating the major components of this type of income the year to year changes
do not present a serious problem. Such, however, is
not the case in the allocation of income derived from
farm operations. Most allocators of farm income
and expense items--there are 11 of each--are taken
from United States Census of Agriculture publications.
This census is taken every five years, the latest in
1950. The published data on income and expense
items, however, are, for the most part, based on the
calendar year 1949. Farm proprietors' income, as
a percentage of total income payments, is the most
important type of income in many Kentucky counties.
It is probable that the farther the estimating year is
removed from the census year the less reliable the
estimates of farm income become. It is also quite
probable, then, that estimates of income from farm
operations are less reliable than estimates of income
from wages and salaries.

Farm proprietors' income is also subject to fluctu-
ation from one year to the next to a greater degree
than is "other income," the income of nonfarm proprietors, or income from property. Especially in the
cases of the latter two types, nonfarm proprietors' income and income from property, this relative stability is conducive to greater reliability in county income
estimates than would otherwise be the case. This is
because of the extensive use of benchmark allocators,
subject to minor adjustments from year to year as new
data become available. In the case of nonfarm proprietors' income, for example, extensive use is made

of the 1948 Census of Business. Unusually reliable
allocators for a large segment of property income
are available for 1950 estimates of county income--
unpublished state income tax return statistics--but
income estimates for subsequent years will probably
have to be made on the basis of these data until other
reliable allocators become available. Allocators for
most of the components of "other income" are usually
directly or closely related to the income components.
There are, for example, very reliable data on the
amount of payments by county for most of the welfare
and social insurance programs. A benchmark allocator
for many of the World War II veterans' payments is currently available, but it is a by-product of distributing
the National Service Life Insurance special dividend
and is not a recurring source of information.

No mention has been made of the fact that the state
estimates of income payments to individuals, published
in summary form and available to researchers in detail, are likewise subject to error. [1] With the exception of interstate situs adjustments, however, the income estimates of the Office of Business Economics
of the United States Department of Commerce are accepted as correct.

The estimates of county income, then, as presented
here must be interpreted in the light of the preceding
points pertaining to reliability. It is extremely unlikely, however, that the data in any case would be
too unreliable for most uses. In the opinion of the author the estimates of nonfarm proprietors' income
and some segments of property income are more subject to error than are those of the other types of income payments. But relative to total income these
two types are small, seldom amounting to more than
25 per cent of the total income received in any county.

Suppose an error overstating these components of
income by 10 per cent is made in a county where, in
combination, they account for 20 per cent of total income. Assuming the other three types of income to
be allocated correctly (or that committed errors would
cancel) the error in total income for this county would
be about 2 per cent. Or in Daviess County, where
wages and salaries were 60 per cent of total income
in 1950, an error of 5 per cent in this component (in
the mind of the author an error of this size is very
unlikely in the wage and salary estimates) would result in an error of about 3 per cent in total income.

In general--and with much emphasis on "general"--
it may be said that the possibility of error increases
as the percentage of total county income derived from
wages and salaries decreases.

Table 46 is a compendium of several items selected to give some further indication of the reliability of
the county income estimates. The counties are ranked
according to per capita income in 1950 and divided into groups of 30 counties each. Included in Group I are
the 30 counties with the lowest per capita income, in
Group II the next 30 counties, and so on. Table 46
does not in any way prove the reliability of the income
estimates for any particular county, and it may be argued that it does not prove the income estimates for
any group of counties as valid. But the various factors used for comparative purposes are chosen because they are, in all probability, closely associated
with income levels. The large decrease in population
in Groups I and II could be logically expected to take
place because of the lack of available local employment and the large number of employment opportunities in other communities during the past ten years.
It is also quite reasonable to assume there should be

Table 46

A COMPENDIUM OF RELATIONSHIPS PERTAINING
TO THE RELIABILITY OF COUNTY PER
CAPITA INCOME ESTIMATES

	Counties Ranked According to Per Capita Income and Divided into Groups of Thirty Counties Each			
	Group I	Group II	Group III	Group IV
Per capita income, 1950 (weighted)	$414	$558	$713	$1,283
Percentage change in population-- 1940 to 1950 (weighted)[a]	-9.2%	-8.0%	1.4%	12.0%
Percentage income reported on state income tax returns--returns with a tax liability (weighted)[b]	13.2%	22.5%	26.5%	45.1%
Recipients of old-age assistance as a percentage of all persons 65 years old and over (weighted)[c]	49.4%	35.0%	29.9%	20.5%
Percentage of population aged 14-17 in school (weighted)[d]	56.6%	67.6%	66.7%	78.4%
Number of passenger car registrations in 1950 per 100 population[e]	10.6	16.9	20.0	24.8

Computed from:

[a]United States Census of Population: 1950, Vol. II, Part 19, Chap. B, Tables 41 and 43. The military population in Hardin and Christian Counties and the inmates of federal and state institutions have been excluded.

[b]Unpublished income statistics from state income tax returns, Kentucky Department of Revenue.

[c]United States Census of Population: 1950, Vol. II, Part 19, Chap. B, Table 41, and unpublished county data on public assistance payments, Kentucky Department of Economic Security.

[d]United States Census of Population: 1950, Vol. II, Part 19, Chap. B, Table 42.

[e]Ibid., Table 43 (see note to footnote "a"), and Kentucky Department of Revenue, Statistical Appendix to the 1951-52 Annual Report.

a direct relationship between the other factors listed
in Table 46 and per capita income level.

AN EVALUATION OF THE METHODOLOGY
EMPLOYED IN DERIVING COUNTY AND
STATE DISTRIBUTIONS OF INCOME
BY SIZE

There is always some question as to whether a
sound evaluation of any statistical analysis can be
made by the same person who decided upon a particular set of definitions and a particular procedure for
making the analysis. Complete objectivity is impossible whenever it is necessary to make assumptions
or choices between usable data; and it may be that
some of the author's biases are overlooked in this
evaluation. But in this section, as well as the other
sections, all effort is directed toward making a ser-
ries of income size distributions for the state and the
counties that will have the greatest possible value.

Time Period Selected

There are several reasons why a single year is selected as the time period and why the year selected is
1950. In the first instance most income data are presented on a calendar year basis; so there is the matter of conformity. Second, a substantial part of the
basic data--individual incomes as reported on state
income tax returns by county--are for a single year,
1950. It is conceivable and highly probable that better
distributions could be made if the time period were
longer; for example, the average income of all recip-

ients over a period of three years, or perhaps the average over an even longer period would be a preferable measure. The point is this: 1950 may not be a typical year, and if it is not typical, then the distributions leave something to be desired. Actually, the year 1950 is, in many respects, not typical because of the Korean war situation. There is a closer economic relationship between the last six months of 1950 and the first six months of 1951 than with the first half of 1950. Another reason why 1950 incomes were chosen for analysis is because more and better data are available with which to make the county total income estimates. These total estimates, of course, are important in the distribution analysis.

As a reminder it is also well to point out that any year selected would be neither a typical year (if there is such a thing) nor a year when all the desired information would be available. If no income size distributions were made until the researcher had at his finger tips all the statistical data needed to do a perfect job, it is quite likely that very few would ever be completed. What is needed most is not a statistically perfect distribution of incomes by size, but a distribution sufficiently reliable for most purposes, and one that may develop into a continuing series.

The Number of Recipients

A fact frequently overlooked by many persons is that the number of recipients is just as important in an income size distribution as the amount of income. Primary interest is in the people who receive incomes, not in the incomes they receive. The definition of the term "income recipients" is made with this axiom in

mind; and the total number of recipients calculated
with extreme care. In spite of this there may be,
and probably is, some error in the calculations. [2]

One possible source of error is in the census estimates of the labor force. "It is estimated that employment status was not reported for approximately
1.2 million persons for the United States as a whole,
or about 1 per cent of the total United States population 14 years old and over. Approximately 45 per cent
of this group might have been added to the labor force
had the necessary information been obtained."[3] Assuming this estimated error for the nation to be representative of the understatement of the civilian labor
force in Kentucky as reported by the census the number of income recipients is understated by about 4,300.
The additions that are made to account for annual turnover in the labor force and increased employment opportunities add to this another 400 recipients, making
a total of 4,700.

The least reliable of all income recipient components is in the estimation of the number of persons
who receive income from property only. Some explanation of this has been made previously, and it is unnecessary to go into further detail here. It is fortu-
nate, however, that there are relatively few persons
in this class, and an underestimate of as much as 50
per cent in this factor would amount to an error of about
0.2 per cent in the total number of income recipients.

It is possible, and perhaps quite likely, that the
number of persons who receive transfer payments on-
ly--retirement payments and the like--is overstated
in spite of the effort to keep the figures as accurate
as possible and to avoid overstating the number of income recipients. There is possible overstatement in
the number of income recipients in the various pro-

grams for which the Kentucky Department of Economic Security has no information, such as railroad retirement, government retirement, and military retirement. The programs for which there is no information on the number of recipients who derived income from other sources accounted for about 55 per cent of the 162,900 recipients in this group. No downward adjustments in the number of recipients are made where specific information is not available. If an adjustment based only on information furnished by the Department of Economic Security is made in the number of recipients receiving incomes under other retirement and welfare programs there would be about 14,000 fewer recipients in this group.

Of the possible errors that may have been committed in determining the number of recipients there appears to be a strong indication that one would compensate for the other. But even though the understatement or the overstatement of recipients in a particular instance is not entirely compensated in other calculations, probably the maximum error in the total is not greater than 1 per cent. [4] And it is also quite likely to be an underestimation rather than an overestimation.

The Amount of Income

There is some difference between the total income payments to individuals as estimated by the Department of Commerce and the total income in the state income size-group distribution. This difference is the result of several factors. About $72 million is added to the Department of Commerce estimate as a result of the interstate situs adjustments previously

explained.   Military wages and salaries totaling $72.4
million are deducted from the estimates.[5] The only
other difference is an overstatement of about 0.2 per
cent in the size distribution total that may properly
be called a statistical discrepancy.   This is the net
accumulated error resulting from the statistical procedure used in deriving the estimated distribution of
incomes for the counties and county groups.

It is erroneous, however, to say that the same degree of accuracy in the state distribution can be maintained in each county income distribution. As a general rule the probability of error in the estimate of total income for a given area is inversely proportional
to the amount of income received by persons living in
the area. County estimates, therefore, are less reliable than the state estimate; and the less income the
persons of a particular county receive, the less reliable are the estimates of total income.   There are
probably many exceptions to this generalization, one
of which may result from the different percentages of
total income derived from wages and salaries.   The
distribution of wages and salaries among the counties
is probably more accurate than the distribution of
some of the other income components, and there is a
great variation in the percentage of total income derived from this source.   Because county income estimates are probably less accurate than the state estimate, and because the accuracy of county income totals probably varies inversely to amount, the distributions of income by size are made for county groups
with the exception of the high income counties.[6] By
grouping some of the counties the distribution data are
made more accurate, but at the expense of complete
detail which for some purposes may be desirable. One
type of possible discrepancy in the total incomes of

counties and county groups may be caused by the
movement of persons from one county to another during 1950. Total county incomes should be estimated
taking into account the residence of the income receiver all during the year; size distributions should
reflect all income received by persons living in a certain county or area on a specified date, no matter
where they lived when the income was earned.

The Allocation Procedure

It is in connection with the allocation procedure
that many of the issues relating to the accuracy of the
size distributions of income are centered. The methodology used in deriving the distributions is the core
of the whole analysis. A high degree of accuracy is
assumed in the estimates of income recipients and in
the estimates of total income payments by county and
also in the amount of income derived from the various
sources (both the cash and imputed items) which are
allocated to recipients in the various income classes
step by step throughout the distribution procedure. Tables 47 and 48 are presented as an aid in the evaluation of the methodology relative to the actual amounts
of income involved in each phase. Table 47 shows,
by county group, the percentage total income reported for tax purposes is of total income payments received; and Table 48 shows, as a percentage of total
income payments to Kentucky residents, the amount
of each nontaxable income component.

The necessity for adjusting the federal income tax
return data to allow for the understatement and nonreporting of incomes is generally recognized by economists seeking to use these data in arriving at a nation-

Table 47
INCOME REPORTED FOR STATE INCOME TAX PURPOSES
AS A PERCENTAGE OF TOTAL INCOME PAYMENTS
BY COUNTY GROUP, 1950[a]

County Group[b]	Percentage of Total Income Payments Reported[c]	County Group[b]	Percentage of Total Income Payments Reported[c]
1	19.7	21	43.1
2	15.9	22	42.1
3	19.7	23	46.6
4	27.5	24	35.2
5	31.5	25	50.3
6	31.0	26	45.5
7	33.5	27	35.7
8	24.3	28	48.1
9	34.4	29	44.0
10	35.3	30	50.0
11	48.7	31	53.9
12	33.8	32	60.1
13	39.7	33	62.7
14	34.5	34	43.4
15	30.8	35	56.1
16	38.6	36	59.5
17	33.9	37	56.3
18	41.8	38	58.9
19	44.3	39	56.3
20	43.3	40	58.1

[a]Reported income is the sum of the reported amounts on pay returns, no-pay returns, and returns filed late exclusive of reported capital gains and losses. It should not be concluded that this table in any way measures the amount of tax evasion. A great amount of income of a taxable nature is not reported because of the minimum filing requirements of the Kentucky income tax law.

[b]For the counties included in each group see Table 44.

[c]Computed from the unpublished state income tax return statistics for 1950, Kentucky Department of Revenue, and the estimates of total income payments.

Table 48

NONTAXABLE COMPONENTS OF INCOME AS A PERCENTAGE
OF TOTAL INCOME PAYMENTS RECEIVED
BY KENTUCKY RESIDENTS, 1950

Component of Income	Percentage of Total Income Payments
Cash items	
Income that accrues exclusively to wage and salary recipients	1. 68
Payments to veterans of World War II that are not based on income or employment status	4. 01
Payments to veterans of all other wars	0. 91
Cash interest and dividends	0. 84
Imputed items	
The value of food and fuel produced and consumed on farms and government payments to owner-operators[a]	3. 48
Imputed interest--"insurance companies".	0. 86
All other imputed interest	1. 29
Subsistence payments to veterans attending college under Public Laws 16 and 346	0. 29
Imputed wages of farm laborers and domestic servants	0. 38
Total	13. 74

Source: Computed from unpublished data on income payments to individuals by source, Office of Business Economics, United States Department of Commerce.

[a]Government payments in cash are included in this item but account
for less than 6 per cent of the total.

al distribution of income by size. [7] The same holds
true, of course, in the use of state income tax return
data in arriving at a state distribution of income by
size. Four separate adjustments are made relative
to the underreporting of taxable incomes and failure
to file returns. The first of these adjustments, that

which is made to bring two northern Kentucky counties up to the level of percentage of total income it is
assumed they should have reported, is one of the adjustments made that affected individual counties. The
reporting level they should have is assumed to be the
average level of three other counties with comparable per capita incomes. It is known, as nearly as
anything can positively be known in such a circumstance, that compliance with the law in these two counties is not as good as compliance in other parts of the
state where income and industrial make-up are comparable. The question to be considered is not whether an adjustment for noncompliance and underreporting is necessary for these two counties, but whether
the amount of adjustment should differ from that made
for other counties in the state. But there may be a
weakness in this assumption because of the different
racial composition of the population or for other un-
identified reasons. It is rather common knowledge
that the average income of Negroes is considerably
below the average income of all persons. [8] In the two
counties for which the adjustment is made less than
3 per cent of the population are Negroes, but in the
three counties on which the adjustment is based they
comprise nearly 13 per cent of the population.[9] This
factor is not considered in making the adjustment. The
other adjustment in compliance that is made on a county basis is for four major coal producing counties.
These adjustments and the considerations upon which
they are based are discussed in detail in an earlier
section. And there is some indication that adjustments should be made for counties other than the six
mentioned, but these indications would not stand up
under close scrutiny; so no further county adjustments
are made.

The third adjustment in the income tax data also has to do with noncompliance--failure to file a return when legally required to do so. Several persons, each of whom have or had a responsibility in the administration of the state income tax law, were asked to make estimates on the amount of noncompliance. There is general agreement among these persons that serious noncompliance exists only in the lower income classes, and that the lower the income class the more serious it becomes. The adjustment percentages used in this study for each size group in which a noncompliance adjustment is made are arbitrary figures for which the author must take full responsibility. But they are not mere guesses--they are based on the best information now available.

The fourth major adjustment in income tax return data is made for underreporting. [10] The same persons consulted in connection with the noncompliance problem were also asked to make estimates of underreporting. In the great majority of cases underreporting is a result of unintentional errors in computing taxable income or allowance deductions. The consensus seemed to be that underreporting is not concentrated in either the high or low income classes, but is spread rather evenly, as a percentage of income, throughout all income size groups and also throughout the state. [11]

The possibilities of error, in the opinion of the author, are greatest in the allocation of nontaxable income--cash and imputed--to the income classes. One such possibility is a result of the different definitions of income recipient used in the different source material employed in making the allocations. As a reminder, the distributions were made by supplementing state income tax return data with data taken from

the 1950 Census of Population. Tax return data are
used as the basic allocator for incomes above $3,000.
Because there is no community property law in Kentucky and because joint returns usually result in a
greater tax liability than separate returns when the
combined incomes are over $3,000, there are prob-
ably few joint returns of a husband and wife who have
separate incomes unless one of these incomes is very
small. "Separate returns usually result in less tax
when combined <u>adjusted gross income</u> is more than
$3,000."[12] Taking into consideration the method
used in computing the number of income recipients,
joint returns could be a source of error only if both
the husband and wife were in the civilian labor force
and if each had a substantial amount of income.

Another possible source of error in this respect
is in the concept of income recipients used in the "Survey of Consumer Finances." "The interview unit of
the survey is the spending unit, defined as all persons
living in the same dwelling and belonging to the same
family who pool their incomes to meet their major expenses."[13] This is somewhat similar in concept to
the combination of families and unrelated individuals
used by the census. The number of income receivers in each spending unit[14] is by no means indicative
of the possible error that may be made in the size distributions resulting from the use of data from this
source in some parts of the allocation process. Many
of the spending units with more than one income receiver would probably not have two or more persons
in the civilian labor force; and, as has been mentioned
before, the term income recipient in this study is not
strictly defined.

In allocating recipients to the three lowest size
groups, after the nontaxable cash income is allocated

to the size groups $3,000--$3,999 and above, no adjustment is made for possible differences in the number of income recipients per family between groups.
The assumption in this case, again, is that very few
families would have more than one person in the civilian labor force if the total cash income of the family unit is less than $3,000. It is an understatement
of fact to say there is no chance for error in the allocation procedure resulting from the various concepts of income recipient; but, at the same time, it
is a pronounced exaggeration to say that the possibility of error will render the distributions valueless.

There are four allocations of nontaxable cash income, five allocations of imputed income, and the allocation of social insurance deductions, all of which
are rather important in the determination of the final
distributions. Each of these allocations is, in part,
based upon the size group totals at a particular point
in the procedure. In theory, to get maximum accuracy, each allocation should be made last; or, to put
it another way, each allocation should be based on the
most complete data possible--the size distributions
as they are after all other allocations are made. In
this phase of the allocation process, a known error is
committed which results in the overestimation of the
number of recipients and income in the lower income
classes by approximately 1 to 3 per cent. Likewise,
there is a compensating underestimation in larger income classes. Since an understatement in the smaller, and an overstatement in the larger, income size
groups is known to occur when "spending unit" data
are used in the allocation, the errors are partially
compensating. No accurate estimate of the amount
of compensation or in what parts of the distributions
any net error is concentrated can be made.

In making the adjustments much use is made of
averages. In some instances, as in allocating nontaxable payments to veterans, it is assumed each veteran receives the same amount. Obviously this is
not the case. The average payment to World War II
veterans in 1950 was $432 (exclusive of subsistence
payments to veterans attending college and veterans'
unemployment compensation). In making the adjustments it is assumed that each veteran in each income
size group receives this amount. The same procedure is followed in other instances; but there is no
way of knowing how much the error is or in which end
of the distribution scales it is greatest.

Other adjustments, also based on averages, are
made but in a somewhat different manner. These are
based on a different average amount of adjustment in
each of the size groups. An illustration is the allocation of nontaxable interest and dividends. This is
a more adequate way of making the allocations and,
in cases such as the one mentioned, is immeasurably
better because of the extreme variation in the average amount of such income received by persons in the
various income classes. More desirable than either
of these methods would be to know, for the recipients
in each income class, the actual amounts of a particular type of income they receive. As an illustration
assume that $1,000,000 is the determined amount that
must be added to the incomes of 10,000 recipients in
the $4,000--$4,999 size group. The average is $100
each, and in making the adjustment about 920 recipients and their incomes are moved into the next higher
size group. But if 100 persons received $1,000 each
and 9,900 persons $91 each an adjustment to the next
higher group is made for about 930 recipients and their
income--an adjustment slightly larger than when it is

assumed each receives the same amount. There is no
way of estimating the amount of error incurred when
averages are employed in making the adjustments;
but the above illustration, even though the estimated
error is small, is no doubt an exaggeration.

Something has already been said about the difficulty of selecting a typical year for which to make an
income distribution. Several reasons were offered
as to why 1950 was selected. But in two important instances the income data from the 1950 Census of Population are used in the allocation procedures--in determining the number of recipients in each of the three
lowest size groups to complete the distribution of cash
income, and in the allocation of imputed income to
farm operators--and these data are based on 1949 incomes. Adjustments are made, however, that have
the effect of changing the data to be more representative of the 1950 distribution. In the process of doing
this some error is undoubtedly made, especially in
the adjustment of farm income statistics, which for
each county are based on the percentage change from
1949 to 1950 for the state as a whole.

For the reasons noted above the accuracy varies
from county to county for both the per capita and the
size distribution estimates, and therefore it is both
inappropriate and impossible to indicate a general
margin of error. But above all it should not be inferred that the possibility for error limits seriously
the use value of the county income estimates.

------

[1]Within the conceptual framework of income payments to individuals the error is probably very small,
but the National Income Division would be the first to
admit the possibility of error in the state estimates.

See U.S. Department of Commerce, <u>National Income and Product of the United States</u>: <u>1929-1950</u>, 56-60.

[2]The fact that the final estimate of the number of income recipients is slightly greater than the preliminary estimate may be indicative of an error.

[3]<u>United States Census of Population</u>: <u>1950</u>, Vol. II, Part 1, Chap. B, x.

[4]This approximation is exclusive of any errors in the basic data and applies only to the total number of recipients for the state as a whole. It is quite possible that the error in the estimated number of recipients in some of the county groups is greater than 1 per cent. If the final number of income recipients estimated as explained in the distribution procedure may be assumed to be approximately correct, the preliminary estimate was understated by a little more than 1 per cent.

[5]The reasons for deducting the military population and pay roll were discussed in Appendix 2.

[6]With a very few exceptions the counties were grouped on the basis of per capita income.

[7]Baird and Fine, "The Use of Income Tax Data in the National Resources Committee Estimate of the Distribution of Income by Size," in <u>Studies in Income and Wealth</u>, Vol. III, 183.

[8]"1951 Survey of Consumer Finances," 927.

[9]<u>United States Census of Population</u>: <u>1950</u>, Vol. II, Part 19, Chap. B, Table 42.

[10]See Hanna, Peckman, and Lerner, "Analysis of Wisconsin Income," in <u>Studies in Income and Wealth</u>, Vol. IX, 47-48. The assumptions made by the differ-

ent researchers exemplifies rather clearly how little is known in the realm of underreporting.

[11]There is an apparent inconsistency between this adjustment and those which followed. No movement of recipients and their income from one size group into the next higher group was made; the number of recipients and the amount of income in all income classes is increased by 3 per cent. This has the net effect of making an adjustment of slightly less than 3 per cent. This is intentional and not through inadvertence, for two reasons. First, even though it is known that an adjustment for underreporting should be made, the amount of the adjustment (like the adjustments for noncompliance) is an arbitrary amount. It may be too large; it may be too small. Complicating the process by making adjustments for movements of recipients from one group to the next would indicate an accuracy in the estimate that does not exist, or, for the time being at least, cannot be proved. The second reason for not making the adjustments that were necessary in later stages of the allocation procedure is simply a matter of efficiency in time allocation.

[12]Kentucky Individual Income Tax Return, form 740, 1951, 4. Gross income subject to tax less any federal income tax paid equals adjusted gross income.

[13]"1951 Survey of Consumer Finances," 920.

[14]Ibid., 927. In 1950, 25 per cent of all spending units had two or more income receivers, ranging from a low of 10 per cent in the "under $1,000" size group to a high of 47 per cent in the $5,000--$7,499 size group.

BIBLIOGRAPHY

BOOKS

Burns, Arthur F. The Instability of Consumer Spending. National Bureau of Economic Research, Inc.,
32nd Annual Report. New York: National Bureau
of Economic Research, 1952.

Income Payments and Retail Sales to Residents of
West Virginia, by Counties, 1929-1946. Charleston:
West Virginia State Chamber of Commerce, 1948.
Current estimates are published in a yearly supplement.

Income Payments to Residents of California by Counties, 1935-1941. California State Chamber of Commerce, 1942. Also Individual Incomes of Civilian
Residents of California by Counties, 1939-1946, 1947;
and Economic Survey Series, 1949-50.

Kentucky Dentists Association. Directory of Licensed
Dentists in the State of Kentucky: 1950. Louisville,
1950.

Kentucky State Medical Association. Kentucky Medical Directory. 2nd ed. and supplements. Louisville:
1949.

Kimmel, Lewis H. Share Ownership in the United
States. Washington: The Brookings Institution, 1952.

Kuznets, Simon. National Income: A Summary of

Findings. New York: National Bureau of Economic
Research, 1946.

—————. Shares of Upper Income Groups in Income
and Savings. New York: National Bureau of Economic Research, 1953.

Martindale-Hubbell Law Directory. Vol. I, 82nd ed.
Summit, N. J.: by author, 1950.

Leven, Maurice, et al., America's Capacity to Consume. Washington: Brookings Institution, 1934.

Studies in Income and Wealth, Vols. III, V, VIII, IX,
X, XIII, and XV. New York: National Bureau of
Economic Research, Inc., annually since 1937.

ARTICLES

Farioletti, Marius. "Some Results from the First
Year's Audit Control Program of Bureau of Internal
Revenue," in National Tax Journal, V (March, 1952).

Hanna, Frank A. "Contribution of Manufacturing
Wages to Regional Differences in Per Capita Income,"
in The Review of Economics and Statistics, XXXIII
(February, 1951).

Johnson, John L. "The Effects of Industry-Mix and
Wage Rates on Per Capita Income in Kentucky," in
Southern Economic Journal, XX (July, 1953).

Journal American Hospital Association: Hospitals,
Part II (June, 1951).

McCracken, Paul W. "A Policy for Prosperity in
1953," in Michigan Business Review, V (January,
1953).

McPherson, W. K. "Some Problems and Opportunities Created by Florida's Changing Population," in
Economic Leaflets, XII (June, 1953).

Miller, Herman P. "An Appraisal of the 1950 Census Income Data," in Journal of the American Statistical Association, XLVIII (March, 1953).

PUBLIC DOCUMENTS

Adamson, W. M. Income in Counties of Alabama,
1929 and 1935. University: Bureau of Business Research, University of Alabama, 1939.

"Additional Report of the Joint Committee on Reduction of Nonessential Federal Expenditures," On Federal Civilian Employment: 1950. 82nd Congress of
the United States. Washington: Government Printing Office, 1950.

Bacon, Marvin A. Income as an Index of the Fiscal
Capacity of Michigan Counties. University of Michigan Government Studies, No. 8. Ann Arbor: Bureau of Government, University of Michigan, 1941.

Bowen, Howard. The Income in the Counties of Iowa.
Iowa State Planning Board. Data are averages for
1927-29 and 1931-33.

Bureau of Agricultural Economics. "Revised Annual
Estimates of Cash Receipts and Home Consumption,
by States, 1949-1950," The Farm Income Situation,
FIS-131 (June, 1951).

Bureau of Agricultural Economics. The Farm Income
Situation, FIS-139 (December, 1952-January, 1953).

California Legislature, Senate Interim Committee on

State and Local Taxation. State and Local Government Finance in California, Part 2. 57th Session,
January, 1947.

Consumer Incomes in the United States. Washington:
National Resources Committee, 1938.

Converse, P. D. County Incomes and Trade Movements in Illinois. Urbana: Bureau of Economic and
Business Research, University of Illinois, 1945.

Coolsen, F. G. , Myers, W. S. , and Martin, J. W. Paducah and Western Kentucky Income, Labor, and Retail Trade Patterns. Frankfort, Ky. : The Agricultural and Industrial Development Board of Kentucky, August, 1952.

Copeland, Lewis C. Methods for Estimating Income
Payments in Counties: A Technical Supplement to
County Income Estimates for Seven Southeastern
States. Charlottesville: Bureau of Population and
Economic Research, University of Virginia, 1952.

————. "Working Papers on a Method for Estimating Family Income Levels in Small Areas." Knox-
ville: Tennessee Valley Authority, 1946 (unpublished).

Covington-Kenton Chamber of Commerce and the Kentucky Agricultural and Industrial Development Board.
Economic and Industrial Survey of Covington, Kentucky. October 30, 1952.

Desk Book of Economic Statistics. Frankfort, Kentucky: Agricultural and Industrial Development
Board, 1952.

Ducoff, L. J. , and Hagood, M. J. Differentials in Productivity and in Farm Income of Agricultural Work-

ers by Size of Enterprise and by Region. U.S. Department of Agriculture, Bureau of Agricultural Economics. Washington: August, 1944.

French, Robert W., and Watters, Elsie. Income Esti-
mates for Louisiana Parishes, 1939 and 1943. Baton
Rouge: Bureau of Business Research, Louisiana
State University, 1945.

Galloway, Robert, and Beers, Howard W. Utilization of Rural Manpower in Eastern Kentucky. Lexington: Kentucky Agricultural Experiment Station,
January, 1953.

Gilliam, Sarah K. Distribution of Income in Virginia,
1947. Charlottesville: Bureau of Population and
Economic Research, University of Virginia, 1947.

Hochwald, Werner, and King, La Verne. "Income
Measures and Their Purpose," Monthly Review,
Federal Reserve Bank of St. Louis, XXXII (August,
1950). Other issues of this publication since January, 1948, have included income studies of various
types.

Hosmer, Joseph B. Preliminary Results of an Economic Evaluation of Georgia Counties. Atlanta: Industrial Development Council, Inc. , Georgia School
of Technology, 1940.

Johnson, John L. The Economy of Northern Kentucky.
Frankfort: The Kentucky Agricultural and Industrial
Development Board, 1954.

Kentucky Crop and Livestock Reporting Service, Bureau of Agricultural Economics, U.S. Department
of Agriculture. Kentucky Agricultural Statistics:
1950. Louisville: 1951.

Kentucky Department of Economic Security. Statistical Journal of Economic Security in Kentucky. Published monthly.

Kentucky Department of Industrial Relations. "Workmen's Compensation Benefits by Industry," Annual
Report: 1950. Frankfort, Ky.

Kentucky Department of Mines and Minerals. Annual Report: 1950. Lexington: 1951.

Kentucky Department of Revenue. Kentucky Property Tax Rates: 1950. Frankfort, Ky.

————. Statistical Appendix to the 1949-50 Annual
Report. Frankfort, Ky.

————. Statistical Appendix to the 1950-51 Annual
Report. Frankfort, Ky.

"Kentucky Public Schools Directory, 1950-51," Kentucky Education Bulletin, XVIII (November, 1950).

Kentucky Revised Statutes, Chaps. 141 and 341.

Kentucky State Committee, Production and Marketing
Administration, U.S. Department of Agriculture,
Kentucky PMA Programs: 1950 Yearbook. Lexing-
ton: 1951.

Kentucky State Department of Health. "Estimated Pop-
lation of Kentucky Counties, as of July 1, 1952" (unpublished).

Lancaster, John L., (ed.) County Income Estimates
for Seven Southeastern States. Charlottesville: Bureau of Population and Economic Research, University of Virginia, 1952.

————. Per Capita Income of Virginia Counties for
1940. Charlottesville: Bureau of Population and Economic Research, University of Virginia.

Lockyer, Charles R.   An Analysis of the Kentucky
Income Tax. Unpublished Ph. D. dissertation, University of Kentucky, 1954.

Martin, James W., and Myers, Will S.   Aspects of the
Louisville Area Economy. Frankfort: The Kentucky Agricultural and Industrial Development Board,
1953.

Mountin, J. W. , and Greve, C. H.   The Role of Grants-
in-Aid in Financing Public Health Programs. Federal
Security Agency, Public Health Bulletin No. 303.
Washington: Government Printing Office, 1949.

Myers, Will S., Johnson, John L. , and Martin, James
W. Kentucky Income Payments by Counties: 1939,
1947, 1950, and 1951. Lexington: Bureau of Business Research, University of Kentucky, '1952.

"Number and Amount of Monthly Benefits in Current
Payment Status as of February 28, 1951, by Type
of Benefit and County Residence of Beneficiary. " Bureau of Old-Age and Survivors' Insurance. Washington, D. C. (unpublished).

Ohio Bureau of Unemployment Compensation, "Hamil-
ton County, Ohio: 1950. Workers Covered under
Ohio Compensation Law. " Tables RS 203. 1-31 and
RS 203. 2-31.

Safley, Edna.   Estimates of North Carolina County
Incomes. Unpublished Master's thesis, University
of North Carolina.

Social Security Board.   Industrial Classification Code,
Description of Industries. Vol. I. Washington: Federal Security Agency, 1942.

"Survey of Consumer Finances, " Federal Reserve
Bulletin. Published annually since 1947.

"Survey of Indiana Commuting Patterns," The Labor Market and Employment Security. September, 1950.

Thompson, Lorin A. Income Payments by Cities and Counties of Virginia, 1947 and 1945. Charlottesville: Bureau of Population and Economic Research, University of Virginia.

United States Code Annotated, 26-1607.

Unpublished data on income payments to individuals by source. Office of Business Economics. U.S. Department of Commerce.

Unpublished data on covered wages and average employment. Kentucky Department of Economic Security, Frankfort, Ky.

Unpublished income statistics from state income tax returns. Kentucky Department of Revenue, Frankfort, Ky.

Unpublished pay roll and enrollment statistics, Office of Education, Washington, D. C.

Unpublished statistics on the number of employees of Class I railroads. Bureau of Railway Economics, Washington, D. C.

U.S. Bureau of the Census. Current Population Reports: Labor Force, Series P-50, No. 31 (March 9, 1951).

————. Current Population Reports: Population Estimates. Series P-25.

————. Governments Division. "City Employment in 1950," Government Employment: 1950, G-GE 50-No. 6 (April, 1951).

————. Statistical Abstract of the United States,

1951. Washington: Government Printing Office, 1951.

—————. United States Census of Agriculture: 1950, Vol. I. Washington: Government Printing Office, 1952.

—————. United States Census of Business: 1948. Washington: Government Printing Office, 1950.

—————. United States Census of Manufacturers: 1947. Vol. III. Washington: Government Printing Office, 1949.

—————. United States Census of Population: 1950. Vols. I and II. Washington: Government Printing Office, 1952.

—————. United States Census of Religious Bodies: 1936. Vol. I. Washington: Government Printing Office, 1937.

U.S. Department of Commerce. "Business Establishments, Employment, and Taxable Pay Rolls, by Industry Groups under Old-Age and Survivors' Insurance Program," County Business Patterns, First Quarter: 1948. Part 1. Washington: Government Printing Office, 1949.

—————. Income Distribution in the United States by Size, 1944-1950. Washington: Government Printing Office, 1953.

—————. National Income and Product of the United States: 1929-1950. A Supplement to the Survey of Current Business. Washington: Government Printing Office, 1951.

—————. Survey of Current Business. An article on "State Income Payments" is published in the July or August issue each year.

U.S. Department of Labor. "Average Employment
and Total Wages," published annually as a statistical supplement to Labor Market and Employment
Security.

U.S. Department of Labor, Bureau of Labor Statistics. "The Consumer Price Index," published monthly in the Monthly Labor Review.

—————. Family Budget of City Workers: October,
1950. Bureau of Labor Statistics, Bulletin No. 1021.
Washington: Government Printing Office, 1951.

Veterans Administration Research Division, Technical Note on County Estimates of Living Veterans in
Civil Life as of June 30, 1951. Washington: December 12, 1951 (mimeographed).

Wardwell, Charles A.R. Regional Trends in the United
States Economy. A Supplement to the Survey of Cur-
rent Business. Washington: Government Printing
Office, 1951.

Wienfeld, William. "Income of Dentists, 1929-1948,"
Survey of Current Business, XXX (January, 1950).

—————. "Income of Lawyers, 1929-1948," Survey
of Current Business, XXIX (August, 1949).

—————. "Income of Physicians, 1929-1949," Sur-
of Current Business, XXXI (July, 1951).